Blackwell Great Minds

Edited by Steven Nadler

The Blackwell Great Minds series gives readers a strong sense of the fundamental views of the great western thinkers and captures the relevance of these figures to the way we think and live today.

blackwell great minds

c. s. lewis

Stewart Goetz

WILEY Blackwell

Registered Office
John Wiley & Sons, Inc., 111 River Street, Hoboken, NJ 07030, USA

Editorial Office
9600 Garsington Road, Oxford, OX4 2DQ, UK

For details of our global editorial offices, customer services, and more
information about Wiley products visit us at www.wiley.com.

Wiley also publishes its books in a variety of electronic formats and by print-on-
demand. Some content that appears in standard print versions of this book may
not be available in other formats.

Library of Congress Cataloging-in-Publication Data

Names: Goetz, Stewart, author.
Title: C.S. Lewis / by Stewart Goetz, Ursinus College, US.
Description: First Edition. | Hoboken : Wiley, 2018. | Series: Blackwell
    great minds ; 16 | Includes bibliographical references and index. |
Identifiers: LCCN 2017037694 (print) | LCCN 2017042737 (ebook) |
    ISBN 9781119190066 (paper) | ISBN 9781119190271 (pdf) |
    ISBN 9781119190172 (cloth)
Subjects: LCSH: Lewis, C. S. (Clive Staples), 1898–1963.
Classification: LCC BX4827.L44 (ebook) | LCC BX4827.L44 G64 2017 (print) |
    DDC 230.092–dc23
LC record available at https://lccn.loc.gov/2017037694

Cover image: Photo by Arthur P. Strong © Ingrid Franzon.
Cover design by Wiley

Set in 9.5/12pt Trump Mediaeval by SPi Global, Pondicherry, India
Printed and bound in Malaysia by Vivar Printing Sdn Bhd

10 9 8 7 6 5 4 3 2 1

To David Charles,
Friend and Mentor,
Who first taught me the importance of philosophy of mind
for philosophy of religion

Contents

acknowledgments

I am indebted to numerous people who helped bring this book to completion. Patrick Casey, Timothy Mawson, and Jerry Walls read and commented on the manuscript in its entirety. Patrick and Jerry "know Lewis," and kept driving me back to reread this or that. Tim helped me clarify various points where Lewis's work intersects with the contemporary philosophical scene. The criticisms and suggestions of all of them reminded me time and again of how important it is to have others read one's work with a critical eye.

Some of the materials needed to write this book are unpublished, and Laura Schmidt of the Marion E. Wade Center at Wheaton College helped me locate what I could not find on my own. I am deeply indebted to her.

Anandan Bommen, Manish Luthra, and Susan Dunsmore each helped with the preparation of the manuscript, and Emily Corkhill and Marissa Koors wisely oversaw its production. Because of them, it is an absolute delight and privilege to publish with Wiley-Blackwell. I am deeply grateful to my wife, Carolyn, who carefully proofread the manuscript.

Finally, I thank Deirdre Ilkson, who approached me about writing this book and commissioned it.

introduction

The first qualification for judging any piece of workmanship from a corkscrew to a cathedral is to know *what* it is—what it was intended to do and how it is meant to be used. After that has been discovered, the temperance reformer may decide that the corkscrew was made for a bad purpose, and the communist may think the same about the cathedral. But such questions come later. The first thing is to understand the object before you: as long as you think the corkscrew was meant for opening tins or the cathedral for entertaining tourists you can say nothing to the purpose about them. The first thing the reader needs to know about *Paradise Lost* is what Milton meant it to be.

(Lewis 1942, 1)

C. S. Lewis distinguished between two kinds of readers, what he termed "the majority" and "the minority." Members of the majority do not put much value on reading, do not think much about and are largely unaffected by what they do read, and never read anything a second time. Members of the minority are contrary in every way. They are constantly looking for periods of leisure and silence in which to read without distraction. For them, reading a certain work is an experience so momentous that the only standard of comparison is provided by experiences of love, religion, or bereavement, and, as a result, what they read is constantly and prominently before their minds. Minority readers will not infrequently read the same book ten, twenty, or thirty times over the course of their lives (Lewis 1961a, 2–3).

Lewis not only wrote about minority readers but was one himself, and what he wrote was read by other minority readers. For example, Sister Penelope of the Community of St. Mary the Virgin penned the following in a letter to Lewis in 1940 about his book *The Problem of Pain*:

> I expected to enjoy myself reading it, & I have done so even beyond my hope. It made me bolt my dinner to get more time for it … & now that I have finished it, reading every word, & a good many bits twice over,

C. S. Lewis, First Edition. Stewart Goetz.
© 2018 John Wiley & Sons, Inc. Published 2018 by John Wiley & Sons, Inc.

I am longing to read it again. That, I think, is a peculiar quality of your writing: I am aching to re-read both *Pilgrim's Regress* & *Out of the Silent Planet*, tho' I have already read the latter twice, once aloud; but this book outstrips even those ... (Lewis 2004b, 449–50)

Sister Penelope's letter made clear that she was a minority kind of reader. For a time, however, the number of readers of Lewis's books, whether minority or majority, was in decline. In 1957, Jocelyn Gibb, the managing director of Geoffrey Bles Ltd., which originally published many of Lewis's less scholarly books, wrote to Lewis about the declining readership of his works: "Sales are not too happy at the moment ... Your older books are falling off in sales which I suppose is bound to happen after some of them have been out for such a long time" (Lewis 2007, 869). But Gibb could not have been more wrong about what was bound to happen. In a recent article in *The Wall Street Journal*, George Marsden, a historian of American Christianity, writes that, since 2001, Lewis's book *Mere Christianity* has sold more than 3.5 million copies in English and been translated into at least 36 languages (Marsden 2016b). Marsden adds that *Mere Christianity* is the book that educated Chinese Christians are most likely to have read after the Bible. And the British philosopher Anthony Kenny points out that by the end of the last century Lewis had become a cultural icon and patron saint of the evangelical wing of American Christianity (Kenny 2013).

Though I am a professional philosopher (I teach philosophy as a subject at the university level) and a lover of books, I was for much of my life a majority reader when it came to the works of C. S. Lewis. I had read a few of them in part, and even fewer in whole. And most certainly, I had not reread them. However, as Lewis wrote, "[t]he two sorts of readers are not cut off by immovable barriers. Individuals who once belonged to the many are converted and join the few" (Lewis 1961a, 6). About a decade ago, I crossed over from the majority into the minority readership of Lewis, having devoured several of his works in a short period of time. Like Sister Penelope, I enjoyed them in a way that I could not have imagined. While the books by Lewis I was reading were not written for a professional philosophical audience, what particularly intrigued me about them was that they were obviously authored by a philosophical mind. It was as a philosopher that I began to buy, read, and, yes, reread, anything and everything written by Lewis.

As a minority reader of Lewis, it did not take me long to discover that there was a significant body of secondary literature about him and his thought. "Having read [my] way so far into his mind ... " (Lewis 1954, 414), I found one thing in particular about this secondary body of work very perplexing: while it had been the philosophical character of Lewis's thought that had initially impressed me, very few of those writing about Lewis and his work recognized and discussed him in terms of the philosopher that he was. Most seemed intent on disregarding or were simply unaware of what Lewis himself had stressed, which was that he had "had a philosophical ... education" (Lewis 2001c, 20). Indeed, Warren Lewis, his brother and only sibling, wrote that "the study of philosophy was to him as inevitable as death will be" (W. Lewis 1982, 161).

Given the prevailing failure to acknowledge Lewis as the philosopher that he was, I have written this book for the purpose of giving him the philosophical attention he deserves. At many points, I have been tempted to interject my own views of matters that Lewis addressed. Dorothy L. Sayers, who was a contemporary of Lewis and an influential literary figure in her own right, understood this temptation all too well and wrote the following to him in 1948:

> There is to-day far too little straightforward interpretive criticism. Everybody insists on doing "creative" criticism—which means that the critic simply uses his author as a spring-board from which to leap off into an exposition of his own views about the universe ... [W]e need the pure interpreter, who will sit down before a poem, or whatever it is, with humility to it and charity to the reader, and begin by finding out and explaining what the author actually did say, before he starts to explain what the author ought to have said and would have said if he had been as enlightened a person as his critic. A friend of mine, after toiling through several unintelligible books about modern poetry, said plaintively: "I want a critic who will say: 'This is a poem about a bus; this is what the poem says about the bus; this is the conclusion the writer draws from his observation about the bus; I think he has said it well (beautifully, badly, etc.) for the following reason.' After that he can say what he likes, and I shall know where I am." (Lewis 2004b, 885)

Although Lewis was a first-rate critic in his own right and not shy about expressing his own views, he wrote in response to Sayers that "I am absolutely with you about criticism: or, should I say, absolutely with you in feeling that we have far too much criticism and far too little *commentary*" (Lewis 2004b, 886). So with the observations of Sayers and Lewis's answer to them as my guide, I have for the most part resisted temptation and authored a straightforward descriptive account of Lewis's philosophical views. I hope I am justified in thinking that what I have written has a bit more life to it than "this is a poem about a bus; this is what the poem says about the bus ... " My thinking this is in part explained by the fact that I often quote Lewis in the course of the exposition of his views. Whatever one might think about the quality of Lewis's philosophical thought, no one can reasonably deny that he was a gifted writer of prose. As Owen Barfield, one of Lewis's closest friends from their undergraduate days together at Oxford, remarked, years after his friend's death, just about everything Lewis

wrote was "so easy to read, because so simply and lucidly written ... "
(1989, 11). Interestingly, Barfield went on to explain this quality of his
friend's written work in terms of the role Lewis's philosophical thought
had played in his development as a writer. But while much of what
Lewis authored was simply and lucidly written, Lewis himself once
pointed out in personal correspondence that he had two ways of writing,
"one for the people (to be used in works of popularized theology) and
one that never aimed at simplicity (in scholarly or imaginative works)"
(Lewis 2004b, 797). So Lewis's own words serve as a bit of a corrective
to Barfield's comments about the simplicity of his friend's works and
forewarn any reader of them that some of what he penned is not all that
straightforward and easy to understand. Hence, at many points, I have
had to reread what Lewis wrote, not as a minority reader but for
the purpose of understanding his philosophical convictions so as to be
able to convey them to readers of this book.

As I stated in the previous paragraph, I have for the most part resisted
the temptation to engage in criticism of Lewis's thought. For the most
part, but not totally. In the spirit of a sympathetic but not servile presentation of Lewis's views, I have occasionally succumbed to temptation and
injected some critical remarks of my own because I believe Lewis would
have appreciated and perhaps, upon reflection, even agreed with them.
I say this because I have been reminded from my rereading of Lewis's
personal correspondence (he was a prolific letter writer) about how
grateful he was for good criticism and, when he was persuaded, openly
acknowledged his change of mind.

I also mentioned a moment ago without explanation that I quote
Lewis frequently in subsequent chapters. My primary reason for quoting
him often and sometimes at length (Lewis himself had a "gift for quoting" (Sayer 1994, 243)) is to make clear to readers that I have not misread
him. Philosophically, Lewis was his own man. As the Lewis scholar
Michael Ward has recently commented, Lewis "was to a certain extent
a 'Free Thinker'; he wasn't trammelled by expectations and conventions
in the same way that most of his contemporaries were" (Ward 2016, 44).
And another serious student of Lewis, Adam Barkman, describes Lewis as
"a lone thinker" (2009, 12). Yet, many try to pigeonhole him as a "this"
or a "that," when in reality he was neither.

Here, for illustrative purposes, it is helpful to consider the issue of
knowledge. In his book *The Allegory of Love*, Lewis wrote about Edmund
Spenser that

> [he was] writing in an age [the sixteenth century] of religious doubt and
> controversy when the avoidance of error [was] a problem as pressing
> as, and in a sense prior to, the conquest of sin: a fact which would have
> rendered his story uninteresting in some centuries, but which should
> recommend it to us. (Lewis 1936, 334)

Recall now Kenny's point, which I mentioned a moment ago, that Lewis has become the patron saint of the evangelical wing of American Christianity, which itself exists in an age that, not unlike Spenser's, is preoccupied with doubt, avoiding error, and, most generally, whether and how we can know. While Lewis was certainly theologically orthodox, he was just as certainly philosophically deeply at odds with a view of our ability to know that a significant segment of the evangelical community espoused and continues to maintain in response to the spirit of the age. As I will make clear in Chapter 2, Lewis believed in the fundamentally unimpaired quality of reason, and he argued that our philosophical views begin with reason because they can begin nowhere else. Contrary to Lewis, the evangelical wing of American Christianity was and remains heavily influenced by what it calls "presuppositionalism." In simplest terms, presuppositionalism is the view that one's ability to know is impaired (often explained in terms of the Fall of Adam and Eve in the Garden of Eden) and, because it is, to avoid error one must have in place certain intellectual commitments before one can know. For many evangelicals, one must rely on what they think of as Christian or biblical presuppositions (regularly referred to as the biblical or Christian worldview, or what God has willed or said as revealed in the Bible) to support one's foundational claims to know and to have reasoned well.

As readers and interpreters of Lewis, evangelical presuppositionalists mistakenly portray Lewis as one of their own. For example, in his short book about Lewis's view of education, entitled *C. S. Lewis: An Apologist for Education*, Louis Markos writes:

> Lewis ... insisted that all conclusions be traced back to their foundational assumptions and presuppositions ... Lewis ... believed ... in the importance of following an argument wherever it leads ... All was open for discussion, though Lewis himself looked to the Bible and the Christian creeds as touchstones for measuring truth claims. (2015, 6, 18–19)

However, as will become obvious in subsequent chapters, Lewis thought that foundational truth claims did not need touchstones by which to be measured. They were simply known to be true. Thus, in discussing our supposed knowledge of the goodness of God, Lewis acknowledged that "some will reply, 'Ah, but we are fallen and don't recognise good when we see it'," to which he replied "But God Himself does not say we are as fallen as all that" (Lewis 2007, 1437). More generally, Lewis reasoned that if one needed to depend on presuppositions (which, by hypothesis, could not themselves just be known to be true, because they would then no longer be presuppositions) in order to know foundational truths, then what justification could one provide to explain one's reliance on those presuppositions? If one reasoned to a presupposition from something one knew, one would have needed a second-order presupposition to validate the reasoning and knowledge which one took respectively to be valid and true and, thereby, supportive of that first-order presupposition. Lewis believed there could be no principled way to stop this regress.

Markos rightly goes on to maintain that:

> [whether Lewis]was writing literature, teaching it, or criticizing it, [he] kept his eye firmly on the work itself, instructing his students and his readers to pay attention to what the work was trying to do and trying to say rather than to impose on the work their own ... presuppositions. (2015, 27)

Thus, Lewis would have instructed us regarding his own work that we should receive it by fairly and squarely laying our minds open to what he wrote and letting it do its work on us. We ought to get ourselves and our views out of the way (Lewis 1961a, 12, 13, 19). In terms of presuppositionalism, we should be careful not to presuppose that Lewis was a presuppositionalist.

So while the theological embrace of Lewis by evangelicals is understandable, it is nevertheless the case that he philosophically parted ways with most of them when it came to questions about the integrity of reason. Lewis thought that Jerusalem (religion) had much to do with Athens (philosophy), but he was convinced that in terms of what we know, one had to start with unaided reason in Athens (without what Christian theologians term "special revelation") and journey to Jerusalem. And while Lewis held that what the biblical authors wrote contains many foundational truths, he believed that when those writers avoided error, they often did so without presupposing anything.

In one of his scholarly books entitled *The Discarded Image*, Lewis wrote:

> [it is] [t]he business of the natural philosopher ... to construct theories which will "save appearances" ... A scientific theory must "save" or "preserve" the appearances, the phenomena, it deals with, in the sense of getting them all in, doing justice to them. (1964, 14)

In writing this book, I have sought in a systematic way within limited space to get in and do justice to the main ideas in Lewis's settled philosophical thought. George Sayer, a student of Lewis's in the mid-1930s, recounted his first meeting with Lewis in Oxford. As he approached the door to Lewis's rooms in Magdalen College, he came upon a man standing outside who was waiting to see Lewis:

> "Are you a pupil come for a tutorial?" he asked.
>
> "No. But Mr. Lewis is going to be my tutor next term." ...
>
> "You're lucky in having him as your tutor," he said ...

As I walked away [after my meeting], I found the man that Lewis had called "Tollers" [he was J. R. R. Tolkien] sitting on one of the stone steps in front of the arcade.

"How did you get on?" he asked.

"I think rather well. I think he will be a most interesting tutor to have."

"Interesting? Yes, he's certainly that. You'll never get to the bottom of him." (Sayer 1994, xvii–xviii, xx)

I am sure I have not gotten to the bottom of Lewis. But I am just as sure that I have gotten below the surface of him in terms of his philosophical views. In getting below the surface, I hope I have managed to avoid committing what Lewis described as "the one sin for which, in literature, no merits can compensate; [that of being] rather dull" (Lewis 1954, 363). Lewis and what he thought were most certainly not dull, as the brief overview of his life and the explanation of the sense in which he was a philosopher in Chapter 1 will begin to make clear. After this overview and explanation, I plunge headfirst in the remaining chapters into the task of setting forth the particulars of Lewis's philosophical ideas. My presentation of them reflects their ordered philosophical importance in Lewis's mind. Thus, I start with longer chapters on Lewis's views of reason, happiness, morality, and free will, and end with shorter treatments of his views of dying to self, God, and the problem of pain. If one does not understand his views of the former, one will have a more difficult time understanding what he had to say about the latter.

"The greatest part of a writer's time is spent in reading, in order to write: a man will turn over half a library to make one book."

(Boswell 2008, 446)

a philosophical mind

Those of us who have been true readers all our life seldom fully realise the enormous extension of our being which we owe to authors. We realise it best when we talk with an unliterary friend. He may be full of goodness and good sense but he inhabits a tiny world. In it, we should be suffocated … My own eyes are not enough for me, I will see through those of others … [I]n reading great literature I become a thousand men and yet remain myself. Like the night sky in the Greek poem, I see with a myriad eyes, but it is I who see. Here, as in worship, in love, in moral action, and in knowing, I transcend myself; and am never more myself than when I do.

(Lewis 1961a, 140–1)

As soon as the mind of the maker has been made manifest in a work, a way of communication is established between other minds and his. That is to say, it is possible for a reader, by reading a book, to discover something about the mind of the writer.

(Sayers 1987, 49)

1.1   A Brief Biography

Clive Staples Lewis was born on November 29, 1898, in Belfast, Ireland. He was the second of two children, his brother Warnie being three years his elder. According to Warnie, one morning during a holiday at the sea, his younger brother, while still a child with the habit of referring to himself in the third person,

> marched up to my mother, put a forefinger on his chest, and announced, "He is Jacksie"; an announcement no doubt received by our mother with an absentminded, "Yes dear". But on the following day he was still Jacksie, and as he refused absolutely to answer to any other name, Jacksie it had to be; a name afterwards contracted to Jacks, and finally

to Jack. So to the family and his intimate friends he remained Jack for the rest of his life. (W. H. Lewis n.d., 8; "Jacksie" was apparently borrowed from the name of a recently-deceased dog of which the young Lewis had been fond. (Gresham 2005, 2))

Jack's parents were Albert and Florence Lewis. Albert was a career solicitor, who by all accounts had a strained relationship with his sons. Florence, an educated woman gifted in logic and mathematics, earned first- and second-class honors respectively in those subjects at the Royal University (now Queen's University) in Belfast. She tutored the young Jack in French and Latin, and he loved her dearly. Tragically, her life was cut short by abdominal cancer in August of 1908, when Jack was nine years of age. He recounted his thoughts about the effects of her demise in the following memorable words:

> With my mother's death all settled happiness, all that was tranquil and reliable, disappeared from my life. There was to be much fun, many pleasures ... ; but no more of the old security. It was sea and islands now; the great continent had sunk like Atlantis. (Lewis 1955, 21)

Though there were certainly pleasures, Lewis tersely wrote in his forties that "I had a not very happy boyhood ... " (Lewis 1967, 57).

With his mother dead not even a month, Jack's unhappiness from her passing was compounded by his being sent off to Wynyard School in England, a boarding school which his parents chose without ever having set eyes on it (Sayer 1994, 57). His life there was nightmarish (Lewis in his later years referred to the school as Belsen, after the World War II German concentration camp). The headmaster of the school was tyrannical and cruel (he regularly flogged his few and decreasing number of students). The school permanently closed in June of 1910, with the headmaster soon thereafter committed to an asylum. In the fall of 1910, Jack was enrolled at Campbell College, a boarding school not far from his home in Belfast. Because of an illness in November of that year and an ensuing convalescence at home, his time at the school was brief. In January of 1911, Jack was sent off again to England and another boarding school, Cherbourg, a preparatory school for entrance into Malvern College, a public school which Albert believed would prepare his son for possible admission to a university like Oxford. Jack's experience in school this time was not as bad as that which he had on the first go-around, and a reader of an examination taken by Jack at Cherbourg for a scholarship at Malvern saw academic promise: "Came into his own in the verse. Some of his rendering truly alpha, with a poetic feeling rare in any boy. I believe he is just the sort to develop to gain a Classics award at Oxford" (Sayer 1994, 75).

Jack entered Malvern College in the fall of 1913. In his first term there, he wrote a poem *CARPE DIEM? After Horace*, which Albert sent to William Kirkpatrick, the former headmaster of a school Albert had attended in his youth. Kirkpatrick was impressed by Jack's work: "It is an amazing performance for a boy of his age—indeed for a boy of any age" (Sayer 1994, 89). Despite his academic development, Lewis was not happy at Malvern, and he more than once petitioned his father to remove him. Much later in his life, Lewis wrote generally about his life at school that "I never hated anything as much, not even the front line trenches in World War I" (2007, 1325). Warnie believed the idea of placing his brother in boarding school was a mistake from the beginning:

> The fact is that Jack should never have been sent to a Public School at all. It would have been a miracle if the boy who in his first term wrote *Carpe Diem* could have found a congenial companion amongst those of his own age, or for that matter at any age level ... [H]e would have found himself much more at home amongst first year undergraduates ... For the main function of the Public School in those days was to produce a standardized article. With two or three notable exceptions they were factories turning out the spare parts and replacements needed to keep Imperial and commercial machinery functioning efficiently, and obviously it was essential that the new part should be identical with the worn-out one. But no polishing, filing, or grinding could have made Jack a cog in any machine ... (W. H. Lewis, n.d., 35–6)

In September, 1914, after only one year at Malvern, Lewis's life in public school was over. Albert sent Jack to live and study with Kirkpatrick, whom Lewis came to refer to as "Kirk" or "The Great Knock." Kirkpatrick was a rationalist and atheist, and Lewis, who also did not believe in God, thrived intellectually under Kirkpatrick's instruction. The Great Knock worked one-on-one with Lewis, schooling him to articulate and defend his views with cold, analytic rigor. By this time, Lewis was proficient in Greek, Latin, and French, with more than a little knowledge of Italian. Kirkpatrick was so impressed with his student that he wrote the following to Albert on January 7, 1915:

> I do not think there can be much doubt as to the genuine and lasting quality of Clive's intellectual abilities. He was born with the literary temperament, and we have to face that fact with all that it implies. This is not a case of early precocity showing itself in rapid assimilation of knowledge ... As I said before, it is the maturity and originality of his literary judgements which is so unusual and surprising. By an unerring instinct he detects first rate quality in literary workmanship, and the second rate does not interest him in any way. Now you will observe that these endowments, in themselves remarkable, do not

in some ways facilitate the work of the teacher, whose business, let us say, is to prepare the pupil for a Classical Scholarship in entering Oxford University. The ideal pupil for that purpose is a boy gifted with memory, receptiveness, patience, and strict attention to grammatical accuracy, and so on … The fact is that a critical and original faculty, whatever may be its promise for the future, is as much of a hindrance as a help in the drudgery of early classical training—Clive has ideas of his own and is not at all the sort of boy to be made a mere receptive machine. (W. H. Lewis 1933, 279)

In December of the same year, Kirkpatrick once again wrote to Albert:

Of Clive himself we may say that it is difficult to conceive of him doing anything else than what he is doing now. Anything else is so repugnant to him that he simply excludes it from his thoughts … In dealing with a natural bias of temperament so strongly accentuated, we must make great allowances, but what is perfectly clear in the case is this: that outside a life of literary study, a career of literary interests, life has neither meaning nor attraction for him … [H]e is adapted for nothing else. You may make up your mind on that. (W. H. Lewis 1934, 39)

About four months later in April, 1916, Kirkpatrick could not refrain from expressing further praise of Lewis in a letter to Albert:

I do not look on Clive as a school boy in any sense of the term. He is a student who has no interest except in reading and study … He hardly realizes – how could he at his age – with what a liberal hand nature has bestowed her bounties upon him … [A]s far as preparation [for university] is concerned, it is difficult to conceive of any candidate who ought to be in better position to face the ordeal. He has read more classics than any boy I ever had – or indeed I might add than any I ever heard of, unless it be an Addison or Landor or Macaulay. These are people we read of, but I have never met any. (W. H. Lewis 1934, 74)

Finally, in December, 1916, toward the end of his time tutoring Lewis, Kirkpatrick penned the following words to Albert: "As a dialectician, an intellectual disputant, I shall miss him, and he will have no successor. Clive can hold his own in any discussion, and the higher the range of the conversation, the more he feels himself at home" (W. H. Lewis 1934, 165). Even though Lewis would write in later years that "we of the teaching professions often exaggerate the influence of teachers" (1954, 350), when he learned of Kirk's death in March, 1921, he spared no praise for his former mentor:

I at least owe to him in the intellectual sphere as much as one human being can owe another. That he enabled me to win a scholarship is the least that he did for me. It was an atmosphere of unrelenting clearness and rigid honesty of thought that one breathed from living with him – and this I shall be the better for as long as I live. (Lewis 2004a, 535)

Summing up his life in school, Lewis wrote: "I was at four schools, and learnt nothing at three of them; but on the other hand I was lucky in having a first class tutor" (2007, 1047).

The scholarship to which Lewis referred in the penultimate quote was in classics at University College, Oxford,[1] where he went to reside as a student in April of 1917. He headed to University College, even though in late March he had failed an Oxford university entrance exam called "Responsions," which included mathematics, a subject at which Lewis was extremely weak. Lewis again failed Responsions in June of that year, and never passed the exam, but was allowed to continue at Oxford nevertheless because of his service in World War I. He entered the war in November, 1917, in the trenches in France, and in the spring of 1918 was wounded there. As to the nature of his war experience, it is best to let Lewis speak for himself:

I have gone to sleep marching and woken again and found myself marching still. One walked in the trenches in thigh gum boots with water above the knee; one remembers the icy stream welling up inside the boot when you punctured it on concealed barbed wire. Familiarity both with the very old and the very recent dead confirmed that view of corpses which had been formed the moment I saw my dead mother. I came to know and pity and reverence the ordinary man: particularly dear Sergeant Ayres, who was (I suppose) killed by the same shell that wounded me ... But for the rest, the war—the frights, the cold, ... the horribly smashed men still moving like half-crushed beetles, the sitting or standing corpses, the landscape of sheer earth without a blade of grass, the boots worn day and night till they seemed to grow to your feet ... "This is War. This is what Homer wrote about." (Lewis 1955, 195–6)

Upon returning to Oxford after the war, Lewis earned three firsts, one in Honours Moderations (mainly a course of study in Greek and Latin texts) in 1920, one in Greats (essentially the study of classics, philosophy, and ancient history) in 1922 (Honours Moderations and Greats were two parts of the single degree *Literae Humaniores*), and one in English language and literature in 1923 (a second degree). It was in part because permanent academic posts in philosophy and classics were hard to come by in Oxford in the early 1920s that Lewis concluded he would do the additional degree in English language and literature. He wrote to Albert in 1922 that

[t]he actual subjects of my own Greats school are a doubtful quality at the moment; for no one quite knows what place Classics and

Philosophy will hold in the educational world in a year's time. On the other hand the prestige of the Greats School is still enormous; so what is wanted everywhere is a man who combines the general qualifications which Greats is supposed to give, with the special qualifications of any other subjects. And English Literature is a "rising" subject. (W. H. Lewis n.d., 114)

John Wain, a former student of Lewis's, succinctly explained Lewis's decision to enter the English school in the following way: "[A]lthough [Lewis] didn't particularly want to teach in the English School, he thought it might be a job" (2015, 244–5).

During this time of uncertainty about his prospects for future academic employment in Oxford, Lewis was in need of money. Albert wrote in his diary on October 11, 1923, that

[w]hile Jacks was at home I repeated my promise to provide for him at Oxford if I possibly could, for a maximum of three years this summer. I again pointed out to him the difficulty of getting anything to do at 28 if he had ultimately to leave Oxford. (W. H. Lewis n.d., 148)

But Lewis did not have to leave. After taking a one-year replacement position in philosophy at University College, Oxford, in 1924–25, about which Lewis wrote to Albert, "Well, it is poorly paid and temporary … but it is better to be inside than out, and is always a beginning" (2004a, 628), Lewis was hired by Magdalen College, Oxford, in 1925 to teach English. He wired his father "Elected fellow of Magdalen. Jack," and Albert wrote in his diary "I went up to his room and burst into tears of joy. I knelt down and thanked God with a full heart" (Lewis 2004a, 642). Lewis wrote to his father the following: "[L]et me thank you from the bottom of my heart for the generous support, extended over six years, which alone has enabled me to hang on till this" (2004a, 642). Though Albert had made it financially possible for Jack to hang on for so long, his son's letters during these years reveal a serious lack of respect for his father. Jack repented of his "many sins" against Albert years after the latter's death and acknowledged more than once in personal correspondence that the relationship with his father was "the blackest chapter in my life" (Lewis 2004b, 340), because he had "treated [his] own father abominably and no sin in [his] whole life now seem[ed] to be so serious" (Lewis 2007, 445).

But Lewis was now a Fellow of Magdalen. According to Warnie, his brother was relieved and "the relief was enormous. It had been a long, wearisome, often heartbreaking struggle to fight his way into that seemingly impregnable fortress which he used to describe as 'the real Oxford'; and now at last the battle was won" (W. H. Lewis, n.d., 161).

But the job was officially in English, not philosophy. Perhaps at least in part as an after-the-fact attempt to convince himself that he would find life in the English faculty more hospitable than a life in philosophy, Lewis wrote to Albert the following in August, 1925:

> As to the other change – from Philosophy to English – I ... think you are mistaken in supposing that the field is less crowded in Philosophy: it seems so to you only because you have more chance of seeing the literary crowd ... On other grounds I am rather glad of the change. I have come to think that if I had the mind, I have not the brain and nerves for a life of pure philosophy. A continued search among the abstract roots of things, a perpetual questioning of all that plain men take for granted ... – is this the best life for temperaments such as ours? ...
>
> I am not condemning philosophy. Indeed in turning from it to literary history and criticism, I am conscious of a descent: and if the air on the heights did not suit me, still I have brought back something of value. (2004a, 648–9)

Although hired *de jure* to teach English language and literature, *de facto* Magdalen College hired Lewis because he could also teach philosophy. According to Lewis biographers, Roger Lancelyn Green and Walter Hooper, "Lewis had to be always ready to 'fill in' with a philosophy tutorial or lecture if required. Of the sixteen pupils Lewis had in 1926 only five were reading English" (2003, 76).

During the years Lewis was struggling to move from the life of an Oxford student to that of an Oxford don, he was also slowly but surely moving intellectually from atheism to theism.[2] He recounted that the "long-evaded encounter [with God] happened at a time when I was making a serious effort to obey my conscience" (Lewis 1967, 169). The date of the momentous "meeting" (it is contested) was in the spring of either 1929 or 1930. The following is Lewis's oft-quoted summary of it:

> You must picture me alone in that room in Magdalen, night after night, feeling, whenever my mind lifted even for a second from my work, the steady, unrelenting approach of Him whom I so earnestly desired not to meet. That which I greatly feared had at last come upon me. In the Trinity Term ... I gave in, and admitted that God was God, and knelt and prayed: perhaps, that night, the most dejected and reluctant convert in all England. (Lewis 1955, 228–9)

Though a dejected and reluctant convert to theism, Lewis wrote not too long afterward to his life-long friend Arthur Greeves that "[i]t is emphatically coming home" (Lewis 2004a, 873). Years later, Lewis recounted that "[i]t must be understood that the conversion ... was only to Theism, pure and simple, not to Christianity" (Lewis 1955, 230). For some time, he had had longstanding reservations about the Christian religion. For example, in October, 1916, Lewis had written to Greeves that

> there was once a Hebrew called Yeshua ... : when I say "Christ" of course I mean the mythological being into whom he was afterwards converted by popular imagination, and I am thinking of the legends about his magic performances and resurrection etc. That the man Yeshua or Jesus did actually exist, is as certain as that the Buddha did actually exist ... But all the other tomfoolery about virgin birth, magic healings, apparitions and so forth is on exactly the same footing as any other mythology. (Lewis 2004a, 234)

But by the time of his conversion to theism, Lewis's views of Christianity were changing. Though not yet a Christian, he acknowledged in writing to his friend Hamilton Jenkin that "it may turn out that way in the end" (Lewis 2004a, 887). And when it finally did turn out that way, Lewis wrote to Greeves that "I have just passed on from believing in God to definitely believing in Christ—in Christianity. I will try to explain this another time. My long night talk with Dyson and Tolkien had a good deal to do with it" (2004a, 974).

The long talk to which Lewis referred was with English colleagues Hugo Dyson and J. R. R. Tolkien and stretched into the wee hours of a morning in September, 1931. The topic of conversation was about the nature of myth and its relationship to the death and resurrection of Jesus Christ. Lewis was familiar with and a lover of pagan stories about dying and rising gods, and up to the time of his discussion with Dyson and Tolkien, he had believed Christianity to be just one more such imaginative myth. As a result of the eventful talk, he became convinced that Christianity was not just another myth like the others, as he had asserted to Greeves in 1916. He was now convinced and wrote to Greeves in October, 1931 that "[t]he story of Christ is simply a true myth: a myth working on us in the same way as the others, but with this tremendous difference that it *really happened*" (Lewis 2004a, 977). The true myth was that to which all others were pointers. Lewis's belief in the significance of the mythology of dying and rising gods was in part a result of his already having become convinced of the importance of dying to self (obeying one's conscience) in living one's life. Many years after his conversion to Christianity, he explained that "[t]he value of myth is that it takes all the things we know and restores to them the rich significance which has been hidden by 'the veil of familiarity'" (Lewis 2013b, 108). The veil of familiarity included the truth that the seed must be buried in order to come to life, and that before there can be spring and summer there must be fall and winter. Thus, the story of

Christ dying and rising was not only the fulfillment of stories about dying and rising gods, but also reflected the philosophical truth about how one ought to approach life. In response to Greeves's frustration with rejection as a writer in 1930, Lewis penned the practical advice that "[a]s you know so well, we have got to *die* … I am writing as I do simply [and] solely because I think the only thing for you to do is absolutely to *kill* the part of you that wants success" (2004a, 926, 927).

Firmly settled in both Oxford and the Christian religion, Lewis began to make a name for himself in academic circles. *The Allegory of Love* was published in 1936. Other academic books of note followed, including *A Preface to Paradise Lost* (1942), the massive *English Literature in the Sixteenth Century: Excluding Drama* in 1954, and *An Experiment in Criticism* in 1961. Prior to any of these academic monographs, Lewis had published in 1933 a semi-autobiographical account of his conversion to Christianity entitled *The Pilgrim's Regress*. The book contained in his own words "needless obscurity" (Lewis 1992b, 200), and it was not until the appearance of *The Problem of Pain* in 1940 that Lewis began to acquire a reputation as a Christian apologist and public intellectual. In light of the book's success, the British Broadcasting Corporation chose Lewis to speak on the radio to the British people during World War II about Christianity. The popular talks were eventually included in the book *Mere Christianity* (1952). In the meantime, publication of *The Screwtape Letters* (1942), *The Great Divorce* (1946), and *Miracles* (1947) solidified Lewis's reputation as a spokesperson for Christianity. Lewis read aloud drafts of many of his works to members of the literary group known as the Inklings, which usually met in Lewis's rooms in Magdalen College on Thursday nights during the academic year, from roughly 1933 through 1949. Members of the group included such notable authors as J. R. R. Tolkien, who read aloud parts of what would become his Ring Trilogy, and Charles Williams.[3]

During the 1950s, Lewis turned to writing children's literature in the form of the Narnia stories. There would be seven books in all, the best-known of which was *The Lion, the Witch, and the Wardrobe*. In 1954, after thirty years as a tutor at Oxford, Lewis accepted the professorship of Medieval and Renaissance English at Cambridge University. In the mid-1950s, he also met an American woman named Joy Davidman, and through a singular series of events ended up marrying her. Lewis told his friend Nevill Coghill that "I never expected to have, in my sixties, the happiness that passed me by in my twenties" (Green and Hooper 1974, 270). But the happiness was short-lived, as Davidman died from cancer in July, 1960. Lewis recounted his sorrow in *A Grief Observed*. He lived for three-and-a-quarter more years after the death of Davidman and passed away on November 22, 1963, the day the American President John F. Kennedy was assassinated.

1.2   Lewis as a Philosopher

Lewis was a most distinguished academic with what in his day was a philosophical pedigree second to none. Yet he was not a member of the professional philosophical guild, and never wrote philosophical books and papers for a strictly professional philosophical audience. In what way, then, was he preeminently a philosopher?

One might think a good way to answer this question would be to query the question itself, which assumes that Lewis was a philosopher. Perhaps despite what he and those who knew him claimed, he was not. But this argumentative move must be dismissed. While Lewis did not write academic philosophical books for professional philosophers, anyone who reads his works knows that many of them are deeply philosophical in nature. Here, *Miracles* immediately comes to mind, along with *The Problem of Pain*, *The Abolition of Man*, and the first part of *Mere Christianity*. Some Lewis scholars have intimated that Lewis likely would have continued producing such philosophical works had it not been for a public debate with the young professional philosopher Elizabeth Anscombe in 1948, at which she criticized his argument against the philosophical view known as "naturalism" (Anscombe 1981, 227). For example, the Lewis scholar Colin Duriez has recently written that in light of Anscombe's critique, Lewis eventually "acknowledge[d] … that philosophy had become increasingly specialized and analytical" (2015, 190) and it had left him behind. Duriez adds that Lewis "felt that if he tried to continue in that more and more rarified world, he would only be communicating with a smaller and smaller audience" (2015, 190).

I will have something to say about the exchange between Anscombe and Lewis in Chapter 2. Here I want to make clear that Duriez is mistaken when he writes that Anscombe's criticism made Lewis realize that philosophy had become increasingly specialized and led him to conclude that he would no longer try to move in that rarified world. Lewis had already come to this realization more than two decades earlier in 1925 when he acknowledged in writing to his father (see the quote in the previous section) that while he had the mind for professional philosophy, he had neither the brain nor temperament for it. Whatever Lewis took away from Anscombe's criticism, it could not have been that it would be wise for him not to continue in the rarified world of philosophy. Lewis could not have ceased at that time to continue in that world because he had walked away from it years earlier.

But Duriez is mistaken only in part. He is also in part correct. As he says, philosophy had become more and more specialized. Since Lewis's days as an undergraduate, the academic discipline had taken a linguistic turn and, among other things, was focused on whether religious, moral, and aesthetic statements are meaningful declarative statements that can be true or false. The accepted view became that assertions like "God exists," "the purpose of life is that we be happy," and "murder is wrong" are strictly speaking neither true nor false, but disguised emotive claims like "Hopefully there is a God!" and "I disapprove of murder and you should too!" Lewis believed this accepted view was seriously mistaken. When he wrote that he had had "a philosophical ... education" (Lewis 2001c, 20), he was referring to a course of study of historical works in which these and similar declarative statements were understood to be genuinely declarative and either true or false. Philosophy, as he learned it, was a discipline concerned with questions about what makes life worth living, what constitutes a good life, what is the nature of the self, and arguments for and against God's existence. Lewis never wavered in his conviction that these "Big Questions" were the real subject matter of philosophy, and the breadth and depth of his education concerning historical thought about them are evidenced by references in his own published works to philosophical luminaries like Plato, Aristotle, Hume, Kant, Confucius, Augustine, Aquinas, Berkeley, Spinoza, Rousseau, Locke, Hegel, Bradley, Bergson, and a veritable host of others. His interactions with the ideas of some of these philosophers are found early on in the unpublished notes for his philosophy lectures (Lewis 1924).

So Lewis's abiding interest in and written work about the Big Questions highlights one important way in which he was first and foremost a philosopher. But there was another way, one which complemented his interest in the Big Questions. This additional way is perhaps best characterized as an issue of personal ownership or livability (cf. Barkman 2009, 1–20). As Robin Lane Fox has recently written, for pagan Greeks and Romans, a conversion to philosophy was a conversion to "its accompanying way of life" (Fox 2015, 6). And Lewis knew as well as anyone else the thought of the pagan Greeks and Romans. An important event in terms of the issue of livability was a lunch conversation Lewis had as a young don at Oxford with his friend Owen Barfield and a pupil Alan Griffiths. Lewis referred to philosophy as a subject, to which Barfield responded:

> "It wasn't a *subject* to Plato ... it was a way." The quiet but fervent agreement of Griffiths, and the quick glance of understanding between these two, revealed to me my own frivolity. Enough had been thought, and said, and felt, and imagined. It was about time that something should be done. (Lewis 1955, 225)

Lewis took Barfield's point to heart. As George Sayer wrote, "[m]any men who read 'Greats' (classical philosophy) at Oxford read it as a subject of academic study, not as something that might affect their conduct. Jack, on the other hand, wanted the study of philosophy to be a road to belief" (1994, 219). At the time of the conversation with Barfield and Griffiths, Lewis espoused philosophical Idealism, which is roughly the view that reality is ultimately spiritual in nature and everything, including seemingly distinct human persons, is a manifestation of Spirit and ultimately identical with it in being. Lewis concluded that one of the major problems with Idealism was that it could not be lived. He acknowledged that "there had long been an ethic (theoretically) attached to my Idealism," but, he continued,

> I thought the business of us finite and half-unreal souls was to multiply the consciousness of Spirit by seeing the world from different positions while yet remaining qualitatively the same as Spirit; to be tied to a particular time and place and set of circumstances, yet there to will and think as Spirit itself does. (Lewis 1955, 225)

Lewis went on to point out that to will and think as Spirit itself does is hard to do. Though he did not straightforwardly explain the difficulty, it is plausible to think he reasoned that if Idealism is true, one is identical with one's neighbor. Thus, in pursuing or not pursuing one's own happiness one is pursuing or not pursuing one's neighbor's happiness, because they are really the same thing. But morality is about how to act when one's interests conflict with those of one's neighbor. How could one choose to live morally when morality presupposed distinctions which were not ultimately real? Lewis concluded that a practical choice had to be made and he started consciously appealing to Spirit for help: "But the fine, philosophical distinction between this and what ordinary people call 'prayer to God' breaks down as soon as you start doing it in earnest. Idealism can be talked, and even felt; it cannot be lived" (Lewis 1955, 226). In Lewis's mind, it could not be lived because to live it he had to avoid praying to God as a Spirit distinct from himself who knew and cared about the petition. Lewis reached the point where he concluded, "I was to be allowed to play at philosophy no longer" (1955, 227). More than two decades later, Lewis would approvingly make reference in personal correspondence to the poet John Keats's point that "axioms in philosophy are not axioms until they are proved upon our pulses" (2007, 425n. 89).

In the end, Lewis rejected Idealism for Christianity and came to believe that not only was professional philosophy's linguistic turn a mistake, but so also was its failure to appreciate that "a philosophy" is something that impacts daily life and not something to be just mentally entertained. In contrast with philosophical academicians of his day (and today, as the philosopher Tim Crane has recently written "[i]t is normal in academic philosophy to separate a philosopher's life sharply from his or her work" (2016, 4)), Lewis joined with those who in much earlier times "still connected thinking with doing and were prepared to alter their way of life as the result of a chain of reasoning" (Lewis 1961b, 7–8). The "doing" extended to one's daily routine, so that Lewis could write about how "[i]t is terrible to find how little progress ones [*sic*] philosophy and charity have made when they are brought to the test of domestic life" (Lewis 2004a, 907–8). In the light of his belief in the importance of the livability of a philosophy, Lewis's insistence in a letter to J. S. A. Ensor in 1944 that "I came to believe in God on purely philosophical grounds" (Lewis 2004b, 605) and in written correspondence with N. Fridama two years later that "I was brought back [to Christianity] … [b]y Philosophy" (Lewis 2004b, 702) makes perfect sense.

1.3   Lewis and Common Sense

When Lewis abandoned Idealism because it could not be lived, he was implicitly acknowledging his respect for and acceptance of common sense. J. A. W. Bennett, who was the successor to Lewis in the Chair of Medieval and Renaissance English at Cambridge, wrote about Lewis that "[t]he whole man was in all his judgments and activities … for [in support of]< common life>" (1992, 74). And Wesley Kort has written recently that "Lewis ha[d] a high regard for what he took to be ordinary experience. He prize[d] attention to … the everyday" (2016, 14). Here are two representative comments from Lewis about living life: "All we can do is to try to follow the plain rules of charity, justice and commonsense and leave the issue [result] to God" (Lewis 2007, 940–1); and "[H]ow right our Lord is about 'sufficient to the day'. Do even pious people in their reverence for the more radiantly divine element in His sayings, sometimes attend too little to their sheer practical common-sense?" (Lewis 2007, 1335).

Lewis clearly thought of common-sense philosophy as that which must be livable. But what about a slightly more expansive conception of common sense? Can something be said about it? According to Arthur J. Balfour in *Theism and Humanism*, one of the books that Lewis claimed most shaped his philosophy of life (Lewis 1962), the following is the creed of common sense:

What *is* the creed of common sense?

It has never been summed up in articles, nor fenced round with definitions. But in our ordinary moments we all hold it; and there should be no insuperable difficulty in coming to an agreement about certain of its characteristics … One such characteristic is that its most important formulas represent beliefs which, whether true or false, whether proved or unproved, are at least inevitable. All men accept them in fact. Even those who criticise them in theory live by them in practice …

But, are there such inevitable beliefs? There certainly are. We cannot … suppose the world to be emptied of persons who think, who feel, who will; or of things which are material, independent, extended, and enduring. We cannot doubt that such entities exist, nor that they act on one another, nor that they are in space or time … (Balfour 2000, 18)

Balfour added that common sense also affirms that

[t]hings are not changed by a mere change of place, but a change of place relative to an observer always changes their appearance for him. Common sense is, therefore, compelled in this, as in countless other cases, to distinguish the appearance of a thing from its reality; and to hold, as an essential article of its working creed, that appearances may alter, leaving realities unchanged.

Common sense … has never held the opinion … that the character or duration of external things in any way depends upon our observations of them … Things in their true reality are not affected by mere observation, still less are they constituted by it. When material objects are in question, common sense never supposes that *esse* [the *being* of material objects] and *percipi* [their being *perceived*] are identical … It is content to say that, though a thing is doubtless always more than the sum of those aspects of it to which we happen to be attending, yet our knowledge that it is and what it is, however imperfect, is, for practical purposes, sufficiently clear and trustworthy, requiring the support neither of metaphysics nor psychology. (Balfour 2000, 91–2)

In Balfour's estimation, then, the world of common sense is a world that contains enduring material entities that exist in space and time independently of the perceivers of them, where, as he intimates, those perceivers are rational souls (beings that think, have experiences, and will (choose). If, like Lewis, we take our lead from Balfour, a respect for common sense would seem to include a healthy respect for beliefs/knowledge that are directly grounded and/or originate in (1) self-awareness (e.g., I believe I am a soul that is distinct from other entities and endures through time; I know I am now experiencing pain; I remember having lunch this noon; I know I want to be happy; I know pleasure is good and pain is bad; I believe I ought to treat others as I would want to be treated); (2) sense perception (e.g., I believe I have a body; I believe there is a car in my driveway that was there yesterday); and (3) reason (e.g., I know that if P then Q, and P, then Q; I know that if A is greater than B, and B is greater than C, then A is greater than C).

In a letter to his friend Leo Baker in July, 1921, Lewis laid out what was coming to be his settled belief in the importance of common sense for assessing the truth of a philosophy of life. The subject matter that elicited his thoughts was a book about Buddhism entitled *The Gospel of Buddha According to Old Records*, provided to him by Baker:

> [T]hanks for the Gospel of Buddha: in so far as it is a gospel, an exposition of ethics etc, it has not perhaps added much to what I know of the subject, tho' it has been very pleasant reading. On the metaphysical presuppositions of Buddhism, it has given me new light: I did not realize, before, his denial of the Atman: that is very interesting. I cannot at present believe it—to me the Self, as really existing, seems involved in everything we think. No use to talk of "a bundle of thoughts" etc for, as you know, I always have to ask "who thinks?" Indeed Buddhism itself does not seem to make much use of the non-Atman doctrine, once it has been stated: and it is only by torture that the theory of rebirth is made compatible with it. Perhaps he has confused a moral truth with a metaphysical fallacy? One sees, of course, its inferiority to Christianity—at any rate as a creed for ordinary men: and though I sometimes feel that complete abnegation is the only real refuge, in my healthier moments I hope that there is something better. This minute I can pine for Nirvana, but when the sky clears I shall prefer something with more positive joy. (Lewis 2004a, 567)

Such was to be the primacy of common sense in Lewis's mind. What, if anything, did he think competes with common sense? Lewis came to believe the major contemporary competitor is a doctrine called "naturalism." As we will see in subsequent chapters, Lewis was well aware of an ongoing effort among a growing number of "naturalistic" philosophers and scientists to reduce or explain away (eliminate) the objects of the world of common sense in terms of the "entities" of the world of science. However, Lewis repeatedly harkened back to the point that our belief in the world presented to us by science ultimately depends upon our belief in and acceptance of the framework of common sense, hence it is impossible to use the former to undermine the integrity of the latter. Because I will be discussing Lewis's convictions about this and related points in subsequent chapters, it will suffice to close this section with Balfour's summation of this point:

> In its most general form the difficulty is this. It is claimed by science that its conclusions are based upon experience. The experience spoken of is unquestionably the familiar perception of external things and their movements as understood by common sense; and, however much our powers of experience be increased by telescopes, microscopes, balances, thermometers, electroscopes, and so forth, this common-sense view suffers no alteration. The perceptions of a man of science are, in essence, the perceptions of ordinary men in their ordinary moments, beset with the same difficulties, accepted with the same assurance. Whatever be the proper way of describing scientific results, the experimental data on which they rest are sought and obtained in the spirit of "naïf realism." (Balfour 2000, 98)

1.4　Reading Lewis

In an essay that he wrote as an Introduction for a translation of a work by the theologian St. Athanasius, who lived in the late third and early fourth centuries, Lewis claimed in his capacity as a tutor in English Literature

> that if the average student wants to find out something about Platonism, the very last thing he thinks of doing is to take a translation of Plato off the library shelf and read the *Symposium*. He would rather read some dreary modern book ten times as long, all about 'isms' and influences and only once in twelve pages telling him what Plato actually said ... The student is half afraid to meet one of the great philosophers face to face. He feels himself inadequate and thinks he will not understand him. But if he only knew, the great man, just because of his greatness, is much more intelligible than his modern commentator ... It has always therefore been one of my main endeavours as a teacher to persuade the young that first-hand knowledge is not only more worth acquiring than second-hand knowledge, but is usually much easier and more delightful to acquire. (1970, 200)

While I have aimed to include what Lewis actually said on just about every page of this book and believe the best thing readers of it can do is read Lewis for themselves, there is nevertheless justification for a book about Lewis's philosophical views. This justification is that Lewis for the most part did not systematically express his philosophical ideas in his written work, which leaves any reader of that work with the task of having to piece together Lewis's philosophy. What makes this project especially difficult to carry out is the fact that Lewis expressed his philosophical views in different literary genres and non-professional venues and, therefore, often did not write with a degree of exactitude most suitable for a clear and precise expression of them.[4] Over two millennia ago, Aristotle wrote that "precision cannot be expected in the treatment of all subjects alike" (1962, 5 [1094b13]) and therefore "one can demand of a discussion only what the subject matter permits" (1962, 35 [1104a2]). In accordance with Aristotle's point, I can only provide the degree of precision in my exposition of Lewis's ideas that his written work allows. For some claims that I make about what Lewis thought, one can find a statement here or an assertion there that seems to contradict it. This is especially the case with his thought about what most would regard as more theological topics. But one need not conclude that Lewis was a careless thinker. More charitably, one might reasonably hold that because he wrote so many different kinds of works for a broadly educated public, he was willing to sacrifice strict accuracy for readability. Therefore, when reading the vast corpus of Lewis's work with the goal of getting to know his mind, one must avoid fixating on isolated sentences or paragraphs.

Lewis himself once protested that one of his academic critics "judges my books *in vacuo*, with no consideration of the audience to whom they were addressed ... " (1970, 182). I am convinced that when one reads Lewis with a charitable spirit, one can for the most part piece together the contents of a well-developed philosophy of life.[5]

1.5 What Is to Come

So where does one begin explaining the philosophical mind of C. S. Lewis? Lewis would have told us to begin with thought and reason. We have already seen that he insisted his conversion to Christianity was philosophical in nature. "I came to it chiefly by Reason ... " (Lewis 2004b, 189). While he was well aware that Christianity undoubtedly included those who "had danced and sung and sacrificed and trembled and adored," it ultimately was acceptable because "the intellect ... " serves as "our guide" (Lewis 1955, 235). The importance for Lewis of the fact that *we*, as *distinct individuals*, are intellects who think, know, and reason cannot be overemphasized. This fact will shed light on so many of the other issues discussed in this book. As Lewis wrote to Leo Baker in the letter quoted above, "to me the Self, as really existing, seems involved in everything we think ... [A]s you know, I always have to ask 'who thinks?'" (2004a, 567). I turn to Chapter 2 to Lewis's treatment of the self which thinks, knows, and reasons.

notes

1 Though Lewis won a scholarship to University College, he had known before taking the scholarship exam that much was at stake in terms of his future livelihood: "I knew very well by now that there was hardly any position in the world save that of a don in which I was fitted to earn a living, and that I was staking everything on a game in which few won and hundreds lost" (Lewis 1955, 183).
2 Though, strictly speaking, "theism" is a genus of which "monotheism" and "polytheism" are species, I will use "theism" to mean "monotheism."
3 Excellent books on the Inklings include Carpenter (1997); Duriez (2015); and Zaleski and Zaleski (2015).
4 Other writers on Lewis are well aware of the problem. Gilbert Meilaender says that

> anyone attempting to write systematically about Lewis' thought faces the great difficulty of coping with the many genres in which Lewis expresses his ideas. He writes theological treatises, short essays on a variety of topics, science fiction and fantasy, children's stories, myth, and literary criticism. (1998, 3)

Interestingly, Meilaender does not list philosophy as one of the genres in which Lewis wrote. I believe this is evidence of the fact that too few have appreciated Lewis as a philosopher.

5   One who does appreciate Lewis as a philosopher is Adam Barkman, and he knows all too well how it is sometimes difficult to piece together Lewis's philosophical thought. For example, Barkman notes how Lewis both seems to embrace and reject the metaphysical categories of substance and accidents, things and qualities. He comments that

> I believe that the answer to these apparent inconsistencies is to be found in *how* Lewis is read ... Thus, in all likelihood, Lewis the philosopher accepted something like the distinction between substance and accident, but Lewis the poet or Lewis the lay pastor rejected it ... (Barkman 2009, 252)

In other words, when reading Lewis, one must pay particular attention to the genre and not be overly concerned with apparent inconsistencies. When one does this, it is possible to get a reasonable sense of what he thought.

the thinking, reasoning, and sensing soul

Yet men go out and gaze in astonishment at high mountains, the huge waves of the sea, the broad reaches of rivers, the ocean that encircles the world, or the stars in their courses. But they pay no attention to themselves.

(Augustine 1961, X. 8; 216)

Aggravate that most useful human characteristic, the horror and neglect of the obvious.

(Lewis 1961b, 16)

2.1 The *Aboutness* of Thought

C. S. Lewis wrote of Edmund Spenser that he "thought … man's nature was given, discoverable, and discovered … " (Lewis 1954, 392). When Lewis introduced the medieval love poem, *The Romance of the Rose*, he described the author Guillaume de Lorris as depicting allegorically "the realities he knows best" (Lewis 1936, 115), which were the thoughts and passions of the "inner world" of the lover. Lewis shared Spenser's and de Lorris's view about our knowledge of ourselves. Indeed, he wrote:

[T]here is one thing, and only one, in the whole universe which we know more about than we could learn from external observation. That one thing is Man. We do not merely observe men, we *are* men. In this case we have, so to speak, inside information; we are in the know. (2001b, 23)

One thing Lewis believed we know about ourselves is that we have thoughts. That we have thoughts is obvious to us because our thoughts are "directly present" (Lewis 2001f, 21) to us in the temporal *now*: "in it alone we perceive, will, enjoy, and suffer [as well as think]" (Lewis 2013b, 203). One thing we know about our thoughts is that they possess the

C. S. Lewis, First Edition. Stewart Goetz.
© 2018 John Wiley & Sons, Inc. Published 2018 by John Wiley & Sons, Inc.

characteristic of *aboutness*. That is, our thoughts are *about* or *refer to* things: "Acts of thinking are … a very special sort of events. They are 'about' something [typically, but not necessarily] other than themselves … " (Lewis 2001c, 25). What our thoughts are often about are objects and events in the world: e.g., a tree, its felling, an automobile, and, perhaps, their relationships to each other—the automobile hitting and damaging the tree so that it must be cut down. Philosophers sometimes refer to the aboutness of our thoughts as the *intentionality* of thought. Thought is intentional insofar as it *represents* or depicts objects by means of its *content*, where the content can be true or false. For example, if one thinks that C. S. Lewis was born in 1898, the content of one's thought is "C. S. Lewis was born in 1898," which accurately represents the year of Lewis's birth. In addition to thinking that C. S. Lewis was born in 1898, one can also *believe* this was the case (thought and belief are different because one can entertain the thought that C. S. Lewis was born in 1898 without believing that he was). Thinking and believing are what philosophers refer to as *attitudes* toward propositions (or sentences) like "C. S. Lewis was born in 1898," so that a propositional attitude is about things in the world (in this case, the birth of C. S. Lewis) by means of its content. Other propositional attitudes with aboutness are hopes, fears, desires, etc. Lewis wrote, "[t]he silence of the eternal spaces terrified Pascal … " (1970, 41). Pascal thought about (he had an attitude toward) a proposition ("The eternal spaces are silent") and he was terrified. Hopes, fears, and desires are different from thoughts and beliefs insofar as they are not true or false. Why they are not true or false is an issue that would take us too far afield relative to the purpose of this chapter to discuss.

Lewis believed that our thought is *inherently* about things. Because it is, we are able to construct *derivative* forms of aboutness that represent things. Lewis used art to illustrate his point:

> The problem here is to represent a three-dimensional world on a flat sheet of paper. The solution is perspective, and perspective means that we must give more than one value to a two-dimensional shape. Thus in a drawing of a cube, we use an acute angle to represent what is a right angle in the real world. But elsewhere an acute angle on the paper may represent what was already an acute angle in the real world, for example, the point of a spear or the gable of a house … [W]e understand pictures only because we know and inhabit the three-dimensional world. If we can imagine a creature who perceived only two dimensions and yet could somehow be aware of the lines as he crawled over them on the paper, we shall easily see how impossible it would be for him to understand … [W]hen we pointed to the lines on the paper and tried to explain, say, that "this is a road," would he not reply that the shape which we were asking him to accept as a revelation of our mysterious other world was the very same shape which, on our own showing, elsewhere meant nothing but a triangle? (2001g, 99–100, 101)

So certain marks on paper can be about or represent things because our thoughts are first about those things, and in light of our thoughts, we make the marks to do their representative work. While individual acts of thinking are often about things in the world other than themselves, they can also be about themselves. For example, I can think about my thought about the weather. According to Lewis, because "a complete philosophy must get in *all* the facts ... one of the facts total thought must think about is Thinking itself" (2001c, 65). And Lewis believed that when we think about thought itself, it is clear to us that our thoughts are not material or physical (Lewis used the terms interchangeably), because "physical events, as such, cannot in any intelligible sense be said to be [inherently] 'about' or to 'refer to' anything" (1964, 166). "[T]o talk of one bit of matter as being [inherently] true about another bit of matter seems to me to be nonsense" (1967, 64).[1]

Lewis, then, was convinced that the aboutness of thought (and other propositional attitudes) makes clear to us the existence of that which is not material in nature. One might ask what it is that makes something material in nature, beyond the fact that it lacks the property or feature of being about anything. Lewis believed this is a hard question to answer, in part, because we are far more familiar with the nature of thought than we are with the nature of what is material:

> In saying that thinking is not matter I am not suggesting that there is anything mysterious about it. In one sense, thinking is the simplest thing in the world. We do it all day long. We know what it is like far better than we know what matter is like. Thought is what we start from: the simple, intimate, immediate *datum*. Matter is the ... mystery. (1967, 64)

Lewis liked to remind his readers that physicists themselves cannot tell us what the material world is really like, beyond informing us about its mathematical properties: "[T]he mathematics may be true about the reality, but it can hardly be the reality itself, any more than contour lines [on a map] are real mountains" (1967, 170). And again,

> [m]any of you have no doubt read Jeans or Eddington. What they do when they want to explain the atom, or something of that sort, is to give you a description out of which you can make a mental picture. But then they warn you that this picture is not what the scientists actually believe. What the scientists believe is a mathematical formula. The pictures are there only to help you to understand the formula. They are not really true in the way the formula is; they do not give you the real thing but only something more or less like it. They are only meant to help, and if they do not help you can drop them. The thing itself cannot be pictured, it can only be expressed mathematically. (2001b, 54–5)

Though Lewis was convinced we know less about the nature of that which is material than we do about the nature of thought, he was well aware that many not only maintained the opposite but also insisted that thought, even if at present we do not see how, must itself be something material in nature. Lewis regarded this philosophical *materialism* as "nonsense, for if [it were] so, that [philosophy] itself would be merely a movement, an event among atoms, which may have speed and direction, but of which it would be meaningless to use the words 'true' or 'false'" (2001g, 103).

Why, then, one might ask, would anyone believe in the truth of materialism, if the aboutness of thought in and of itself falsifies it? Lewis wondered too, in part because he believed another feature of ourselves, namely, our reasoning, which involves thought with its aboutness, was problematic for materialism. This additional characteristic, which Lewis considered in his treatment of the philosophical theory called "naturalism," is the subject of the next section.

2.2 Reasoning and the Falsity of Naturalism

Lewis sometimes distinguished between reason as *intellectus* and reason as *ratio*:

> We are enjoying *intellectus* when we "just see" a self-evident truth; we are exercising *ratio* when we proceed step by step to prove a truth which is not self-evident ... When *ratio* is used with this precision and distinguished from *intellectus*, it is ... very much what we mean by "reason" today ... (Lewis 1964, 157–8)

In this section, I focus on Lewis's treatment of *ratio*, which he referred to as "the connecting by inference of propositions [contents] ... with further propositions ... " (Lewis 2001d, 31). Connecting contents by inference is a change, transition, or movement that occurs when we apprehend (grasp, see, or know) certain contents and their connections with other contents. For example, we experience the relevant inferential movement from awareness of "If the train is late, then I will have to change my schedule" and "The train is late" to awareness of "I will have to change my schedule," and we say that we *infer* the third proposition from the first two. Like Lewis, I will often refer to reason in the sense of making inferences as *reasoning*.

Lewis believed that reasoning, like thought, is something directly present to us. He placed much stock in reasoning because he believed one could not put much stock in anything else without first putting it in reasoning. In particular, he argued that one cannot reason against putting stock in reasoning without drawing upon the stock one already has in reasoning. In his view, one must simply acknowledge that we reason, and any view of reality that implies that we do not reason is indefensible and unacceptable from the get-go.

Though Lewis stressed the importance of reasoning, he recognized that some disregard or dismiss its significance. He recounted a time when

> in argument with an intelligent man I [had] pointed out that the posi-tion he took up would logically involve a denial of the validity of thought, and he ... understood, and agreed with me, but [did not regard] this as any objection to his original position. He accept[ed] without dis-may the conclusion that all our thoughts are invalid. (1986a, 65–6)

But Lewis also knew that many people claimed to reason their way to the philosophical views they held, and they regarded the fact that their views were so reasoned as validation of their truth. One such view was the philosophical position known as "naturalism," and Lewis used it as his target to set forth his views about the status of reasoning.

Some of Lewis's readers in his own day undoubtedly asked "What is naturalism?" More than a few readers of this book will probably ask the same question. Before explaining Lewis's understanding of it, I must stress that the majority of philosophers today are, as they were in Lewis's day, naturalists. For example, the philosopher Timothy Williamson (2011) writes that "[m]any contemporary philosophers describe them-selves as naturalists." Another philosopher, Barry Stroud, states that "'Naturalism' seems to me ... rather like 'World Peace.' Almost everyone swears allegiance to it, and is willing to march under its banner" (2004, 22). And the philosopher Peter van Inwagen acknowledges that "Naturalism was a popular doctrine (popular among scientifically minded philosophers and philosophically minded scientists) in the 1940s when Lewis devised his argument against it, and it is if anything even more popular today" (2011, 28).

So, what is naturalism? According to Williamson (2011), naturalists "believe something like this: there is only the natural world ..." But what is the natural world? Lewis thought that to have a view about what it is, one must have a concept of nature. But "you cannot have [that] concept until you have begun to abstract" (Lewis 1964, 38) and, like the pre-Socratic philosophers of Greece, classify "the great variety of phenomena which surrounds us ... under a name [so that it can be] talked about as a single object" (Lewis 1964, 37). According to Lewis, when the naturalist thinks abstractly about the natural world as a single object, he comes to think of it as a connected material (physical) *system*. For the naturalist, then, "nature" means "the system of events in space-time governed by interlocking laws ..." (Lewis 1970, 133), where this system makes up *everything* or *all* that there is: "*Nature* means to him [a naturalist] merely 'everything' or 'the whole show' or 'whatever there is'" (Lewis 2001c, 6). Because nature is the whole show, whatever happens in it is "an inevitable result of the character of the whole system" (Lewis 2001c, 15). So naturalism is the view that whatever happens in the material world, which is the only world, must ultimately be explicable exclusively in terms of that which is material in nature. When all is said and done in terms of the explanatory story, one must not, and never need, go outside the material series of events to explain what happens in that series of events. For any event in the material world, to the extent that it is explicable, the explanation of it must be in terms of other material events. The material world is, in naturalist language, *causally closed* to or excludes any explanation that is not material in nature.

To illustrate an implication of naturalism for the explanation of what happens in this world, consider the epigraph of the Introduction, which is from Lewis's (1942) book, *A Preface to Paradise Lost*. Lewis stated that the first qualification for judging any piece of workmanship from a corkscrew to a cathedral is to know *what* it is for. Of course, Lewis's statement presupposes that pieces of workmanship like corkscrews and cathedrals are artefacts whose existences are adequately explained in terms of *purposes*.

Here, it is helpful to reflect briefly on my typing of these sentences (I will discuss this issue at much greater length in Chapter 5). The movements of my fingers on the keyboard are events in the material world, and one might think that they are ultimately (finally, or, in the end) adequately explained by the purpose that I have for writing this book, which is that I inform you, the reader, about the philosophical thought of C. S. Lewis. Lewis put the point as follows:

> Every object you see before you at this moment—the walls, ceiling, and furniture, the book, your own washed hands and cut fingernails, bears witness to the colonisation of Nature by Reason: for none of this matter would have been in these states if Nature had had her way. (2001c, 39)

These arrangements of matter, including the present movements of my fingers, are all ultimately explained in terms of purposes. However, *if* naturalism is true, these arrangements ultimately cannot be explained in this way. They ultimately cannot be explained in this way because a purpose is something *mental* in nature (for something to be mental in nature just is for it to have aboutness) and, thereby, psychological in nature, where the psychological is regarded by many philosophers as a genus that divides into mental and nonmental species (examples of the latter are pleasures and pains, which are intrinsically not about anything). But, according to naturalism, any material event (the movements of my fingers in typing this manuscript, which are events in this world) must ultimately be completely explicable in terms of other material (non-psychological) events. The following is the naturalist Alex Rosenberg's statement of this implication of naturalism:

> Our conscious thoughts are very crude indicators of what is going on in our brain. We fool ourselves into treating these conscious markers as thoughts about what we want and about how to achieve it, about plans and purposes. We are even tricked into thinking they somehow bring about behavior. We are mistaken about all of these things ... You cannot treat the interpretation of behavior in terms of purposes and meaning as conveying real understanding ... [T]he individual acts of human beings [are] unguided by purpose ... What individuals do, alone or together, over a moment or a month or a lifetime, is really just the product of the process of blind variation and environmental filtration operating on neural circuits in their heads. (2011a, 210, 213, 244, 255)

According to Rosenberg, real (correct) understanding (which, Lewis would have interjected, seems to be something mental in nature) of our behavior must be explanations that do not include what is mental in nature. The naturalist Richard Rorty agrees with Rosenberg, and provides the following concise summary of the implications of naturalism:

> Every speech, thought, theory, poem, composition and philosophy will turn out to be completely predictable in purely naturalistic terms. Some atoms-and-the-void account of micro-processes within individual human beings will permit the prediction of every sound or inscription which will ever be uttered. (1979, 387)

And here is what one other naturalist, David Papineau, has to say about explaining events in the material world:

> We may not know enough about physics to know exactly what a complete "physics" might include. But as long as we are confident that, whatever it includes, it will have no ineliminable need for any distinctively mental categorizations, we can be confident that mental properties must be identical with (or realized by) certain non-mentally identifiable properties. (2002, 41)

And

> When I say that a complete physics excludes psychology, and that psychological antecedents are therefore never needed to explain physical effects, the emphasis here is on "needed". I am quite happy to allow that psychological categories *can* be used to explain physical effects, as when I tell you that my arm rose because I wanted to lift it. My claim is only that in all such cases an alternative specification of a sufficient antecedent, which does not mention psychological categories, will also be available. (1993, 31, n. 26)

As I discussed in the first section of this chapter, Lewis believed that the aboutness of thought makes it immaterial in nature, and the naturalists whom I have just quoted confirm Lewis's conception of things insofar as they think of the nature of the material (physical) as that which is non-mental and non-psychological. But our focus now is on the implications of naturalism for explaining our reasoning, where our reasoning is something that is part of the "whole show," "everything," or "whatever there is." According to the naturalist, Georges Rey, one significant implication is the following:

> Any ultimate explanation of mental phenomena will have to be in *non-mental* terms, or else it won't be an *explanation* of it. There might be an explanation of some mental phenomena in terms of others—perhaps *hope* in terms of *belief* and *desire*—but if we are to provide an explanation of all mental phenomena, we would in turn have to explain such mentalistic explainers until finally we reached entirely non-mental terms. (1997, 21)

Lewis believed that a view like naturalism, which implies that a mental phenomenon like reasoning must and will ultimately be entirely explicable in nonmental and non-psychological terms,[2] "is really a theory that there is no reasoning" (Lewis 2001c, 27). Or, stated slightly differently, Lewis was convinced that if naturalism is true, then "what we thought to be our inferences" (2001c, 32) are not. The following was his argument against naturalism: When we reason, we are passive. We are patients. What this means is that when we are aware of, apprehend, or understand "If the train is late, then I will have to change my schedule" and "The train is late," we cannot help being aware of, apprehending, or understanding and inferring "I will have to change my schedule." We cannot help inferring this because we are *causally determined* to infer it; one event of awareness causes another. We do not choose to infer what we do because we cannot help inferring it. Given the one apprehension, the other will follow, whether we like it or not: "I am quite convinced that my acts of thought ... are not free but determined. E.g. if the truths A > B and B > C are both present to my mind I *must* think A > C. I have no choice" (Lewis 2007, 1351).[3] In short, when we reason there is mental-to-mental explanation in the form of awareness-to-awareness causation, and this causation is not reducible to (cannot be rightly stated in terms of) either non-awareness (material)-to-awareness causation or non-awareness (material)-to-non-awareness (material) causation.

One other illustration of Lewis's point about the nature of reasoning should suffice. Those who teach formal logic often begin with the inference rule known as *modus ponens*, which is as follows: From if A then B, and A, it follows that B. Lewis held that if one grasps If A then B, and A, one cannot help but believe that B follows. One cannot help but believe that B follows from If A then B, and A, because awareness of the latter causes the belief that B follows from them.

"But do we not sometimes reason wrongly?" one might ask. Lewis acknowledged that we sometimes reason incorrectly, and held that when we do, a belief in a conclusion has a mental cause other than apprehensions of contents of premises and an inference rule that support the belief: "To be caused is not to be proved" (Lewis 2001c, 24). Lewis cited prejudice and wishful thinking as examples of mental causes that do not justify beliefs. In more complicated inferential sequences, misremembering what came before can cause the arrival at a wrong conclusion. And the attention and apprehension required for reasoning well might be interrupted by a loud explosion, a desire to get a cup of tea, or fatigue, so that no conclusion is reached. Lewis claimed only that *if* one successfully attends to and apprehends A > B and B > C, then one will be causally determined by that apprehension to apprehend A > C. Moreover, it seems he would have regarded the purpose of teaching a logical rule like *modus ponens* as that of getting a student to attend to and apprehend the nature of the connective "If A then B." Once a student understands it and apprehends A, he must conclude B.

According to Lewis, then, apprehensions (Lewis also refers to them as graspings, seeings, knowings, perceivings, understandings) and believings are all mental events: they are events with aboutness and contents. So when one event of apprehending causes another, there is mental-to-mental causation. But this is precisely the kind of explanation that naturalism declares is impossible. Hence, Lewis concluded, naturalism must be false, because it is a philosophical view that entails that there is no reasoning:

> Any thing which professes to explain our reasoning fully without introducing an act of knowing thus solely determined by what is known, is really a theory that there is no reasoning.

> But this, as it seems to me, is what Naturalism is bound to do. It offers what professes to be a full account of our mental behaviour; but this account, on inspection, leaves no room for the acts of knowing or insight on which the whole value of our thinking, as a means to truth, depends. (Lewis 2001c, 27)

Given naturalism's popularity, Lewis's "argument from reason" against it was bound to receive scrutiny. One of the most well-known objections to it was put forth in 1948 by the young non-naturalist philosopher Elizabeth Anscombe at a meeting of the Oxford Socratic Club of which Lewis was the president. Anscombe wrote that, according to Lewis:

> [O]n [the naturalistic] hypothesis there would be no difference between the conclusions of the finest scientific reasoning and the thoughts a

man has because a bit of bone is pressing on his brain. In one way, this is true. Suppose that the kind of account which the "naturalist" imagines, were actually given in the two cases. We should have two accounts [explanations] of processes in the human organism. "Valid", "true", "false" would not come into either of the accounts. That shows, you say, that the conclusions of the scientist would be just as irrational as those of the other man. But that does not follow at all. Whether his conclusions are rational or irrational is settled by considering the chain of reasoning that he gives and whether his conclusions follow from it. When we are giving a causal account of this thought, e.g. an account of the physiological processes which issue in the utterance of his reasoning, we are not considering his utterances from the point of view of evidence, reasoning, valid argument, truth, at all; we are considering them merely as events. Just *because* that is how we are considering them, our description has in itself no bearing on the question of "valid", "invalid", "rational", "irrational", and so on. (1981, 226–7)[4]

In her reply to Lewis's argument, Anscombe distinguished between validity and invalidity as features of logical relations between propositions (what Lewis referred to as ground-consequent relationships)—what are sometimes called forms of argument, e.g., *modus ponens*, and a particular occurrence of reasoning that moves from an awareness of If P then Q, and P, to a particular awareness of Q. An explanation of the particular instance of awareness of Q in the reasoning process is, unlike the explanation of the relationship of the conclusion Q to the premises If P then Q, and P in the argument form *modus ponens*, causal in nature. That is, there is a causal relationship that occurs in time between an awareness of If P then Q, and P, and an awareness of Q that tracks or maps the non-temporal logical relationship.

Lewis believed Anscombe's rejoinder to his argument assumed a position on the very question at issue, which was whether or not all causation is physical in nature. He believed she simply took for granted that when giving a causal account of the relationship between instances of awareness in a process of reasoning, one is giving an account in terms of physiological (physical) processes. But, he insisted, that is what is being disputed. Lewis agreed with Anscombe that reasoning involves causation, but because the causation is between events of awareness, apprehension, seeing, or understanding, it is not physical but mental in nature.[5] Here is Lewis's statement of the issue:

[A]cts of inference can, and must, be considered in two different lights. On the one hand they are subjective events, items in somebody's psychological history. On the other hand, they are insights into, or knowings of, something [e.g., argument forms] other than themselves. What from the first point of view is the psychological transition from thought A to thought B, at some particular moment in some particular mind, is, from the thinker's point of view a perception of an implication (if A, then B). When we are adopting the psychological point of view we may use the past tense. "B *followed* A in my thoughts." [This is the mental-to-mental cause and effect relation.] But when we assert the implication we always use the present—"B *follows* from A". If it ever "follows from" in the logical sense, it does so always. [This is the ground-consequent relation.] (2001c, 26)

It looks therefore, as if, in order for a train of thought to have any value, these two systems of connection [the cause-effect and the ground-consequent] must apply simultaneously to the same series of mental acts. (Lewis 2001c, 24)[6]

So far, we have seen how Lewis believed that if naturalism were true, then we would not reason. But we know that we reason. Therefore, naturalism must be false because of the apprehension-to-apprehension causation that is involved in reasoning. However, Lewis was convinced that something else is also the case in light of the fact that we reason. What is also the case is that our reasoning alters the physical world. That is, there is mental-to-mental causation which leads to mental-to-physical causation: "Nature (at any rate on the surface of our own planet) is perforated or pock-marked all over by little orifices at each of which something of a different kind from herself—namely reason—can do things to her" (Lewis 2001c, 40). In other words, it is the case that "whenever we think rationally we are, by direct spiritual power, forcing certain atoms in our brain … to do what they would never have done if left to Nature" (Lewis 2001c, 205). Lewis also stated this point about the causal influence of reasoning in terms of our being spirits or souls (more about this in a later section of this chapter):

If we are in fact spirits, not Nature's offspring, then there must be some point (probably the brain) at which created spirit even now can produce effects on matter not by manipulation or technics but simply by the wish to do so. If that is what you mean by Magic then Magic is a reality manifested every time you … think a thought. (2001c, 245)[7]

In response to Lewis's argument, one might try to find a kind of halfway house for reasoning. For example, one might admit thought's reality as irreducibly mental but hold that its occurrence in reasoning is completely determined by physical goings-on. Lewis responded that in this case thought would be "the … irrelevant product of cerebral motions … " (Lewis 1970, 21). At this point, he was fond of citing the following words from J. B. S. Haldane: "If my mental processes are determined wholly by the motions of atoms in my brain, I have no reason to suppose that my beliefs are true … and hence I have no reason for supposing my brain to be composed of atoms" (Lewis 2001c, 22).[8] In other words, to suppose that thought involved in reasoning is really about something but nevertheless completely explicable in terms of material causes would imply that there is no reasoning. I will return briefly to Lewis's belief that thought involved in reasoning cannot be explicable in terms of material causes in Chapter 4 when I discuss his view of epiphenomenalism.

If naturalism has the implications pointed out by Lewis for the mental-to-mental causation involved in reasoning and the mental-to-physical causation that results from it (and given what naturalists themselves say about naturalism, it is difficult to argue that he was creating a false characterization of their understanding of it), why believe naturalism? According to many, if not all, naturalists, a belief in naturalism arises out of and is necessitated by an understanding of the explanatory power of science. For example, Rosenberg (2011b) writes: "[n]aturalism is the philosophical theory that treats science as our most reliable source of knowledge," and Williamson (2011) confirms that naturalists believe "the best way to find out about [the natural world] is by the scientific method." Lewis pointed out that naturalists believe a complete account of our existence can in principle be provided by science in terms of physics, chemistry, biochemistry, and evolutionary biology:

> On the fully naturalistic view all events are determined by laws. Our logical behaviour, in other words, our thoughts … are governed by biochemical laws; these, in turn, by physical laws which are themselves actuarial statements about the lawless movements of matter. These units never intended to produce the regular universe we see: the law of averages … has produced it out of the collision of these random variations in movement. The physical universe never intended to produce organisms. The relevant chemicals on earth, and the sun's heat, thus juxtaposed, gave rise to this disquieting disease of matter: organization. Natural selection, operating on the minute differences between one organism and another, blundered into that sort of phosphorescence or mirage which we call consciousness—and that, in some cortexes beneath some skulls, at certain moments, still in obedience to physical laws, but to physical laws now filtered through laws of a more complicated kind, takes the form we call thought. Such, for instance, is the origin of this paper: such was the origin of Professor Price's paper [to which Lewis was responding]. What we should speak of as his "thoughts" were merely the last link of a causal chain in which all the previous links were irrational. He spoke as he did because the matter of his brain was behaving in a certain way … (1970, 136)

But, responded Lewis, how can one *reason* to a belief in naturalism on the basis of a supposed scientific account of our origins and thought, if naturalism implies there is no reasoning? A belief in naturalism is allegedly arrived at by an occurrence of reasoning that it excludes from explanatory reality. To illustrate his point, Lewis wrote that we infer our belief in evolution from our belief in fossils: e.g., if the skeletal remains of X, Y, and Z vary only slightly and those of Y appear to be intermediate between X and Z, then Z evolved from X through Y; the skeletal remains of X, Y, and Z vary only slightly and those of Y appear to be intermediate between X and Z; therefore, Z evolved from X through Y (cf. Lewis 2001c, 21). Here we have an instance of reasoning in the form of *modus ponens*. Lewis concluded that "[u]nless human reasoning is valid no science can be true" (2001c, 21). But naturalism makes reasoning of any kind impossible. Hence, naturalism makes it impossible to do science.

I will set forth in more detail Lewis's response to naturalism's account of our existence in Chapter 5. At this juncture, one can hear a chorus of antagonists invoking a kind of "X-of-the-gaps" objection. The most common species of this form of objection is the "God-of-the-gaps" argument. Roughly, according to it, it is methodologically impermissible to appeal to God to explain some event in or feature of the material world for which no natural explanation can be discovered. Were such an appeal to be allowed, science might stop seeking a natural explanation of a certain natural phenomenon in light of repeated failures to find such an explanation. And this would inhibit the progress of science. In the case of our reasoning, a proponent of a "mind-of-the-gaps" objection would claim that it is methodologically impermissible to appeal to a mental explanation of a thought or belief in cases where no nonmental (material) explanation can at present be had. Were such an appeal to be allowed, the progress of a brain science like neuroscience would be impeded when it failed in its quest to find the neurological causes of a thought or belief.

Lewis, we can reasonably conclude, would have responded that his argument from reason is *not* a mind-of-the-gaps argument, because we do not *postulate* a mental explanation for the occurrence of a thought or belief arrived at in reasoning on the basis of being unable to find a nonmental explanation of it. On the contrary, he believed that we are in the know about ourselves and, because we are, we are directly aware of the mental causes of the resultant beliefs in instances of reasoning. No postulation here is necessary.

So far, in arguing against naturalism, Lewis assumed we know that we reason: "The naturalist and I both admit this" (Lewis 2001c, 31). And he sought to show that naturalism cannot explain our reasoning as an occurrence within nature. But what if we were in doubt about whether we reason? What if inference "[i]tself [were] on trial" (Lewis 2001c, 32)? Could we seek to establish that we reason by arguing that what "we now call rational thinking or inference must ... have 'evolved' by natural selection, by the gradual weeding out of types less fitted to survive" (Lewis 2001c, 28)? Lewis maintained that we could not, for three reasons.

First, aboutness and the reasoning process that depends upon it are immaterial in nature. The evolutionary process works solely on that which is material in nature. Because it does, and because what is immaterial and what is material in nature have their respective natures (they are what they are) essentially, Lewis insisted it is impossible, through "eliminating responses that were biologically hurtful and multiplying those which tended to survival" (Lewis 2001c, 28), to convert through incremental change what is material in nature into what is immaterial in nature (e.g., a material stimulus-and-response relationship cannot incrementally be changed into an immaterial inferential relationship). To illustrate his point, Lewis distinguished between the idea of sight and knowledge of light, and pointed out that the former cannot be changed into the latter:

> Our physical vision is a far more useful response to light than that of the cruder organisms which have only a photo-sensitive spot. But neither this improvement nor any possible improvements [in sight] we can suppose could bring it an inch nearer to being a knowledge of light. It is admittedly something without which we could not have had that knowledge. But the knowledge is achieved by experiments and inferences from them, not by refinement of the response. It is not men with specially good eyes who know about light, but men who have studied the relevant sciences. (Lewis 2001c, 28–9)

Second, because evolutionary processes, by hypothesis, are part of an interlocked system of blind, nonmental causes which ultimately result in the survival of some entities to the exclusion of others, survival could be achieved by processes that were non-inferential in nature. Hence, Lewis believed that the principle "If useful for survival, then inferential in nature" is false. Thus, he concluded there is no way to establish on the assumption of naturalism and natural selection that human beings would have to get to a point where they made inferences in order to survive. Indeed, naturalists themselves believe that many organisms have survived without ever getting to that point.

Third, Lewis insisted that if the question is genuinely about whether we reason or not, one cannot establish the conclusion that we do reason by *reasoning* from the assumption of naturalism and evolutionary theory. To do that would be to make use of the very thing in question.

Is it, then, impossible to believe naturalism? Lewis thought not, because a belief in its truth (assuming, for the sake of argument, the reality of the aboutness of thought) might be a fluke or accidental effect of material causes, in which case one would find oneself being caused to believe in naturalism without any reasoning (Lewis 2001c, 23). Given that no naturalist considers his belief in naturalism a fluke, Lewis concluded that "the claim of Reasoning to be valid [because ultimately arrived at through the mental-to-mental causation of reasoning] is the only [claim] which the Naturalist cannot [reasonably] deny without (philosophically speaking) cutting his own throat" (2001c, 53). But to accept its validity also amounts to cutting his throat. So, concluded Lewis, there is no "flukeless" way to believe in naturalism.

Lewis's discussion of naturalism makes clear that he fully recognized and appreciated the existence of different philosophical systems or worldviews about which we think and reason. Given our ability to think and reason, we are able to perch ourselves on an intellectual mountaintop and consider the landscape of worldviews below. Lewis tells us in his autobiography *Surprised by Joy* of an important intellectual moment when he read Samuel Alexander's *Space, Time, and Deity* and discovered the author's distinction between "enjoyment" (a term of art for Alexander and not what we typically mean by "enjoyment") and "contemplation." According to Lewis's presentation of Alexander, "[w]hen you see a table you 'enjoy' the act of seeing and 'contemplate' the table. Later, if you took up Optics and thought about Seeing itself, you would be contemplating the seeing and enjoying the thought [about the seeing]" (1955, 217). Similarly, when you grieve the loss of a loved one, you contemplate the one beloved while enjoying the grief. Again,

> [w]e do not "think a thought" in the same sense in which we "think that Herodotus is unreliable." When we think a thought, "thought" is a cognate accusative (like "blow" in "strike a blow"). We enjoy the thought (that Herodotus is unreliable) and, in so doing, contemplate the unreliability of Herodotus. (Lewis 1955, 217–18)

As applied to reasoning about naturalism, the distinction between enjoyment and contemplation yields the following result: When we reason about naturalism, we contemplate naturalism for its truth or falsity and enjoy our reasoning about it. When we think and reason about the nature of our reasoning about naturalism itself and make our reasoning the object of contemplation, we discover that the nature of our reasoning is such that engagement in it is something that itself falsifies naturalism. From what we discover about the nature of reasoning we conclude that naturalism is not capable of refuting anything "except itself" (Lewis 1970, 138).

Lewis argued that when all has been said that can be said about the fact that we reason, we see clearly that we cannot reason against reason. Therefore, he insisted that "[r]eason is our starting point. There can be no question either of attacking or defending it" (Lewis 2001c, 33). Nevertheless, Lewis is sometimes charged with having failed to do what he claimed he would do, which is provide an argument for reason. For example, Peter Schakel writes the following about Lewis's argument from reason:

> It is a tight and carefully articulated argument ... But it too leaves the unavoidable gap, for Lewis does not actually establish in positive terms the existence of reason ... Lewis shows that Naturalism can offer no

substantive arguments against reason; but a negative proof is not the same as a positive one. Thus when he says "If any thought is valid, such a Reason must exist ... ," we are inclined to accept the conditional clause as self-evident, but it has not been proved. (1984, 135–6)

One can sense Lewis would have been thoroughly exasperated at this point. In terms of Schakel's criticism, Lewis would have responded that we *begin* with reason, because any attempt to "establish in positive terms the existence of reason" is an exercise in futility, given that such an attempt would involve the use of reason to establish reason. Given our "inside information about ourselves," we simply know we reason on the grounds that we are directly aware of doing so. Reasoning is our starting point, not an endpoint. Stated slightly differently, it is futile to claim that our reasoning is trustworthy on the grounds of some argument, because any attempt to establish its trustworthiness by argumentation would make use of the ability to reason that is supposedly in question.

Lewis believed that one of the important conclusions that follows from his argument from reason is that an occurrence of reasoning is *supernatural* in nature, because it goes on or occurs outside of and invades nature. The philosopher John Cottingham has recently written that "'[s]upernatural' seems to me a very unsatisfactory term ... One of the problems with 'supernatural' is that it is a kind of blank, a placeholder ... : it purports to classify or inform, but actually tells us little or nothing about the item so described" (2016, 48). Lewis admitted that calling reasoning "supernatural" does "some violence to our ordinary linguistic usage" (2001c, 35). What he meant by calling reasoning "supernatural" was that

> it "won't fit in" [the material causal story]; that such an act ... cannot be merely the exhibition [causal result] at a particular place and time of that total ... system of events called "Nature". It must break sufficiently free from that universal chain in order to be [causally] determined by what it knows. (Lewis 2001c, 35)

Hence, "every instance of human reason is miraculous ... " (Lewis 2001c, 226). Lewis, who early in life aspired to be a poet, enjoyed illustrating the implications of naturalism and, thereby, the meaning of "supernatural," in the following comments about the materialism of the typical modern literary critic:

> [T]he typical modern critic is usually a half-hearted materialist. He accepts, or thinks he accepts, that picture of the world which popularized science gives him. He thinks that everything except the buzzing electrons is subjective fancy; and he therefore believes that all poetry must come out of the poet's head and express (of course) his pure, uncontaminated, undivided "personality", because outside the poet's

head there is nothing but the interplay of blind forces. But he forgets that if materialism is true, there is nothing else inside the poet's head either. (Tillyard and Lewis 1939, 28)

Lewis's mention of what is inside the poet's head makes clear that he thought the term "supernatural" is more than just a blank or placeholder, as Cottingham suggests. Lewis the philosopher maintained "supernatural" positively refers to the psychological nature of events such as thinking, reasoning, experiencing pleasure, and experiencing pain. Hence, while he might have been somewhat sympathetic with Cottingham's claim that a description of God as a supernatural person "is unlikely to do much more for most people than ... conjure up some vague and distinctly unhelpful notion of a ... disembodied spirit" (Cottingham 2016, 48), Lewis was confident that "supernatural" conveyed a great deal of content against the backdrop of philosophical naturalism.

2.3 A Possible Quibble

Lewis believed we know we live in a world that includes what is supernatural in nature, because we know we reason. However, he was well aware that for "some people the great trouble about any argument for the Supernatural is simply the fact that argument should be needed at all. If so stupendous a thing exists, ought it not to be obvious as the sun in the sky?" (Lewis 2001c, 63). And if it is that obvious, are not arguments against naturalism really wasted effort? Lewis believed they were not, for two reasons.

First, Lewis thought it was important to keep clear the distinction between science and naturalism. The former is a kind of empirical human inquiry that when used properly is of great value for mastering nature and improving the quality of our lives. The latter is a philosophical view that takes the material causal explanatory categories of the former and insists that they are applicable to anything and everything, even to things to which they are not suited. When "the 'scientific' habit of mind" (Lewis 2001c, 66), which, since the sixteenth century, has been used to understand and master nature, is wrongly extended into the domain of reasoning, we end up eliminating reasoning itself. When this happens, all is lost:

> [Naturalism] goes on claiming territory after territory: first the inorganic, then the lower organisms, then man's body, then his emotions. But when it takes the final step and we attempt a naturalistic account of thought itself, suddenly the whole thing unravels. The last fatal step has invalidated all the preceding ones: for they were all reasonings and reason itself has been discredited. (Lewis 1970, 138)

Second, Lewis believed it was important to make clear that in light of the naturalist's blindness to and/or denial of the nature of reasoning and the kind of explanation that genuinely accounts for it, we should not be surprised that the naturalist has "forgotten the evidence for the Supernatural" (Lewis 2001c, 66). After all, forgetfulness of what is most obvious is part and parcel of the human condition:

> When you are looking at a garden from a room upstairs it is obvious (once you think about it) that you are looking through a window. But if it is the garden that interests you, you may look at it for a long time without thinking of the window. When you are reading a book it is obvious (once you attend to it) that you are using your eyes: but unless your eyes begin to hurt you, or the book is a text on optics, you may read all evening without once thinking of eyes ...

> All these instances show that the fact which is in one respect the most obvious and primary fact, and through which alone you have access to all the other facts, may be precisely the one that is most easily forgotten—forgotten not because it is so remote or abstruse but because it is so near and so obvious. And this is exactly how the Supernatural has been forgotten. The Naturalists have been engaged in thinking about Nature. They have not attended to the fact that they were *thinking* ... The Supernatural is not remote and abstruse: it is a matter of daily and hourly experience, as intimate as breathing. Denial of it depends on a certain absent-mindedness. But this absent-mindedness is in no way surprising. (Lewis 2001c, 63–5)

2.4 Caveat: Bulverism

Lewis believed what is obvious is too easily overlooked and forgotten, so we should not be surprised that naturalists are blind to the supernatural nature of reasoning. But Lewis was also aware that not all naturalists are simply absent-minded and forgetful. Some muster arguments against belief in the reality of the supernatural. I will present them and what Lewis would likely have said in response in Chapter 5. Other naturalists reject anything supernatural without argument. Lewis was particularly concerned with those who resorted to a "you-only-say-that-because ... " kind of position. Examples in Lewis's day were Freudians, who might say that those who believed Queen Elizabeth I was a great queen did so because they had a mother complex, and Marxists, who might maintain that those who supported capitalism did so because they were all members of the bourgeoisie who profited from a policy of laissez-faire. In other words, the views of those who supported the Queen and of those who believed in capitalism were allegedly false because of their causal source. The beliefs were mentally caused, but they had the wrong kind of mental cause, and thus were irrational. When it came to Christianity, Lewis wrote, "I see my religion dismissed on the grounds that the 'comfortable parson had every reason for assuring the nineteenth century worker that poverty would be rewarded in another world'" (1970, 273). Lewis encountered this "you-say-that-because … " riposte so often that he concluded he had to invent a name for it. "I call it Bulverism" (1970, 273).

Lewis claimed there are two fundamental problems with Bulverism. First, it "is a truly democratic game in the sense that all can play it all day long … " (1970, 273). Thus, Lewis could have come back at his opponent's Bulveristic dismissal of the parson's religion with his own Bulveristic charge that his opponent dismissed the parson's religion because he (the opponent) wanted to live without accountability to God. Similarly, the Marxist could have been Bulveristically told that he believed what he did because he wanted a piece of the estate-owner's fortune without having to work for it. Lewis believed that to elevate discussion to a higher level, a level that involved reasoning, the Bulverizer would have to maintain "that some thoughts are tainted and others are not---which has the advantage . . . of being what every sane man has always believed. But if that is so, we must then ask how you find out which are tainted and which are not" (Lewis 1970, 272). And the only way to find out which, if any, are tainted would be

[to] find out on purely logical grounds which of them do, in fact, break down as arguments. Afterwards, if you like, [you may] go on and discover the psychological causes of the error. In other words, you must show *that* a man is wrong before you start explaining *why* he is wrong. (Lewis 1970, 273)

So, according to Lewis, the Bulverizer has it backwards: he first assumes without argument that his opponent is wrong and then distracts the attention of his opponent and others who might be listening by allegedly explaining what the causes of the ridiculously mistaken belief are, all the while hoping that no one else wants to play the game with him. Regardless of whether others catch on to the Bulverizer's *modus operandi*, Lewis made it clear what he thought of the Bulverizer's method: "Any man would much rather be called names than proved wrong" (Lewis 2007, 1232).

But Lewis believed there is a second problem with Bulverism: "You must reason even to Bulverize" (Lewis 1970, 274). Here, I think Lewis thought the Bulverizer had to be engaged in some form of reasoning like the following: If person P says X because he is a member of group M, then what P says is discredited; P says X because he is a member of M; therefore, what P says is discredited. So Lewis held that in the end Bulverizing is parasitic on reasoning in the sense that the Bulverizer can only engage in his *ad hominem* practice in light of having first reasoned about how to discredit the position of his opponent.

2.5 First- and Third-Person Points of View

So far, I have explained how Lewis believed the aboutness of thought and the nature of reasoning falsify naturalism and the materialism it typically presupposes. He was persuaded that there is yet another way of making clear that materialism is false. This way makes use of the distinction between the first-person point of view, that of the subject or "I" of experience, and the third-person point of view, that of the external observer. To elucidate the difference between these two perspectives, he wrote "Meditation in a Toolshed" in which he recounted an experience from his own life:

> I was standing today in the dark toolshed. The sun was shining outside and through the crack at the top of the door there came a sunbeam. From where I stood that beam of light, with the specks of dust floating in it, was the most striking thing in the place. Everything else was almost pitch-black. I was seeing the beam, not seeing things by it.
>
> Then I moved, so that the beam fell on my eyes. Instantly the whole previous picture vanished. I saw no toolshed, and (above all) no beam. Instead I saw, framed in the irregular cranny at the top of the door, green leaves moving on the branches of a tree outside and beyond that, 90 odd million miles away, the sun. Looking along the beam [the latter experience], and looking at the beam [the former experience] are very different experiences. (Lewis 1970, 212)

With the distinction between looking along and looking at having been made, where looking along and looking at are respectively Alexander's enjoyment and contemplation (see Feinendegen and Smilde 2015, 22–3), Lewis considered what it is like to experience pain:

> A physiologist … can study pain and find out that it "is" (whatever *is* means) such and such neural events. But the word *pain* would have no meaning for him unless he had "been inside" by actually suffering. If he had never looked *along* pain he simply wouldn't know what he was looking *at*. The very subject for his inquiries from outside exists for him only because he has, at least once, been inside. (1970, 214)

Edward Dell wrote a letter to Lewis in which he asked what Lewis meant by "experience." Lewis responded:

> [B]y *experience* I mean "That part or result of any event which is presented to consciousness". Thus in a Toothache the total event is a complex physiological, bio-chemical, and (in the long run) atomic event: what is presented to consciousness, i.e. the *Pain*, I call an *experience*. (2004b, 928–9)

Lewis believed the physiologist can study neural events and learn about the correlations between them and experiences of pain from the third-person perspective (he can look at pain) only because he has experienced pain from the first-person perspective (he has looked along pain). Lewis made the same point about correlation with regard to neural events and thoughts, and emphasized that when we are looking along thought, we are attentive to events that are different from those that are looked at:

> The cerebral physiologist may say, if he chooses, that the mathematician's thought is "only" tiny physical movements of the grey matter. But then what about the cerebral physiologist's own thought at that very moment? A second physiologist, looking at it, could pronounce it also to be only tiny physical movements in the first physiologist's skull. Where is the rot to end?

> The answer is that we must never allow the rot to begin. We must, on pain of idiocy, deny from the very outset the idea that looking *at* is, by its own nature, intrinsically truer or better than looking *along*. (Lewis 1970, 215)

Lewis held that what a physiologist sees when looking at a mathematician's brain is not the thought that the mathematician looks along. The events looked at and along are *correlated but not identical* with each other. However, at some point, causal interaction between the two occurs. An instance of one kind of event produces an instance of the other:

> All sorts of things are, in fact, doing just what the actor does when he comes through the wings. Photons or waves (or whatever it is) come towards us from the sun through space. They are, in a scientific sense, "light". But as they enter the air they become "light" in a different sense: what ordinary people call *sunlight* or *day*, the bubble of blue or grey or greenish luminosity in which we walk about and see. Day is thus a kind of stage set.

> Other waves (this time, of air) reach my eardrum and travel up a nerve and tickle my brain. All this is behind the scenes; as soundless as the whitewashed passages are undramatic. Then somehow (I've never seen it explained) they step on the stage (no one can tell me *where* this stage is) and become, say, a friend's voice or the *Ninth Symphony*. Or, of course, my neighbor's wireless—the actor may come on stage to play a driveling part in a bad play. But there is always the transformation.

> Biological needs, producing, or stimulated by, temporary physiological states, climb into a young man's brain, pass on to the mysterious stage and appear as "Love" ... (Lewis 1970, 247–8)

It is appropriate to draw this brief section to a close by making clear that the points Lewis made decades ago about the nature of thought and pain and the differences between looking along and looking at are now the bread and butter of a family of contemporary philosophical arguments confronting materialism/physicalism. For example, David Chalmers, who writes that "we are surer of the existence of conscious experience than we are of anything else in the world" (1996, xii; recall Lewis's assertion that we know what thought is like far better than we know what matter is like), claims that there is no way to overcome the "hard problem" of consciousness, which is the problem of explaining how and why physical processes are accompanied by qualitative experience: "We have good reason to believe that consciousness arises from physical systems such as brains, but we have little idea how it arises ... " (Chalmers 1996, xi). Joseph Levine is well known among contemporary philosophers for posing the problem of the explanatory gap: there is no explanation for how a physical event like the firing of C-fibers gives rise to the experience of pain, with the result that we can conceive of C-fibers firing without experiencing pain, and vice versa (Levine 2001; 2002). And Frank Jackson's "Mary Argument" describes a situation in which a brilliant female scientist confined to a black and white room learns everything there is to know about the neurophysiology of vision and then is released to experience the world outside with its red roses and blue sky:

> Will she *learn* anything or not? It seems just obvious that she will learn something about the world and our visual experience of it. But then it is inescapable that her previous knowledge was incomplete. But she had *all* the physical information. Ergo there is more to have than that, and Physicalism is false. (Jackson 2002, 275)

What these contemporary philosophers focus on in their arguments was on the radar of C. S. Lewis many decades earlier.

2.6 The Soul

According to Lewis, sound, in the scientific sense of waves in motion, somehow, through physical–to-mental causation, steps on to the stage as a friend's voice or the *Ninth Symphony* of Beethoven. Lewis believed the "stage" is the soul, and the distinction between a soul and a material body provides the basis for what philosophers term soul-body or mind-body "substance dualism," or simply "dualism." One of Lewis's colleagues at Magdalen College, Oxford, was the philosopher Gilbert Ryle, who was well known for his book *The Concept of Mind* in which he argued with "deliberate abusiveness" that belief in "the dogma of the Ghost [the soul] in the Machine [the body]" is a philosophical mistake (1949, 15–16). The well-known contemporary naturalistic philosopher Daniel Dennett, who was a student of Ryle's, has continued his mentor's assault against the truth of dualism by attacking the idea of the "Cartesian Theater" (Dennett 1991, 17). Lewis was well aware of the philosophical climate of his day and its hostility to dualism. He believed it was the culmination of a centuries-long and much bigger project to disenchant the world:

> At the outset the universe appears packed with will, intelligence, life and positive qualities; every tree is a nymph and every planet a god. Man himself is akin to the gods. The advance of knowledge gradually empties this rich and genial universe: first of the gods, then of its colours, smells, sounds and tastes, finally of solidity itself as solidity was originally imagined. As these items are taken from the world, they are transferred to the subjective side of the account: classified as our sensations, thoughts, images or emotions. The Subject becomes gorged, inflated, at the expense of the Object. But the matter does not rest there. The same method which has emptied the world now proceeds to empty ourselves. The masters of the method soon announce that we were just as mistaken (and mistaken in much the same way) when we attributed "souls", or "selves" or "minds" to human organisms, as when we attributed Dryads to the trees. Animism, apparently, begins at home. We, who have personified all other things, turn out to be ourselves mere personifications. Man is indeed akin to the gods: that is, he is no less phantasmal than they. (Lewis 1986a, 81–2)

Lewis responded to the disenchantment project that "[t]he real difficulty for most of us is … we find it impossible to keep our minds, even for ten seconds at a stretch, twisted into the shape that this philosophy [of disenchantment] demands" (Lewis 1986a, 83–4). In other words, in terms of living life it is not possible to take seriously for any length of time the idea that we are nothing more than material "stuff" causally interacting with other material "stuff." We cannot take this idea seriously because we are directly acquainted with ourselves as souls. That is the essence of Lewis's position as he articulated it in his reflections on the nature of thought, reasoning, and the distinction between looking along and looking at. Hence, he insisted that to disenchant the world completely by ultimately denying the existence of ourselves as souls makes no more sense than reasoning to the conclusion that we do not reason:

> But if [man] were [a natural organism], then, as we have seen, all thoughts would be equally nonsensical, for all would have irrational causes [there would be no mental-to-mental causation]. Man must therefore be a composite being—a natural organism tenanted by, or in a state of *symbiosis* with, a supernatural spirit. (Lewis 2001c, 204)

Though man is a composite being, Lewis likely believed the soul, which is one half of the composite, is not itself composite. He would have thought it is simple in the sense that it has no separable parts that compose it. Lewis wrote in the margin of his edition of Aristotle's *Ethica Nicomachea* that "the 'parts of the soul' are only a metaphor" (quoted in Barkman 2009, 269). And when he was discussing the novelist's interest in treating the inner world of the passions and the emotions which contend for supremacy against reason, Lewis described the subject matter in terms of the "unitary 'soul' ... which ... is ... the arena in which the combatants meet: it is to the combatants—those 'accidents occurring in a substance'—that he must attend" (Lewis 1936, 61). In his *Commentarium in Tractatum De Toto et Parte* (probably written between 1928 and 1930), Lewis mentioned what the ancient Greeks termed *akrasia* (the phenomenon where one chooses (acts) against one's better judgment), and he wrote that "[t]he single subject of many experiences seems to remain intact on the cognitive side—temptation given in to leaves me well aware where I am & what I am doing—but it is the single will that is disintegrated" (Feinendegen and Smilde, 2015, 148).

Mrs. Frank L. Jones once wrote Lewis and asked "What is a soul?," to which he responded "*What is a soul*? I am. (This is the only possible answer: or expanded, 'A soul is that which can say I am')" (Lewis 2007, 10). And moving from the first- to the third-person plural, Lewis wrote of "our souls, that is, ourselves" (2001d, 72).[9] One sometimes hears the query "Can you provide me with a positive characterization of a soul?" (A strictly negative characterization would be "A soul is not material; a soul is not visible; etc.") Lewis would have responded: "A soul is that thing which thinks and reasons, chooses, experiences pleasure and pain, etc." He believed it is important to stress that all these kinds of transitory events of which we are directly aware, namely, thoughts, reasonings, experiences of pleasure, etc., presuppose that the soul or "I" is "the stage" on which they appear, where this stage is substantial and endures through time:

> Suppose that three sensations follow one another—first A, then B, then C. When this happens to you, you have the experience of passing through the process ABC. But note what this implies. It implies that there is something in you which stands sufficiently outside B to notice B now beginning and coming to fill the place which A has vacated; and something which recognizes itself as the same through the transition from A to B and B to C, so it can say "I have had the experience of ABC". Now this something is what I call Consciousness or Soul ... The simplest experience of ABC as a succession demands a soul which is not itself a mere succession of states, but rather a permanent bed along which these different portions of the stream of sensation roll, and which recognizes itself as the same beneath them all. (Lewis 2001f, 135)

While the simplest self-conscious experience of a sequence ABC requires the existence of a soul, so do thoughtful changes like religious conversion,

the thinking, reasoning, and sensing soul

in which "the new man must still be in some sense the same, or else salvation has no meaning. The very idea of *conversion* and *regeneration* are essentially different from the idea of substitution [of one thing for another]" (Lewis 2004b, 201). Because most philosophers and other members of academia today are, as they were in Lewis's heyday, naturalists, they seek to explain away the reality of not only religious conversion but also the soul that undergoes it. Nevertheless, there is widespread agreement among them that all of us, the converted and unconverted alike, at least start out believing in the existence of the soul-body distinction (dualism). For example, the experimental cognitive scientist Jesse Bering writes that human beings are believers in dualism (Bering 2006), and the psychologist Nicholas Humphrey insists that there is a human inclination to believe in dualism. Toward the end of his book *Soul Dust*, Humphrey mentions other scholars who also acknowledge this ordinary belief in dualism:

> Thus, development psychologist Paul Bloom aptly describes human beings as "natural-born dualists." Anthropologist Alfred Gell writes: "It seems that ordinary human beings are 'natural dualists,' inclined more or less from day one, to believe in some kind of 'ghost in the machine' ... " Neuropsychologist Paul Broks writes: "The separateness of body and mind is a primordial intuition ... Human beings are natural born soul makers, adept at extracting unobservable minds from the behaviour of observable bodies, including their own." (Humphrey 2011, 195)

Bering, Humphrey, Bloom, Gell, and Broks, even though they no longer affirm the truth of dualism, nevertheless acknowledge that human beings naturally believe it. While Lewis, as we have seen, argued explicitly against naturalism and for supernaturalism and, thereby, implicitly for dualism, he also believed, like Bering, *et al.*, that ordinary people affirm dualism without any argument. Indeed, he often drew attention to the fact that people for millennia have been dualists:

> From the earliest times the Jews, like many other nations, had believed that man possessed a "soul" or *Nephesh* separable from the body, which went at death into the shadowy world called *Sheol*: a land of forgetfulness and imbecility where none called upon Jehovah any more, a land half unreal and melancholy like the Hades of the Greeks or the Niflheim of the Norsemen. From it shades could return and appear to the living, as Samuel's shade had done at the command of the Witch of Endor. (Lewis 2001c, 237)

Lewis reminded his readers that early Christians also believed in ghost survival: "they believed in it so firmly that, on more than one occasion, Christ had had to assure them that He was *not* a ghost" (Lewis 1970, 159).

What, then, is the relationship between a belief in ghosts and a belief in dualism? Lewis would have had us understand that a belief in ghosts is a belief in a certain kind or version of dualism. But, someone might ask, aren't ghosts themselves something material? And if they are, how could ancient peoples who believed in ghosts be dualists? Is not dualism a belief that there are material bodies and immaterial souls?

Lewis thought not. He was well aware of the distinction between "popular beliefs" and the developments of them by philosophers. He was convinced that a belief in dualism is essentially an ordinary belief in a distinction between a soul and its body. Beliefs about the natures of the body and the soul have to await philosophical reflection. Common sense itself is philosophically idle. Here is Lewis's treatment of the issue:

> We are often told that primitive man could not conceive pure spirit; but then neither could he conceive mere matter. A throne and a local habitation are attributed to God only at that stage when it is still impossible to regard the throne, or palace even of an earthly king as merely physical objects. In earthly thrones and palaces it was the spiritual significance—as we should say, the "atmosphere"—that mattered to the ancient mind. As soon as the contrast of "spiritual" and "material" was before their minds, they knew God to be "spiritual" and realised that their religion had implied this all along. But at an earlier stage that contrast was not there. To regard that earlier stage as unspiritual because we find there no clear assertion of unembodied spirit, is a real misunderstanding … [I]t is quite erroneous to think that man started with a "material" God or "Heaven" and gradually spiritualised them. He could not have started with something "material" for the "material", as we understand it, comes to be realised only by contrast to the "immaterial", and the two sides of the contrast grow at the same speed. He started with something which was neither and both. As long as we are trying to read back into that ancient unity either the one or the other of the two opposites which have since been analysed out of it, we shall misread all early literature and ignore many states of consciousness which we ourselves still from time to time experience. The point is crucial … for … any sound … philosophy. (2001c, 122–4)

With regard to dualism, it was a philosopher like Plato who began to draw out the distinctions between soul and body that led to thinking of the one as immaterial and the other as material. Lewis maintained that as soon as the question about the difference in natures between soul and body was known, the answer to it became clear. But until the question was raised, no one had a belief about the issue. Moreover, Lewis emphasized that the distinction between the natures of the soul and body implied nothing like what Plato thought about the disvalue of the latter: "I fear Plato thought the concrete flesh … bad, and have no doubt he was wrong" (2004b, 326).

Lewis is well known for his book *Mere Christianity*, where mere Christianity is the idea of a core set of beliefs that are shared by a variety of Christian communions: Roman Catholic, Protestant, Eastern Orthodox, etc. He likened mere Christianity to "a hall out of which doors open into several rooms" (Lewis 2001b, xv), some of the rooms being Methodism, Anglicanism, Lutheranism, etc. When it came to the nature of a human being, he advocated what might be called "mere dualism," which is a core set of beliefs about the soul-body distinction that is shared by a variety of dualist denominations: Platonic, Cartesian, Thomist, etc. It, too, can be likened to a hall out of which open a multitude of doors into various rooms (see Goetz 2015a). To those who doubted the reality of a mere Christianity, Lewis appealed to his experience with Christianity from the outside as an atheist:

> But those who have always lived within the Christian fold may be too easily dispirited by [the divisions of Christendom]. They are bad, but such people do not know what it looks like from without. Seen from there, what is left intact despite all the divisions, still appears (as it truly is) an immensely formidable unity. I know, for I saw it; and well our enemies know it. That unity any of us can find by going out of his own age. (1996, 7)

Because Lewis believed mere Christianity itself presupposed a belief in mere dualism, where mere dualism is the commonsensical view about the nature of a human being, I think he would have recommended to doubters of the reality of mere dualism that they focus on their own first-person experience and, if they needed third-person confirmation of that experience (a kind of stepping outside their own age), that they consult the work of people like Bering, Humphrey, Bloom, Gell, and Broks mentioned above.

2.7 Thought, Image, and the Immaterial

I began this chapter with Lewis's claim that we know ourselves better than anything else in the universe. We have inside information about ourselves. What we know is that we are immaterial souls who are able to reason, experience pleasure and pain, etc. Given knowledge about ourselves, we also think about ourselves. According to Lewis, "[i]t is of the very nature of thought and language to represent what is immaterial in picturable terms" (1936, 44). Thus, "anyone who [thinks] about things that cannot be seen, or touched, or heard, or the like, must inevitably talk as *if they could be* seen or touched or heard … " (Lewis 2001c, 115).

But given his argument from reason and the distinction between looking along and looking at, it is hard to understand why Lewis insisted that anyone who thinks about what cannot be sensed must do so in terms of that which can. To support his claim, Lewis pointed out that when he thought of London he usually had a mental image of Euston Station, and he described a young girl who, when she thought of poison, had a mental picture of horrid red things (Lewis 2001c, 114). He also stressed that having an image along with one's thought did not necessarily prevent him or the young girl from thinking true things about London and poison respectively. And he regarded this as an important point for our thought about God: even though our thought about God must always be accompanied by an image of something sensible (e.g., the idea that Christ came down from and ascends to heaven is attended by the image of his moving downwards through space), we can nevertheless think true thoughts about Him (e.g., that Christ oversees and governs the whole field of reality).

But is it really the case that every time we think about what is immaterial our thought must be accompanied by an image derived from our sense experience? It is hard to see why Lewis believed this is the case. For example, consider the issue of understanding an argument. Lewis said a person will claim to grasp the argument or see the point, where "grasps" suggests taking something in one's hands and "seeing" connotes, well, seeing. But while it is the case that one can express understanding an argument in terms of grasping it or seeing the point, one can also simply *understand* an argument without any accompanying imagery. Certainly, one does not have the image of *standing under* the argument or of standing among others in the sense of "I am with you." One simply understands it and understands what understanding the argument is. The same point can be made about the idea of making an inference. While one might say inference involves moving from premises to conclusion, "moving" here in no way involves an image of spatial movement. Rather, it refers to the idea of understanding, in a momentary temporal succession, the connections of content between the premises and the conclusion. And if one thinks about the pleasure one might derive from such an inference, one certainly has no image of that experience of pleasure.

So while Lewis seems to have been on solid ground when he claimed that the presence of images does not necessarily undermine the integrity of the thoughts that they accompany, his claim that all thought about what is immaterial must involve an image of what can be seen, or touched, or heard, etc., seems groundless. And perhaps in the end he believed this himself. More than a decade after the publication of *Miracles*, from which the quote at the outset of this section is taken, Lewis wrote to Mary Van Deusen about belief and imagination and claimed, "I can picture [very] few of the things I believe in—I can't picture will, thought, time, atoms … " (2007, 1086). Lewis might well then have agreed with the following: While we often do make use of picturable terms when referring to immaterial events, we need not do so in order to think of them.

2.8 Pleasurable Reason

The following words of Lewis capture at a general level the main points of this chapter:

> [T]he naturalistic conclusion is unbelievable. For one thing, it is only through trusting our own minds that we have come to know Nature herself. If Nature when fully known seems to teach us (that is, if the sciences teach us) that our own minds are chance arrangements of atoms, then there must have been some mistake; for if that were so, then the sciences themselves would be chance arrangements of atoms and we should have no reason for believing them. There is only one way to avoid this deadlock. We must go back to a much earlier view. We must simply accept it that we are spirits, free and rational beings, at present inhabiting an irrational universe, and must draw the conclusion that we are *not derived from it* ... We have come from somewhere else. Nature is not the only thing that exists. There is "another world", and that is where we come from. And that explains why we do not feel at home here. (Lewis 1986a, 78)

Lewis would say naturalism is false. We ourselves are not material beings but souls that have an origin outside this world. He would have stressed that up to this point in his anti-naturalist argument, "[t]here [has been] no reason ... to bring in ... Christianity [God] ... We [have not needed it] to refute naturalism" (Lewis 1970, 138). But things are about to change. As we will see in Chapter 3, Lewis thought that we came from another place in the sense that we were created by God for a purpose, where this purpose is the meaning of life. David Gelernter has recently written: "[m]ost ... philosophers identify human thought with rationality, reasoning, logic. Even if they see emotion as important, they rarely see it as central ... " (2016, C2). With Lewis's emphasis on thought and reason, one might understandably think he believed the purpose of life is knowing, reasoning, or something of the sort, where this is achieved in part in this life with its full realization or perfection coming in the next. But this was not Lewis's view. Even before he had become a theist, Lewis had concluded that "[w]hatever else the human race was made for, it at least was not made to know" (2004a, 640). "No one is more convinced than I that reason is utterly inadequate to the richness and spirituality of real things: indeed this is itself a deliverance of reason" (2004a, 670). So while Lewis wrote in defense of the supernatural nature of thought and reason, he was convinced that what life is ultimately concerned with, what is its ultimate meaning or purpose, is something other than the exercise of the intellect: "I'm all for a planet without aches or pains ... but I doubt if I'd care for one of pure intelligence" (2007, 623). What Lewis ultimately cared for in addition to the absence of pain was the experience of pleasure. It was Lewis's experience of pleasure which helped convince him that what life is ultimately all about, its meaning, is what is psychological yet nonmental in nature.

notes

1 Sean Carroll writes the following about physicalism: "The most difficult problem is a philosophical one: how is it even possible that inner experience, the uniquely experiential *aboutness* of our lives inside our heads, can be reduced to matter in motion?" (2016, 5).

2 In order to avoid undue repetition, from here on I assume that what is nonmental is also non-psychological in nature, though strictly speaking this is false (e.g., an experience of pleasure is nonmental but also psychological in nature).

3 Lewis contrasted reason with imagination in terms of determinism and freedom:

> For the character of reasoning is that every judgment rigidly determines and is determined by others; but the character of imagining is that it is free—at least within very wide bounds indeed. If you imagine a tower, even a solid tower, foundations and builders are not necessarily implied: for you are at perfect liberty if you choose to suppose that it was produced by the fiat of a magician and is supported by four buried Jinns. (2013b, 47)

4 I would be remiss not to mention a controversy among Lewis scholars that concerns Anscombe's criticism of the argument from reason. The controversy is about whether Lewis continued to believe in the soundness of the argument from reason against naturalism, after Anscombe's criticism of it. Along with Victor Reppert (2003), I think it must be concluded that Lewis continued to believe in the argument's soundness. This is because the most extensive presentation of the argument appears in the book *Miracles* of which there are two editions, and there are two editions because Lewis revised the argument from reason in light of Anscombe's critique of it. There is no plausible explanation for his having revised the argument for a second edition of *Miracles*, if he had ceased to believe in the argument's soundness. One must conclude that his discouragement coming out of the exchange with Anscombe was not that she had shown the argument to be unsound but that he had failed to present it correctly in what turned out to be the first edition of *Miracles*. My presentation of the argument is of the reworked version in the second edition of *Miracles*.

Marcel Sarot (Sarot 2011, 43 footnote 4) rightly points out that one of the main changes Lewis introduced into his revised formulation of his argument against naturalism in the second edition of *Miracles* was the substitution of "non-rational" for "irrational," because Anscombe convinced Lewis that an irrational belief is one that is mentally caused, though wrongly, while a non-rational belief is one that is naturally caused and, therefore, neither rational nor irrational.

5   Van Inwagen criticizes Lewis's argument in the following way:

> In Lewis' view, a "Cause-effect 'because'" explanation of a belief fact
> [a belief that C. S. Lewis was a Cambridge professor is a belief fact] implies
> that the proposition [C. S. Lewis was a Cambridge professor] that is the
> object of the belief fact is not accepted rationally by its subject *simply in
> virtue* of its being a "Cause-effect 'because'" explanation. (2011, 35)

Van Inwagen seemingly believes Lewis held that the mere fact that a
belief is caused excludes the possibility of that belief being accepted rationally. But this was not Lewis's view. Lewis believed the problem created
by naturalism for reasoning was not that a belief fact has a cause but that
the truth of naturalism excludes a certain kind of cause of the belief fact,
namely, a mental cause of apprehension.

Van Inwagen also writes, "[i]f a human being ... can have beliefs, there
seems to be no reason to deny that that human being's believing certain
things might be the *cause* of his or her believing certain other things"
(2011, 36). Lewis would have agreed with this statement, but added that
believing something involves an apprehension of content, and an apprehension of content is a mental event. Hence, Lewis would have had us
pause when van Inwagen claims that Lewis failed to show that a belief
fact cannot be fully explained naturalistically in terms of the way the
universe was in the past and the laws of physics (van Inwagen 2011, 34–8).
Lewis would have wanted to know whether mental apprehensions are
part of the explanatory apparatus of the laws of physics. Do we find physicists describing the world in terms of apprehensions? If not (as seems to be
the case with any traditional physics), then Lewis would have responded
that a full explanation of a belief fact in terms of the way the universe was
in the past and the laws of physics would ensure that the belief fact was
not a result of reasoning. If naturalism is compatible with a "physics" that
includes mental explanations, then Lewis would have answered that he
was not attacking this "version" of naturalism.

And, finally, if physical events have two "aspects" in virtue of
having two kinds of properties, nonmental and mental (a view that
Lewis seems never to have taken seriously), and naturalism implies
that a belief fact can be fully explained under the nonmental aspect of
physical events, then Lewis would once again have insisted that naturalism excludes reasoning. But if the belief fact is explicable in terms of
the mental aspect of apprehension exemplified by physical events, then
Lewis would have made clear that he was not attacking that version of
naturalism.

A philosopher who is willing to countenance a more expansive meaning
of "naturalism" is Graham Oppy. According to Oppy:

> Naturalism says that causal reality is natural reality: the domain of causes
> is nothing more nor less than the natural world ... Supernaturalism says
> that causal reality outstrips natural reality: there are supernatural causes ...
> Supernaturalists who believe in ghosts ... but who deny that God exists,
> are not theists. (2013, 6)

So Oppy regards those who believe in ghosts as supernaturalists. Yet later in the same book, he writes the following:

> Clearly, if we suppose that non-physical souls are non-natural, then the hypothesis that there are non-physical souls is inconsistent with naturalism ... However, in that case, there is a revision of the naturalist position—call it [the] naturalist* position ... On ... the naturalist* view— global causal reality includes two different kinds of natural* causal entities: physical entities (such as brains) and non-physical entities (such as souls) that interact causally with one another. (2013, 54–5)

Lewis would have regarded naturalism* as supernaturalism.

6 Arend Smilde (2011, 23) suggests one might wish that Lewis could and would have explained the causal connection between the apprehension of a ground and the occurrence of a belief. He rightly responds that if Lewis could have explained this in naturalistic terms, he would have reduced the connection to a natural occurrence and, thereby, undermined his argument from reason. The point of the argument is that the connection cannot be explained naturalistically because it is ultimate and irreducible.

7 Lewis said that created spirit "probably" affects matter directly, without making use of any intervening mechanism ("technics"), in the brain. In personal correspondence with Mrs. Robert Manly in February, 1960, Lewis wrote: "I take it [that] the point at which Rational Soul has purchase on the body—the starting platform from which she controls the whole engine—is the brain" (2007, 1136).

8 The Haldane quote comes from Haldane (1928, 220.) Haldane agreed with Lewis:

> I don't think thought is a mere by-product of physical or chemical processes in [brains]. But if Mr. Lewis has ever been anaesthetized, or even drunk, he must admit that, at least in the present wicked world, his capacity for thought depends on the chemical state of his brain. On the other hand, the chemical state of his brain does not depend, except to a very slight extent, on what he is thinking. (lewisiana.nl/haldane/)

Lewis would likely have retorted that the more one thinks, the more the chemical state of one's brain does depend on what one is thinking.

9 Timothy Cleveland writes:

> C. S. Lewis, being an orthodox Christian, is of course committed to *talk* of "souls." However. it is far from clear that anyone who takes talk of souls seriously must be committed to the metaphysics of the soul theory [the theory of the existence of souls]. By "soul," Lewis may only intend whatever is essential to the "self." (2005, 186n. 2)

It is reasonable to think Lewis would have made at least three points in response to Cleveland. First, belief in the soul is not (and is not part of) a theory of the soul. It is a commonsense basic belief, one that is not inferred from other beliefs. Lewis held that this belief arises out of a first-person awareness of oneself as a soul. Second, a Christian is committed to talk of souls because there are souls. Third,

> I (Lewis) believe I am a soul and that there are souls. If you, Cleveland, do not, so be it. But please respect what I say about the soul and do not change it to agree with what seems to be your belief in the non-existence of the soul.

the meaning of life

What is the meaning of it, Watson?" said Holmes solemnly ... "What object is served by this circle of misery and violence and fear? It must tend to some end, or else our universe is ruled by chance, which is unthinkable. But what end? There is the great standing perennial problem to which human reason is as far from an answer as ever.

(Conan Doyle 1930, 901)

[N]o man is a hypocrite in his pleasures.

(Boswell 2008, 938)

[N]o man can enjoy happiness without thinking that he enjoys it.

(Johnson 1969, 35)

Human beings never enjoy complete happiness in this world.

(Brontë 1997, 262)

3.1 Setting the Stage

When he was an atheist in the 1920s, C. S. Lewis wrote that "[n]early all that I loved I believed to be imaginary; nearly all that I believed to be real I thought grim and meaningless" (1955, 170). In his *"De Futilitate,"* which was an address given as a Christian at Magdalen College during World War II, he said that most of us sometimes think and feel that the universe is futile. Lewis suggested we might try to show that this thought and feeling result from presupposing, in line with our being artificers (designers and makers of objects), that the universe, too, is an artefact, but one which does not fulfill its purpose:

> "Futility" is the opposite of "utility". A machine or plan is futile when it does not serve the purpose for which it was devised. In calling the universe futile, therefore, we are really ... treating it as if it were a thing

manufactured ... for some purpose [and concluding that it does not serve, or fails to fulfill, the purpose for which it was made]. (Lewis 1967, 59–60)

Lewis believed this line of thinking, when pushed to its limit, would result in the view that thought and reasoning themselves are futile and, respectively, neither true nor false, nor valid nor invalid. Thus, thought and reasoning would tell us nothing about the nature of the world. We saw in Chapter 2 that he concluded this position was intellectually indefensible. He could find no way to rationally escape an acknowledgment that our thought is really about things and that we validly reason from one thought to another. So our thought and our reasoning are revelatory about the nature of the universe, at least to the following extent: they reveal a supernatural dimension of reality that, on some occasions, functions well.

While Lewis believed there is no rationally principled escape from the view that the universe contains supernatural beings which successfully think and reason, he recognized that some might still think that "though the ultimate reality is logical it has no regard for values [because of waste and cruelty], or at any rate for the values we recognize. And so we could still accuse it of futility" (Lewis 1967, 65). However, he believed this accusation would itself be futile, because to make it we would have to invoke what we regard as an objective standard of value to which we believe the universe fails to measure up:

> Unless we judge this waste and cruelty [of the universe] to be real evils we cannot of course condemn the universe for exhibiting them. Unless we take our own standard of goodness to be valid in principle (however fallible our particular applications of it) we cannot mean anything by calling waste and cruelty evils ... In a word, unless we allow ultimate reality to be moral, we cannot morally condemn it. The more seriously we take our own charge of futility the more we are committed to the implication that reality in the last resort is not futile at all. (Lewis 1967, 69–70)

Lewis went on to point out that recognizing the objectivity of our values still leaves open the question about how the actual course of events in the world can be reconciled with those values. As will become clearer in subsequent sections of this chapter, he concluded this reconciliation requires the reality of an afterlife. But some individuals during the high point of Lewis's years in Oxford (roughly, the mid-1930s through the mid-1950s) thought it pointless to rail against the universe for failing to cooperate fully with our values. This was because they believed our thoughts about values were neither true nor false. These individuals affirmed that all statements about values, about things that are good and things that are evil (bad), are, strictly speaking, meaningless. Their philosophy was known as *logical positivism*, which was roughly the idea that a statement is meaningless if it cannot be empirically—i.e., by means of one or more of the five senses—verified or falsified. Lewis probably encountered at least the spirit of logical positivism in his tutor William Kirkpatrick. In his autobiography of his early life *Surprised by Joy*, Lewis described his first meeting with the Great Knock, upon disembarking from a train:

> At Bookham I was met by my new teacher—"Kirk" or "Knock" or the Great Knock as my father, my brother, and I all called him ... We shook hands, and ... [a] few minutes later we were walking away from the station.

> "You are now," said Kirk, "proceeding along the principal artery between Great and Little Bookham." .... I said I was surprised at the "scenery" of Surrey; it was much "wilder" than I had expected.

> "Stop!" shouted Kirk with a suddenness that made me jump. "What do you mean by wildness and what grounds had you for not expecting it?" ... A few passes sufficed to show that I had no clear and distinct idea corresponding to the word "wildness," and that, in so far as I had any idea at all, "wildness" was a singularly inept word. "Do you not see, then," concluded the Great Knock, "that your remark was meaningless?" (1955, 133–4)

Kirkpatrick pressed Lewis to explain what he meant by his off-the-cuff comment about scenery. One can imagine what Kirkpatrick would have said had Lewis been in a bit more philosophical frame of mind and queried of his new tutor something like "What is the meaning of life?" In a letter in 1920 to his friend Arthur Greeves, Lewis actually wrote about an epic poem that was "a sort of journey into the underworld, where various ancient sages [were] interviewed on the meaning of life ... " (Lewis 2004a, 476). One can imagine Kirkpatrick, upon hearing the phrase "the meaning of life," having retorted "What do you mean by 'the meaning of life'?" Were Lewis to have stumbled verbally, one can almost hear the old man vigorously stating "Your question was meaningless!"

Regardless of whether or not Kirkpatrick was an incipient logical positivist (Lewis wrote: "Born a little later, he would have been a Logical Positivist" (Lewis 1955, 135)), adherents of the view treated any declaration about the meaning of life just as they treated statements about value: all were nonsense, or at least not declarative statements that were true or false. For example, the Oxford academic and logical positivist, A. J. Ayer, wrote in 1947 that life "has for each of us whatever meaning we severally choose to give it. The purpose of a man's existence is constituted by the ends to which he ... devotes himself" (2008, 201). Ayer went on to claim that happiness is not this end, "unless the word 'happiness' is used merely as a description of any end that is in fact pursued" (2008, 201). Moreover, "[s]ince judgments of value are not reducible to statements of fact, they are strictly speaking neither true nor false … " (Ayer 2008, 202). Ayer maintained it was tempting to infer from this that "no course of conduct is better or worse than any other. But this would be a mistake. For the judgment that no course of conduct is better or worse than any other is itself a judgment of value and consequently neither true nor false" (2008, 202). Ayer concluded that whatever values one chooses as ends, it is only necessary that they be consistent. Otherwise, they could not be achieved. "But," he added, "once their consistency is established, they can be criticized only on practical grounds [whether they are achievable, and not whether they are true or false] … " (2008, 202). The upshot was that any statement that identifies a certain end or purpose that is good as the meaning of life is neither true nor false.

Were logical positivists treating the question of life's meaning reasonably? The contemporary philosopher Susan Wolf has her doubts:

> [W]hen people do ask about the meaning of life, they are evidently expressing some concern or other, and it would be disingenuous to insist that the rest of us haven't the faintest idea what that is … Rather than dismiss a question with which many people have been passionately occupied as pure and simple nonsense, it seems more appropriate to try to interpret it and reformulate it in a way that can be more clearly and unambiguously understood. Though there may be many things going on when people ask, "What is the meaning of life?", the most central among them seems to be a search to find a purpose or a point to human existence. (2013, 304–5)

Ayer, as we have seen, thought of the question "What is the meaning of life?" as a question about the purpose of life, which he believed is answered in terms of the ends an individual chooses to pursue. But he also insisted that if the ends are thought to be things of value, things that are good or evil, then statements about them cannot be true or false. Lewis explicitly mentioned Ayer in personal correspondence, and was not too impressed by him, writing, "I live among these … linguistic birds, and have quite enough of them" (Lewis 2007, 447). Ayer was no more complimentary about Lewis:

> While the analytic movement [in philosophy], in one form or another, took increasing control of the English philosophical scene, there were some pockets of resistance to it. One of those who fought a rearguard action against it in Oxford was the English scholar C. S. Lewis, who had once had the ambition to become a tutor in philosophy and still took a lively interest in the subject. He presided over the Socratic Club, which then drew a large audience to meetings at which the principal speakers usually struck a religious note. At one of these meetings … I undertook a reply to a paper by Michael Foster … I dealt with his paper rather harshly, and when he made little effort to defend

it, C. S. Lewis took over from him. Lewis and I then engaged in a flashy debate, which entertained the audience but did neither of us much credit … (1977, 296–7)

According to Ayer, Lewis was a resistance fighter. In the present context, this means that Lewis believed statements about value can be true or false. Not surprisingly, Lewis also believed that a statement about the purpose of life can be true or false. His views about the purpose of life are the subject of the next section.

3.2 The Purpose of Life

During World War II, Lewis was a member of the Oxford Home Guard, which the British government had established in part out of concern that Germany might invade Britain. Lewis wrote that he was "patrolling" Oxford one night in 1940 (his shift was from 1:30 a.m. until about 4:30 a.m.) when he persuaded a fellow sentry to "realise for the first time in his life that 'nature' can't have 'purposes' unless it is a rational substance [a soul which thinks and reasons], and if it is you'd much better call it God, or the gods, or a god, or the devil" (Lewis 2004b, 448). Lewis himself believed that nature does not have its own purposes. Instead, he thought God created the natural world, and the human beings which inhabit it, for a purpose. According to the non-theist Kurt Baier, the mere idea that there is a purpose of life for a human being is demeaning and/or degrading:

> To attribute to a human being a purpose in [the sense of the purpose of an artefact] is not neutral, let alone complimentary: it is offensive. It is degrading for a man to be regarded as merely serving a purpose. If, at a garden party, I ask a man in livery, "What is your purpose?" I am insulting him. I might as well have asked, "What are you *for*?" Such questions reduce him to the level of a gadget, a domestic animal, or perhaps a slave. I imply that *we* allot to *him* the tasks, the goals, the aims which he is to pursue; that *his* wishes and desires and aspirations and purposes are to count for little or nothing. (2000, 120)

Lewis would likely have conceded to Baier that some purposes of life would be degrading and offensive. An example that is often discussed in contemporary literature concerns the Greek myth of Sisyphus, where Sisyphus, a king who betrayed divine secrets to mortals, was condemned by the gods to roll a stone up a hill, only to have it roll back down, and to roll it up again, only to have it roll back down, *ad infinitum*. If one removes the idea of punishment and thinks of Sisyphus as being created by the gods for the purpose of repeatedly rolling a stone up a hill, one will appreciate Baier's point.

But Lewis would have wondered how it follows from the fact that one or more purposes are degrading that all are. For him, the issue would have turned on what the purpose is. At this point, we do not have to speculate about what he believed. In a letter from September, 1933, to his friend Greeves, Lewis wrote: "God not only understands but *shares* the desire ... for complete and ecstatic happiness. He made me for no other purpose than to enjoy it" (2004b, 123). In *The Great Divorce*, which is about a fantastical bus trip to heaven, one of the ghostly visitors says "I wish I'd never been born ... What *are* we born for?" To which a Spirit answers, "For infinite happiness ... " (Lewis 2001e, 61). Lewis wrote elsewhere that infinite, complete, or ecstatic happiness is the life of the blessed and he stated that we must suppose "the life of the blessed to be an end in itself, indeed The End ... " (Lewis, 1992a, 92). And in personal correspondence at the outset of World War II, Lewis made clear that God not only made him for no other purpose than the experience of perfect happiness, but He also made others for the same purpose, even members of the Gestapo:

> In fact I provisionally define Agapë as "steadily remembering that inside the Gestapo-man there is a thing [which] says I and Me just as you do, which has just the same grounds (neither more nor less) as your 'Me' for being distinguished from all its sins however numerous, which, like you, was made by God for eternal happiness ... " (Lewis 2004b, 409)

In sum, Lewis believed the purpose of life is that we experience a happiness that he variably described as eternal, infinite, complete, or perfect. The experience of this happiness is the life of the blessed. That we experience it is the purpose for which God created us, and that we are created for it implies "that a continual looking forward to the eternal world is not (as some modern people think) a form of escapism or wishful thinking, but one of the things a Christian is meant to do" (Lewis 2001b, 134). We are meant to look ahead like this because "infinite happiness really is there, waiting for us ... " (Lewis 2001b, 136). Lewis believed that even if "old age and death had been made optional ... it [would] still be true that our real destiny was elsewhere, that we have no abiding city here and no true happiness ... " (Lewis 2004b, 986). We would have no true happiness here because even without death and old age, there would still be pain and suffering. Thus,

> [o]ne ought not to need the gloomy moments of life for beginning detachment [from this world], nor be re-entangled by the bright ones. One ought to be able to enjoy the bright ones to the full and at that very same moment have the perfect readiness to leave them, confident that what calls one away is better. (Lewis 2004b, 987)

Of course, what calls one away is perfect happiness.

But what is happiness? Being told that we are made for it in a perfect form does not tell us what it is. Ayer, as I have already indicated, maintained it is *whatever* end a person happens to choose to pursue. Lewis, we must remember, was a man of common sense. So, what, if anything, would Lewis say common sense tells us about happiness? Certainly not whatever someone happens to decide. Aristotle, in his *Nicomachean Ethics*, which Lewis had read, said that most people would agree that the highest good attainable by action is happiness:

> for both the common run of people and cultivated men call it happiness ... But when it comes to defining what happiness is, they disagree, and the account given by the common run differs from that of the philosophers. The former say it is some clear and obvious good, such as pleasure ... (Aristotle 1962, 6 [1095a17–23])

The ordinary person, insofar as he identifies happiness with experiences of pleasure, is, in philosophical terms, a hedonist about happiness. Philosophers are not hedonists about happiness, or so Aristotle wrote (roughly, he identified happiness with virtuous activity of the soul). And Lewis? He unequivocally stood with the *hoi polloi*. In the *The Screwtape Letters*, he had the devil Screwtape complain that God is

> a hedonist at heart. All those fasts and vigils and stakes and crosses are only a façade. Or only like foam on the seashore. Out at sea, out in His sea, there is pleasure, and more pleasure. He makes no secret of it; at His right hand are 'pleasures for evermore.' ... He's vulgar ... He has a bourgeois mind. (Lewis 1961b, 101)

And in response to a letter from Canon Quick about *The Problem of Pain*, Lewis wrote:

> I wasn't writing on the Problem of Pleasure! If I had been you might find my views *too* hedonistic. I [would] say that every pleasure (even the lowest) is a likeness to, even, in its restricted mode, a foretaste of, the end for [which] we exist, the fruition of God ... [T]he normal value judgement of all unsophisticated people ... seems to hold [what] philosophers are always neglecting ... That pleasure is simply good ... (2004b, 463)

So in Lewis's mind, every pleasure that a person experiences in this life is an indication of the purpose for which he or she was created, which is the enjoyment of God, where enjoying God is experiencing pleasure. When he referred in a letter to the Protestant Westminster Catechism, he emphasized that "Man was created 'to glorify God and *enjoy* Him forever'" (Lewis 2007, 856), and he believed glorifying God is itself enjoyed. Lewis thought a Christian "believes that men are going to live forever, [and] that they were created by God and so built that they can find their true and lasting happiness only by being united to God ... " (Lewis 1970, 109).

In sum, Lewis thought happiness is experiencing pleasure, where experiencing pleasure is the purpose for which God created us.[1]

3.3 What Makes Life Worth Living

In *An Experiment in Criticism*, Lewis wrote that as a psychological term, "fantasy" has three meanings, the second of which is a

> "pleasing imaginative construction entertained incessantly ... without the delusion that it is a reality ... It becomes the prime consolation, and almost the only pleasure, of the dreamer's life ... He becomes incapable of all the efforts needed to achieve a happiness not merely notional" (1961a, 51).

One sees in these few statements (as in so many others throughout the Lewis corpus) how pleasure connoted happiness in Lewis's mind. Where there is the former to some degree, there is the latter to an equal degree. In opposition to Baier, Lewis would have wondered how anyone could reasonably think that a person's experiencing nothing but pleasure, as the purpose of life, is offensive or degrading. If someone needed an explanation for why it is not, Lewis would likely have maintained that experiencing pleasure is not offensive because it is what *makes life worth living*. At one point, Lewis expressed the idea of life's being worth living in terms of life's being worth having: "Let the doctor tell me I shall die, unless I do so-and-so; but whether life is worth having on those terms is no more a question for him than for any other man" (1970, 315).

To Lewis, it was because experiencing pleasure is what makes life worth living that it is the essence of happiness. But what is it about experiencing pleasure that led Lewis to believe it is that which makes life worth living? At this juncture, we must enter into what he took to be the intellectual space of value judgments that was vacated by Ayer and other logical positivists. Lewis believed that pleasure is good, as he stated in the letter to Canon Quick that I quoted in Section 3.2. In slightly more philosophical terminology, Lewis believed pleasure is *intrinsically* good, where something is intrinsically good if it is good in and of itself or, in different words, it is good independent of its relationship to anything else (it does not derive its goodness from its relationship to anything else, where goodness that is derived in this way is *extrinsic* in nature). Earlier in the same letter to Canon Quick, Lewis stressed that he thought "*all* pleasure simply good: what we call bad pleasures are pleasures produced by actions, or inactions, [which] break the moral law, and it is those actions or inactions [which] are bad, not the pleasures" (2004b, 462–3). Elsewhere, he affirmed "I have no doubt at all that pleasure is in itself a good ... (1967, 21). And in a letter to Mary van Deusen, Lewis approvingly exclaimed about God's provision of pleasure described in Psalm 38:8 "And what unabashed Hedonism in 8!" (2007, 685).

So Lewis held that God creates persons for the purpose that they experience perfect happiness, where happiness consists of experiences of pleasure which are intrinsically good. Thus, if one understands the question "What is the meaning of life?" as the question "What, if anything, makes life worth living?," Lewis would have answered "Pleasure." Here, it is worth making two additional points.

First, Lewis was a hedonist about happiness. He was not a hedonist *simpliciter*. The distinction is important. A hedonist *simpliciter* is someone who maintains that pleasure *and pleasure alone* is intrinsically good. Lewis did not believe that pleasure is the only intrinsic good. For example, he believed justice is also an intrinsic good. So when Lewis affirmed hedonism, he was affirming it only about happiness.

Second, though pleasure, like thought, is psychological in nature, it lacks the aboutness of the latter. Pleasure is not something mental because it is not directed at or does not refer to anything, whether itself or something else. While one might say "I am pleased about your engagement," what one means is that one experiences pleasure upon learning about your engagement. The learning is what is mental in nature, not the pleasure. So on Lewis's view, that which life is ultimately about, both in the sense of being life's purpose and what makes life worth living, is itself not about anything. But while not about anything, pleasures "are unmistakably real, and therefore, as far as they go, give the man who feels them a touchstone of reality" (Lewis 1961b, 58).

3.4   Pain, Pleasure, and Happiness

The purpose of life is to experience perfect happiness. Or so thought Lewis. But what makes happiness perfect, as opposed to imperfect? Here, we need to turn to the notion of hedonism once again. A hedonist about happiness is someone who believes not only that pleasure is intrinsically good but also holds that pain is intrinsically evil. To say that the experience of pain is intrinsically evil is to say that pain is evil and does not derive its evilness from its relationship to anything else. It is evil in and of itself. Thus, Lewis wrote the following: "I have no doubt at all that ... pain in itself [is] an evil ... " (Lewis 1967, 21). "Pain is unmasked, unmistakable evil ... " (Lewis 2001f, 90). If happiness is perfect, then it must exclude any experience of pain because pain is intrinsically evil. The upshot is that perfect happiness consists of nothing but experiences of pleasure.

To understand the purpose of life as Lewis saw it, it is helpful to consider very briefly the philosophical issue known as the problem of, or argument from, evil against the existence of God. The philosopher John Mackie, who was an atheist and a student at Oxford while Lewis taught there, raised this issue in his classic paper "Evil and Omnipotence" (Mackie 1990). Mackie claimed that pleasures and pains are respectively goods and evils and that if God (an omnibenevolent, omnipotent, and omniscient being) existed, there would be experiences of pleasure but no experiences of pain in the world. Given that there are experiences of pain, Mackie concluded that God does not exist.

Lewis was well aware of the problem of evil (see Chapter 8). Here is his formulation of it: "If God were good, He would wish to make His creatures perfectly happy, and if God were almighty He would be able to do what He wished. But the creatures are not happy. Therefore God lacks either goodness, or power, or both" (Lewis 2001f, 16). One senses from Lewis's personal correspondence that his conceptualization of the problem of evil in terms of the lack of happiness was deeply rooted in his personal experience: "Sometimes I am very unhappy" (Lewis 2004b, 595). And in describing his friend Charles Williams's advice for dealing with the discontents of young people, Lewis wrote that Williams insisted "the worst thing we could do was to tell them that they were not so unhappy as they thought ... For young people usually are unhappy ... The world is painful ... " (Lewis 2013b, 121).

In asserting that pleasure is intrinsically good and pain is intrinsically evil, Lewis was implicitly recognizing the distinction between nonmoral (amoral) good and evil and moral good and evil (the distinction between nonmoral and moral values).[2] He believed that if there were no nonmoral value in the world, there would be no moral value. As I will elaborate in Chapter 4, Lewis thought that morality was first and foremost concerned with nonmoral value in the form of the happiness of others, and he wanted others to understand that the distinction between nonmoral and moral value was not something in which he believed because of his conversion to Christianity: "The difference I am drawing between moral and nonmoral good comes rather from secular ethics [thought]" (Lewis 2004b, 447).

3.5 An Alternative Rejected

As I have argued at length elsewhere, very few readers of Lewis have read him with an eye on the topics of this chapter and those who have had their eye on these issues have largely misunderstood and/or misrepresented his views (Goetz 2015a). These latter few have for the most part claimed that Lewis espoused the privationist view of evil of the medieval Christian theologian and philosopher St. Augustine, despite everything that Lewis said to the contrary. This misunderstanding of what Lewis thought is so prevalent that it warrants a brief treatment here.

In the late fourth and early fifth centuries, Augustine struggled to understand the origins and nature of evil. Early in his philosophical life, he was attracted to the thought of a person named Mani, the founder of Manichaeism, who held that there are two ultimate and eternal powers or principles in the universe: one good and the other evil. Within this dualism of ultimate powers, what is evil is thought of as a thing, entity, or substance in its own right. After much intellectual labor, Augustine came to the conclusion that Manichaeism is false because there is only one ultimate power, God, who is good. What, then, about evil? What is its nature? Augustine arrived at the view that it is not anything positive at all. It has no real existence in the sense of its being a positive reality. Rather, it is a privation or lack of good, conceived of as measure, form, and order:

> For what else is that which we call evil but a removal of good? In the bodies of animals, to be afflicted with diseases and wounds is nothing other than to be deprived of health: the aim of treatment is not to make the evils which were in the body, such as diseases and wounds, move from where they were to somewhere else, but rather that they should cease to exist, since a wound or a disease is not in itself a substance but a defect in the substance of flesh. The flesh itself is the substance, a good thing to which those evil things, those removals of the good, known as health, occur. In the same way all evils that affect the mind are removals of natural goods: when they are cured they are not moved to somewhere else, but when they are no longer in the mind once it has been restored to health, they will be nowhere. (Augustine 1999, XI; 41)

Etienne Gilson, the famous scholar of medieval philosophy, summarized Augustine's understanding of the nature of evil as follows:

> [E]vil can only be the corruption of one or other of these perfections in the nature possessing them. An evil nature is one in which measure, form or order is vitiated, and it is only evil in exact proportion to the degree in which they are vitiated. If the nature were not vitiated, it would be all order, form and measure, i.e. it would be good; even when vitiated, as nature it is still good, and evil only in so far as it is vitiated. (1960, 144)

But what are measure, form, and order? By "measure, form, and order," Augustine seems to have meant the structure and proportion that is definitive of or proper to an object as a member of its kind. For example, the human body is one that should be symmetrical with respect to the contralateral positioning of its legs, arms, eyes, etc. As properly situated and functioning, these organs contribute to the measure, form, and order of the human organism and, therefore, increase its good. Augustine believed the created order of the universe is a gradation of mutable entities, with spiritual beings occupying a higher place in the order of being than material entities. Measure, form, and order go downward in a hierarchical scale of gradations among kinds of beings, yet members of all types of created objects, because they possess some degree of proper structure and proportionality, are good.

According to Augustine, evil is a disruption or privation of good as measure, form, and order. To the extent that evil is a disruption of this kind, it is disorder and corruption. Wherever there is less measure, form, and order than there ought to be, there evil exists. But whatever is disrupted in this way retains some good to the extent that it maintains some degree of proper structure and proportionality. It is important to make clear that on the privationist view of evil, nothing—no entity—can be completely evil. Evil as privation is parasitic on good in the sense that it requires for its presence some degree of measure, form, and order. To the degree that this proper structure and proportionality are present, there goodness is present. To the degree that this proper structure and proportionality are absent, there evil is present. But it must be stressed that although evil is a privative parasite, it is not a thing. It is not an entity in its own right. Its status as a privative parasite consists in its being a lack of measure, form, and order.

Equally important for Augustine's view of evil is the idea that evil is not privation or lack *per se*. For example, it is not evil that a stone cannot see. The stone's lack of sight is not evil because it was never intended that a stone should possess the structure and order that facilitate sight. Blindness is only evil in an entity that is supposed to be able to see. Similarly, it is not evil that a tree cannot hear. It was never intended that a tree should be able to hear. Hence, the lack in a tree of the measure, form, and order that facilitate hearing is not evil. A human being, however, should have the requisite structures that promote sight and hearing. Hence, damage to an eye or an ear that results in blindness or deafness in a person is a real evil.

In conclusion, on the Augustinian view of evil, evil cannot exist in and of itself but only as a parasite on what is good. Should all measure, form, and order cease to be, evil would cease to be. All creation is good, some parts containing more structure and order than others. But wherever there is a lack of measure, form, and order that should be present, there is evil. On the privationist understanding of evil, pain cannot be intrinsically evil because evil is a lack or privation of measure, form, and order. For Lewis, while "[e]vil is certainly not a 'Thing'" (2007, 8), pain is intrinsically evil because the evilness of an experience of pain, where an experience of pain is an event in a soul, is not a lack but a positive property (characteristic, feature) of that experience.

3.6 Space, Time, and Meaning

At the outset of *The Problem of Pain*, Lewis wrote about why he was not a theist in his earlier life:

> Not many years ago when I was an atheist, if anyone had asked me, "Why do you not believe in God?" my reply would have run something like this: "Look at the universe we live in. By far the greatest part of it consists of empty space, completely dark and unimaginably cold. The bodies which move in this space are so few and so small in comparison with the space itself that even if every one of them were known to be crowded as full as it could hold with perfectly happy creatures, it would still be difficult to believe that life and happiness were more than a by-product to the power that made the universe. As it is, however, the scientists think it likely that very few of the suns of space—perhaps none of them except our own—have any planets; and in our own system it is improbable that any planet except the Earth sustains life. And Earth herself existed without life for millions of years and may exist for millions more when life has left her ... The [human] race is doomed. Every race that comes into being in any part of the universe is doomed; for the universe, they tell us, is running down, and will sometime be a uniform infinity of homogeneous matter at a low temperature. All stories will come to nothing: all life will turn out in the end to have been a transitory and senseless contortion upon the idiotic face of infinite matter." (2001f, 1–2, 3)

Before becoming a theist, then, Lewis believed the insignificant size of our earth and other celestial bodies relative to the vast reaches of empty space, as well as the extreme brevity of life compared to the vast stretches of time, implied negative judgments about the meaningfulness of life (and the existence of God). But as he continued to think about these issues, he came to believe that the issue of size was irrelevant to the question of life's meaning, understood as that which makes life worth living. The following is Lewis's view after he became a Christian:

> The real question is why the spatial insignificance of the earth, after being known for centuries [at least all the way back to Ptolemy in the second century CE], should suddenly in the last century [the nineteenth] have become an argument against Christianity. I do not know why this has happened; but I am sure it does not mark an increased clarity of thought, for the argument from size is ... very feeble.

> When the doctor at a post-mortem diagnoses poison, pointing to the state of the dead man's organs, his argument is rational because he has a clear idea of that opposite state in which the organs would have been if no poison were present. In the same way, if we use the vastness of space and the smallness of earth to disprove the existence of God, we ought to have a clear idea of the sort of universe we should expect if

God did exist. But have we? Whatever space may be in itself ... we certainly perceive it as three-dimensional, and to three-dimensional space we can conceive no boundaries. By the very forms of our perceptions, therefore, we must feel as if we lived somewhere in infinite space. If we discovered no objects in this infinite space except those which are of use to man (our own sun and moon), then this vast emptiness would certainly be used as a strong argument against the existence of God. If we discover other bodies, they must be habitable or uninhabitable: and the odd thing is that both these hypotheses are used as grounds for rejecting Christianity. If the universe is teeming with life, this, we are told, reduces to absurdity the Christian claim—or what is thought to be the Christian claim—that man is unique ... If, on the other hand, the earth is really unique, then that proves that life is only an accidental by-product in the universe, and so again disproves our religion. (1970, 39–40)

Lewis concluded that an objection from the size of the earth against the meaningfulness of life is not, contrary to what one might think, an argument based "on the observed nature of the actual universe at all. [One] can make it without waiting to find out what the universe is like, for it will fit any kind of universe we choose to imagine" (2001c, 80). But if the objection from size is not based on empirical observation, what, then, explains the raising of it? After he had suggested that bafflement about existence *per se* is an inherent feature of the way we think of things, Lewis went on to mention that the claim that difference of size determines differences of value is erroneous and rests on no more than a non-rational assumption:

I suspect there is something in our very mode of thought which makes it inevitable that we should always be baffled by actual existence, *whatever* character actual existence may have. Perhaps a finite and contingent creature—a creature that might not have existed—will always find it hard to acquiesce in the brute fact that it is, here and now, attached to an actual order of things.

However that may be, it is certain that the whole argument from size rests on the assumption that differences of size ought to coincide with differences of value: for unless they do, there is, of course, no reason why the minute earth and the yet smaller human creatures upon it should not be the most important things in a universe that contains the spiral nebulae. Now, is this assumption rational or emotional? ... I ... conclude that the importance attached to the great differences of size is an affair, not of reason but of emotion ... (1970, 40–1)

Lewis believed that the meaningfulness of our lives is a function of our experiences of what is good, where what is good is something of positive value. He affirmed that what ultimately matters is that God created us to be happy, and happiness is a good that can be experienced regardless of how large or small the experiencer is in comparison with other things. A person who is short can be just as happy as someone who is tall. A person who exists on a tiny planet can be just as happy as someone who exists on a large one. So if the meaning of life is about happiness, arguments about life's meaninglessness from considerations of size are really red herrings.

So much, then, for Lewis's treatment of size and its relationship to the meaning of life as the experience of perfect happiness. What about the relationship between the meaning of life as the experience of perfect happiness and time? Here, Lewis believed there is an important connection. To understand what it is, consider the following objection to the idea of everlasting life raised by the contemporary atheist, Julian Baggini, in his book *What's It All About?*:

> An eternal life might turn out to be the most meaningless of all. What would be the point of doing anything today if you could just as easily do it tomorrow? As Albert Camus put it in *The Plague*, "The order of the world is shaped by death." The very fact that one day life will end is what propels us to act at all … Life must be finite to have meaning, and if finite life can have meaning, then this life can have meaning … [L]ife's meaning has to be found in the living of life itself, and the promise of eventual death is necessary to make any action worthwhile at all. (2004, 54–5)

Is death needed to make any action both possible and worthwhile and to provide life with meaning? Lewis believed that it is not. On many occasions, the purpose for which we act is that we experience the pleasure that comes from what we do, where the pleasure is intrinsically good. For example, Lewis insisted that reading is a source of pleasure. He wrote to his friend Arthur Greeves in February, 1932, that "re-reading old favourites is one of the things we differ on, isn't it, and you do it very rarely. I probably do it too much. It is one of my greatest pleasures: indeed I can't imagine a man really enjoying a book and reading it only once" (2004b, 54). Writing, too, was a source of pleasure for Lewis. In a letter from April, 1936, to his former student Dom Bede (Alan) Griffiths, Lewis confessed "that I have a constant temptation to over asperity as soon as I get a pen in my hand, even when there is no subjective anger to prompt me: it comes, I think, simply from the pleasure of using the English language forcibly … " (2004b, 187). In addition to mental sources of pleasure like reading and writing, Lewis knew bodily sources of pleasure just as well. Walking tours with friends that frequently lasted several days were some of them. As a caricature of himself, Lewis had Ransom, the central figure in his science fiction story *Out of the Silent Planet*, explain why he was where he was in the dark of night:

> "How do you come to be in this benighted part of the country?"
>
> "I'm on a walking-tour, said Ransom … "

"God!" exclaimed Devine ... Do you do it for money, or is it sheer masochism?"

"Pleasure, of course," said Ransom ... (Lewis 2003a, 18)

And some bodily sources of pleasure could be mixed with mental pleasures of remembrance. Lewis related the following to Mary van Deusen in a letter from March, 1955:

> I feel strongly, with you, that there was something more than a physical pleasure in those youthful activities. Even now, at my age, do we often have a *purely* physical pleasure? Well, perhaps, a few of the more hopelessly prosaic ones: say, scratching or getting one's shoes off when one's feet are tired. I'm sure my meals are not a purely physical pleasure. All the associations of every other time one has had the same food (every rasher of bacon is now 56 years thick with me) come in: and with things like Bread, Wine, Honey, Apples, there are all the echoes of myth, fairy-tale, poetry, [and] scripture. (2007, 583)

So Lewis believed that death is not needed to explain why it is that we act. Pleasure is intrinsically good and its attractiveness leads us to want it and, in not a few cases, to act to experience it *now*. In a half-hearted concession to the idea that we act for pleasure, Baggini writes: "[m]oments of pleasure are precious *because* they pass, because we cannot make them last any longer than they do" (2004, 133). Lewis acknowledged the evanescent nature of the pleasure of listening to opera on the gramophone in a letter to Greeves in February, 1916: "like every other pleasure it just slips out of your hand when you think you've got it. The most striking example of this is the holiday which one looks forward to all the term and which is over and gone while one is still thinking how best to enjoy it" (Lewis 2004a, 164). But while Lewis knew first-hand the fleeting nature of experiences of pleasure, he would have responded that Baggini is mistaken about what makes moments of pleasure precious. Moments of pleasure are not precious because they pass but because they are intrinsically good. But most importantly for present purposes, Lewis would have added that not only would moments of pleasure be precious even if they never passed, but also we would wish that they never pass precisely because they are intrinsically good. In the following comment to Greeves in March, 1916, Lewis connects the fleetingness of pleasure with the notion of perfect happiness:

> I well remember the glorious walk of which you speak, how we ... were for a short time perfectly happy—which is a rare enough condition, God knows. As Keats says "Rarely, rarely comest thou, spirit of Delight". I do hope we shall have many more pleasant hours ... (2004a, 171)

Lewis's comment to Greeves intimates why the experience of perfect happiness as something that never ends is the purpose of life. Were it to end, as moments of such happiness do in this life, something would be deeply amiss. In the thralls of some of the happiest days of his life as a married man, Lewis wrote: "O God, if there were no such thing as the Future!" (Lewis 2007, 864). The future in this life, he knew all too well, spelled the end of the happiness he enjoyed in the present.

In Lewis's mind, then, it is the intrinsic goodness of pleasure and our being created to experience it without end that explain why there is a significant connection between time and the meaning of life. Not only is death not needed to explain why we act, but also, given that the perfect happiness for which we were created and which we desire cannot be had in this life, there must be life after death where it can be experienced. Lewis believed that one of the deceits foisted upon us by modernity is the idea "that Earth can be turned into Heaven at some future date by politics or eugenics or ... psychology or what not" (1961b, 133). He thought this notion ludicrous, and concluded that, as I will discuss in Section 3.9, life ultimately does not make sense without the experience of the perfect happiness we so deeply desire. So while issues of size are not relevant for the meaning of life as the experience of the perfect happiness which makes life worth living, the fact that perfect happiness is that which makes life worth living has important temporal implications in the form of the requirement that there be life after death.

3.7   Another Alternative Rejected

The Lewis scholar Peter Kreeft writes: "Hedonism identifies the good with pleasure. Lewis does not deny that pleasure is good ... Pleasure is good, but goodness is not the same as pleasure" (1994, 78). Lewis would have agreed: pleasure is good (indeed, it is intrinsically good) without being identical with good, just as a ball is red without being identical with redness. Kreeft goes on to assert that "[i]n pursuing happiness, even if we are shallow enough to identify it with pleasure ... we do not have the right to lie, cheat, steal, betray, and harm" (1994, 78). Even if we are shallow enough to identify happiness with pleasure? At this point, not only does Kreeft misunderstand Lewis, but Lewis would likely have accused him of Bulverizing. While Lewis believed we ordinarily think of happiness as experiences of pleasure, ordinariness is not identical with shallowness. The philosopher of happiness, Nicholas White, has written that the hedonistic understanding of happiness "takes happiness to be constituted by something [pleasure] that ... everyone finds attractive, or even attractive in the extreme. It's so attractive, in fact, that virtually every philosopher who's not a hedonist [about happiness] has felt obliged to explain why not" (2006, 53–4). Lewis believed that no philosopher has convincingly explained why the commonsensical identification of happiness with pleasure is mistaken.

Most who write about Lewis have not felt obliged to explain why he was, or was not, a hedonist about happiness. Indeed, as I have already stated, most who write about him do not spend any significant time explaining what he thought about happiness, period. A few, like Kreeft, mention that Lewis believed pleasure is good, but then proceed, without any explanation, to deny that Lewis believed happiness is experiences of pleasure. Some go a step further to claim or intimate that Lewis was a eudaemonist about happiness. While I have addressed this issue at length elsewhere (Goetz 2015a), it is important to devote some space here to explaining why Lewis was not a eudaemonist about happiness.

What is a eudaemonist? According to the philosopher, Nicholas Wolterstorff,

> [t]he eudaimonist holds that ... the well-lived life [is], by definition, the happy life, the *eudaimōn* life ... It is important to understand what sort of goal happiness is [according to the eudaimonist]. "Happiness" is not the name of experience of a certain sort. "Pleasure" names experiences of a certain sort; "happiness" does not. The eudaimonist is not saying that one's sole end in itself is or should be bringing about experiences of a certain sort, everything else being a means ... [T]he ancient eudaimonists insisted that *eudaimonia* is activity. Happiness does not consist in what happens to one but in what one makes of what happens to one. (2008, 150, 151, 152)

In light of Wolterstorff's remarks, there are three considerations that weigh against the view that Lewis espoused eudaemonism.

First, there are Lewis's own statements about hedonism which I have already quoted (e.g., that God is a hedonist, and that if he (Lewis) had written a book on the problem of pleasure, a reader might have found his views too hedonistic). When read straightforwardly, these statements support the view that he thought of happiness as experiences of pleasure. Indeed, anyone who takes the time to carefully read Lewis cannot help but notice how often he mentions and discusses pleasure and pain.

Those who either completely neglect or give passing mention to Lewis's view of pleasure and happiness sometimes mistakenly take his mention of virtue, which is a disposition to virtuous action, as sufficient for his being a eudaemonist. For example, Adam Barkman writes: "Lewis agreed with Plato (and ... also with Aristotle) that although virtue is a means to happiness, it is also an essential part of happiness ... True Happiness always requires virtue ... " (2009, 395). The problem here is that while Lewis did believe that perfect happiness requires virtue in the sense that only those who justly choose a virtuous life should experience perfect happiness (see Chapter 8), and once in heaven they will enjoy the activity which flows from their virtuous character (see Chapter 4), so far as I know he *never* stated (and Barkman never provides a reference where he stated) that virtuous activity is an essential *part of* happiness. At one point, Barkman claims that eudaemonism is the view that "makes the desire for happiness prior to duty to the moral law" (2009, 322). If someone who believes this general statement qualifies as a eudaemonist, then Lewis was a eudaemonist. But a person can believe this statement without in any way believing that virtuous activity is an essential part of happiness, which Wolterstorff and Barkman (at other points) maintain is the belief of a eudaemonist.

Second, Lewis was commonsensical. The hedonist's concept of happiness is that of ordinary people. The eudaemonist's concept of happiness is not. The eudaemonist philosopher Julia Annas has this to say about ancient eudaemonist theories vis-à-vis common sense:

> [A]ncient [eudaemonistic] theories are all more or less revisionary, and some of them are highly counter-intuitive. They give an account of happiness which, if baldly presented to a non-philosopher without any of the supporting arguments, sounds wrong, even absurd ... [A]ncient theories greatly expand and modify the ordinary non-philosophical understanding of happiness, opening themselves up to criticism from non-philosophers on this score.
>
> It is in fact common ground to the ancient theories that, on the one hand, we are all right to assume that our final end is happiness of some kind, and to try to achieve happiness in reflecting systematically on our final end; but that, on the other hand, we are very far astray in our initial assumptions about what happiness is ... So we should not be surprised that ancient theories have counter-intuitive consequences about happiness. (1993, 331)

Third, Lewis emphasized he believed that happiness directly involves the subject as a patient, not an agent. As Wolterstorff points out in the earlier quote, eudaemonists believe happiness is an activity, with the subject as an agent, in opposition to hedonists who believe it is something that happens to one. Because I will have much to say about this issue in Chapter 6, I will say no more about it here.[3]

3.8 Joy or *Sehnsucht*

Closely related to perfect happiness is what Lewis referred to as Joy or *Sehnsucht*, a concept that "[p]oets have said more about ... than philosophers" (2007, 996). Lewis thought of *Sehnsucht* as a ceaseless longing or desire for a place that cannot be satisfied by anything in this life. In Wesley Kort's words, Joy "is the sense of something expansive and appealing that evokes a strong sense of longing, as toward something that summons and completes" (2016, 34). Once again, it is best to let Lewis speak for himself. The following are some of the things he had to say about Joy:

[It] is that of an unsatisfied desire which is itself more desirable than any other satisfaction. I call it Joy, which is here a technical term and must be sharply distinguished both from Happiness and from Pleasure. Joy (in my sense) has indeed one characteristic, and one only, in common with them; the fact that anyone who has experienced it will want it again. Apart from that, and considered only in its quality, it might almost equally well be called a particular kind of unhappiness or grief. But then it is a kind we want. I doubt whether anyone who has tasted it would ever, if both were in his power, exchange it for all the pleasures in the world. But then Joy is never in our power and pleasure often is. (1955, 17–18)

All Joy reminds. It is never a possession, always a desire for something longer ago or further away or still "about to be." (1955, 78)

Joy is distinct not only from pleasure in general but even from aesthetic pleasure. It must have the stab, the pang, the inconsolable longing. (1955, 72)

I came to know by experience that [Joy] is not a disguise of sexual desire. Those who think that if adolescents were all provided with suitable mistresses we should soon hear no more of "immortal longings" are certainly wrong. I learned this mistake to be a mistake by the simple, if discreditable, process of repeatedly making it. From the Northernness one could not easily have slid into erotic fantasies without noticing the difference; but when the world of Morris became the frequent medium of Joy, this transition became possible. It was quite easy to think that one desired those forests for the sake of their female inhabitants, the garden of Hesperus for the sake of his daughters, Hylas' river for the river nymphs. I repeatedly followed that path—to the end. And at the end one found pleasure; which immediately resulted in the discovery that pleasure (whether that pleasure or any other) was not what you had been looking for ... Joy is not a substitute for sex; sex is very often a substitute for Joy. I sometimes wonder whether all pleasures are not substitutes for Joy. (1955, 169–70)

Lewis, then, held that Joy is a *desire*. As Stephen Logan points out, Lewis did not say that "the unsatisfied desire is more satisfying [than any other satisfied desire], but that it is more *desirable* [than any other satisfaction]" (2010, 37). According to Lewis, "considered only in its quality, [Joy] might almost equally well be called a particular kind of unhappiness ... " (1955, 18). Given that something with extrinsic value gets that value from something else of value to which it is related, these statements by Logan and Lewis about Joy imply that it might itself be simultaneously both extrinsically evil (its present failure to be satisfied produces pain) and extrinsically good (the idea of someday possessing that at which Joy is directed produces pleasure in the present). Though Joy might be pleasurable in this way, it is not identical with pleasure (and, therefore, also not identical with happiness). Beyond not being identical with pleasure, Joy differs from pleasure by not being even indirectly subject to the will (choice). One can choose a multitude of activities that will produce pleasure, but not so with Joy: "Thence arose the fatal determination to recover the old thrill [Joy], and at last the moment when I was compelled to realize that all such efforts were failures. I had no lure to which the bird would come" (Lewis 1955, 166). Lewis claimed that the source of the error of thinking that Joy is obtainable by an act of will is the deeper error of thinking that the object of Joy, what it is about, is a *state of mind*:

> The first [blunder] was made at the very moment when I formulated the complaint that the "old thrill" was becoming rarer and rarer. For by that complaint I smuggled in the assumption that what I wanted was a "thrill," a state of my own mind. And there lies the deadly error. Only when your whole attention and desire are fixed on something else ... does the "thrill" arise. It is a by-product. Its very existence presupposes that you desire not it but something other and outer. If by any perverse askesis [training] or the use of any drug it could be produced from within, it would at once be seen to be of no value. For take away the object, and what, after all, would be left? ... And the second error is, having thus falsely made a state of mind your aim, to attempt to produce it. From the fading of the Northernness I ought to have drawn the conclusion that the Object, the Desirable, was further away, more external, less subjective, than even such a comparatively public and external thing as a system of mythology—had, in fact, only shone through that system ... But far more often I frightened [Joy] away by my greedy impatience to snare it, and, even when it came, instantly destroyed it by introspection, and at all times vulgarized it by my false assumption about its nature. (Lewis 1955, 168–9)

> Joy itself, considered simply as an event in my own mind, turned out to be of no value at all. All the value lay in that of which Joy was the desiring. And that object, quite clearly, was no state of my own mind or body at all. In a way, I had proved this by elimination. I had tried everything in my own mind and body; as it were, asking myself, "Is it this you want? Is it this?" Last of all I had asked if Joy itself was what I wanted; and, labeling it "aesthetic experience," had pretended I could answer Yes. But that answer too had broken down. Inexorably Joy proclaimed, "You want—I myself am your want of—something other, outside, not you nor any state of you." (Lewis 1955, 220–1)

So Joy is a desire whose object is not a state of mind. There is much evidence in support of the view that Lewis thought of the direct object of Joy as a *place*. In *The Pilgrim's Regress*, which was published in 1933 not long after his conversion to Christianity, Lewis described the object of an intense longing as a mysterious distant island:

> [T]here came to him [John, the pilgrim and main character] from beyond the wood a sweetness and a pang so piercing ... It seemed to him that a mist which hung at the far end of the wood had parted for a moment, and through the rift he had seen a calm sea, and in the sea an island, where the smooth turf sloped down unbroken to the bays ... (1992b, 8)

As the Lewis scholar, Alister McGrath says:

> Although "the Landlord" – God – features prominently in [*The Pilgrim's Regress*], it is quite clear that the sense of longing experienced by John, the pilgrim, concerns this island. Desire is not associated primarily with finding the Landlord; it is the island that John seeks, believing it to be the source of his heart's desire. (2014, 115)

Almost a decade after writing *The Pilgrim's Regress*, we still find Lewis referring to Joy's object as a place, as "our own far-off country" (2001g, 29), "Heaven" (2001g, 33), and "another world" (2001b, 137).[4]

In an Afterword to the third edition of *The Pilgrim's Regress* in 1943, Lewis wrote:

> if a man diligently followed this desire, pursuing the false objects until their falsity appeared and then resolutely abandoning them, he must come out at last into the clear knowledge that the human soul was made to enjoy some object that is never fully given—nay, cannot even be imagined as given—in our present mode of subjective and spatio-temporal existence. (1992b, 204–5)

And speaking of *Sehnsucht* in the works of Edmund Spenser, Lewis wrote that it would not be regarded by a Christian Platonist "as a horrible form of spiritual dram-drinking," but "would logically appear as among the sanest and most fruitful experiences we have," because the longed-for object "really exists and really draws us to itself" (Lewis 2002, 357).

Two questions loom large. First, where does God fit into Lewis' account of Joy? Is God the "object" the soul was made to enjoy? McGrath provides a thoroughly reasonable answer: "Lewis clearly assumes that 'heaven' entails God, so that an argument for the existence of heaven is an indirect argument for the existence of God" (2014, 117).

Second, where do pleasure and happiness fit into Lewis' account of Joy? Could someone as thoughtful as Lewis, who claimed that "We know we are being touched by a finger of that right hand at which there are pleasures for evermore" (Lewis 1992a, 90) and that "God not only understands but *shares* the desire ... for complete and ecstatic happiness ... [and]

made me for no other purpose than to enjoy it" (Lewis 2004b, 123), also claim that Joy is directly aimed at a place and indirectly at a person, but has nothing to do with pleasure and happiness? Any charitable reader must answer "No." Surely Lewis believed that the pleasures that are for evermore and comprise complete and ecstatic happiness are to be had if and only if one makes peace with and finds one's rest in God in heaven. In short, the object of Joy is not a state of mind but an idyllic place (heaven) where one can experience a state of mind (perfect happiness) through a personal relationship with the being (God) who provides that happiness:

> The happiness which God designs for His higher creatures is the happiness of being ... united to Him ... That is why it is just no good asking God to make us happy in our own way without bothering about religion. God cannot give us a happiness and peace apart from Himself, because it is not there. There is no such thing. (Lewis 2001b, 48, 50)

As Barkman writes, "[Lewis] felt that Joy ... is valuable only insofar as it leads us to its proper object, which is God *qua* Happiness; indeed it is for this reason that Lewis clearly distinguished between Joy and Happiness, for the former leads to the latter" (2009, 82).

Here, Lewis's exposition of "Appreciative pleasures" deserves brief discussion (Lewis 1988, 12–17). A pleasure of appreciation is a pleasure experienced with the understanding that the source of the pleasure deserves to be appreciated:

> This judgment that the object is very good, this attention (almost homage) offered to it as a kind of debt, this wish that it should be and should continue being what it is even if we were never to enjoy it, can go out not only to things but to persons. When it is offered to a woman we call it admiration; when to a man, hero-worship; when to God, worship simply. (Lewis 1988, 16–17)

So a person can delight/take pleasure in God upon an appreciation of the fact that God created him for the purpose of experiencing the pleasure that he is having. This person desires to give glory to the appreciated source of the pleasure. Indeed, Lewis thought of glorifying God as praising Him for the pleasure that comes from being in a relationship with Him. In his book *Reflections on the Psalms*, he described how it finally occurred to him that praising God is itself a pleasurable act that consummates the enjoyment of Him:

> [A]ll enjoyment spontaneously overflows into praise unless ... shyness or the fear of boring others is deliberately brought in to check it. The world rings with praise—lovers praising their mistresses, readers their favorite poet, walkers praising the countryside ... I had not noticed how

the humblest, and at the same time most balanced and capacious, minds, praised most ... I had not noticed either that just as men spontaneously praise whatever they value, so they spontaneously urge us to join them in praising it ... The Psalmists in telling everyone to praise God are doing what all men do when they speak of what they care about ... [W]e delight to praise what we enjoy because the praise not merely expresses but completes the enjoyment; it is its appointed consummation ... [T]he delight is incomplete till it is expressed. (Lewis 1986b, 94–5)

In Lewis's estimation, then, God made all people for perfect happiness, and the experiences of pleasure in this life are an early taste of what is in store for believers in their far-off heavenly country in God's presence. Joy is a desire for a paradisal place with its God, who, when He is thanked, praised, and served for his goodness, ultimately provides the pleasure that constitutes ecstatic happiness:

[B]ut the mind and, still more, the body receives life from Him at a thousand removes—through our ancestors, through our food, through the elements. The faint, far-off results of those energies which God's creative rapture implanted in matter when He made the worlds are what we now call physical pleasures; and even thus filtered, they are too much for our present management. What would it be to taste at the fountainhead of that stream of which even these lower reaches prove so intoxicating? Yet that, I believe, is what lies before us. The whole man is to drink joy from the fountain of joy. As St. Augustine said, the rapture of the saved soul will "flow over" into the glorified body. In the light of our present specialised and depraved appetites, we cannot imagine this *torrens voluptatis* [torrent of pleasure] ... (Lewis 2001g, 44)

The Scotch catechism says that man's chief end is "to glorify God and enjoy Him forever". But we shall then know that these are the same thing. Fully to enjoy is to glorify. In commanding us to glorify Him, God is inviting us to enjoy Him. (Lewis 1986b, 96–7)

[The Christian] believes ... that [men] were created by God and so built that they can find their true and lasting happiness only by being united to God ... (Lewis 1970, 109)

So rather than Joy being at odds with the idea of perfect happiness as nothing but experiences of pleasure, the existence of Joy or *Sehnsucht* is, as Peter Kreeft says, a strong clue "that infinite happiness exists and that you are designed to enjoy it" (1989, 254). John Beversluis puts it this way: "As a Christian Romantic, Lewis was convinced that all men desire God, since all men desire happiness and true happiness can be found in God alone" (1985, 27). Ultimately, then, the explanation for why Joy, as an unsatisfied desire, is more desirable than any satisfaction of another desire is because its satisfaction, when it occurs, will be a thoroughly pleasurable state of existence that never ends and to which the pleasures of satisfied desire in this world are but pointers.

3.9 Things Making Sense

According to Lewis, all of us seek unity among the multiplicity of things in our lives. Thus, when he discussed the idea of the unity of a human work of art like a poem in the medieval world, Lewis insisted that the demand for unity was not a medieval oddity but part of "the nature of consciousness itself" (1936, 141). And if works of art "lack unity, they lack it not because they are medieval, but because they are, so far, bad" (Lewis 1936, 141).

Lewis believed that just as human artifacts as such require unity, so also a human life, as an artifact, requires unity if it is to be intelligible and understood. But while the unity of a life is necessary if events in it are to make sense, it is not sufficient. There must be a *certain kind* of unity in which the events are arranged a certain way. And to understand how this unity is ultimately achieved, we must return to the purpose of life, where a life "ends" with a non-ending experience of nothing but the intrinsic goodness of pleasure, where that goodness makes life worth living. Given that Lewis thought this is the purpose of life, he believed it is perfectly understandable why we have a desire for perfect happiness. And, he concluded, if this desire can ultimately be justly satisfied, things will ultimately make sense. They will ultimately fit together in the right way. If this desire cannot ultimately be justly satisfied, then life will ultimately not make sense. Things will not finally come together as they should. In a letter to Greeves in mid-1930, Lewis described what one of his favorite authors, William Morris, missed about the importance of unsatisfied desire:

> You know I always thought Morris the most essentially *pagan* of all poets. The beauty of the actual world, the vague longings [which] it excites, the inevitable failure to satisfy these longings ... [B]ut of what this longing really pointed to, of the reason why beauty made us home-sick, of the reality *behind*, I thought he had no inkling. And for that reason his poetry always seemed to me dangerous and apt to lead to sensuality—for it is the frustrated longing that drives us to the *pis aller*, and as we lose hope of our real immortal mistress we turn to harlots. (2004a, 911)

And, thus, Lewis ended up with a third way of understanding the meaning of life (in addition to those concerned with being created for a purpose and experiencing that which makes life worth living). According to this third way, to ask "What is the meaning of life?" is to ask "Do things ultimately make sense?" We find Lewis explicitly linking meaning with sense in his account of his trying to prove God's nonexistence:

> Thus in the very act of trying to prove that God did not exist—in other words, that the whole of reality was senseless—I found I was forced to assume that one part of reality—namely my idea of justice—was full of sense ... If the whole universe has no meaning, we should never have found out that it has no meaning ... (2001b, 38–9)

Another way of capturing this third way of understanding life's meaning is in terms of the concept of things fitting together in the right way. Thus, when he wrote about the medieval model of the universe as conveyed through the minds of poets and artists, Lewis commented that they "rejoiced also in that great imagined structure [of the universe] which gave [the particulars] all their place. Every particular fact and story became more interesting and more pleasurable if, by being properly fitted in, it carried one's mind back to the Model as a whole" (Lewis 1964, 203).

As will become clear in Chapter 6, Lewis believed that the idea of things ultimately making sense consisted of our lives being stories or narratives that end the right way with perfect happiness. In a Godless universe, "[a]ll stories will come to nothing: all life will turn out in the end to have been a transitory and senseless contortion upon the idiotic face of infinite matter" (Lewis 2001f, 3). However, in a universe created by God, no story need come to nothing, because each person's life can end with the perfect happiness for which he or she was created.

In discussing which big picture or overall framework makes the most sense of our lives, Alister McGrath suggests that Lewis disagreed with

> a "glib and shallow rationalism" which holds that the great truths about the purpose and value of human existence can be solved by unaided human reason. For Lewis, the kind of "sense making" offered by the Christian vision of reality is about discerning a resonance between its theory and the way the world seems to be. Its theoretical spectacles seem to bring reality into sharp focus, just as a false theory prevents us from seeing what is really there. (2014, 136)

I am not sure what McGrath thinks a "glib and shallow rationalism" is (Lewis used the phrase to describe the life of his intellect as a materialistic atheist (Lewis 1955, 170) whose goal was to justify what really "mattered most of all" to him, which was his "deep-seated hatred of authority, [his] monstrous individualism, [and his] lawlessness" (Lewis 1955, 172)). What I am sure of is that Lewis wrote at length in defense of reason. And I am also sure that he believed that reason made it vividly clear that the purpose of life is that an individual be perfectly happy, and that this happiness is identical with experiences of pleasure, with the value of being intrinsically good. Lewis believed not only that this is the way things seem to be, but also that it is the way things are. And an individual need not know anything about Christianity in order to know these things. For Lewis, Christianity was itself reasonable because it affirmed what we know about ourselves on the basis of our reason alone.

Yet, Lewis knew all too well that there would be individuals who questioned the reasonableness of their own or others' values merely on the ground that they had learned them from their elders, Christian or not. Lewis remained convinced that there was no need to cede ground to these deniers of the reasonableness of the goodness of pleasure and happiness. He insisted that no one's values "are invalidated by the fact that they have a history in which nursemaids play a part—any more than reason collapses when you realise that you learned most of it from your elders" (Lewis 2004b, 373). After all, if the learning of reason and values were sufficient to invalidate them, then the judgment that one's reason and values were unsound because they had been learned from one's elders would itself be unsound.

The question about the meaning of life can be reasonably understood in a variety of ways. Lewis understood it as "What is the purpose of life?," "What makes life worth living?," and "What is the way in which life makes sense?" In answering these different questions, he made use of such concepts as happiness, pleasure and pain, and intrinsic good and evil. But where did he think morality fitted into all of this? This is the subject of Chapter 4.

notes

1   Some have verbally expressed consternation at my claims that Lewis believed we know the purpose for which God created us and that this purpose is hedonistic in nature. The burden of this chapter is to answer the second concern. As to the first worry, those who raise it might be surprised to learn that Lewis was part of mainstream Christian tradition. For example, Heiko Oberman, a scholar of the Reformed tradition, writes that, according to John Calvin,

> redemption is far more than just restoration, and grace does not merely repair nature, but reopens the intended path of evolution towards fulfillment and happiness. "Eternal bliss" is not merely the end of the road, but its goal, its *finis*, best understood as an immense magnet which "directs" all preceding stages ... [I]t must be emphasized that Calvin's understanding of happiness should not be spiritualized. After all, the creation "'in all its parts" has only one purpose: to serve mankind as source and resource of happiness ... [I]t is granted—day by day—in a most earthly fashion: in the taste of food and in the afterglow of wine ... Augustine's dualistic dialectic between *frui* and *uti*, between enjoyment of God and use of the world, is transcended [by Calvin] to make space for,

and lend legitimacy to, the pursuit of pleasure in the "sweet delicacies" of the world ... [F]or Calvin [the pursuit of happiness] belongs to the original purpose of human life on this earth. (Oberman 1993, 272–3, 280)

For another example of someone in the mainstream Christian tradition who held that God created us for the purpose that we be perfectly happy, see my discussion of Thomas Aquinas in Goetz (2015a).

2   That Lewis understood the distinction is evidenced by his comment about Machiavelli, whom he claimed was not aware of it: "Machiavelli had no more notion of the amoral as distinct from the immoral than of the steam-engine" (Lewis 1954, 51); and by his recapitulation of Hugo of St. Victor's view that pleasure is "evil, but not morally evil ... " (Lewis 1936, 15).

3   Justin Dyer and Micah Watson point out that "[p]leasure [is] important in Lewis' view of the world," while stressing that Lewis did not embrace "full-blown consequentialism or utilitarianism" about politics and government (2016, 119). They maintain (2016, 116–23) that Lewis believed government is justified in interfering with the liberty and interests of its citizens on the basis of the harm principle of the utilitarian philosopher, John Stuart Mill. This principle holds that the state can justifiably interfere with a citizen's interests if his actions in promoting those interests interfere with or harm the interests of others. Dyer and Watson maintain that Lewis rejected the classical/ancient view that government has an interest in the well-being of its citizens and is therefore justified in interfering in their lives to help them realize the good life. Mill was a hedonist about happiness and the classical/ancient view of government was espoused by eudaemonists. So Dyer and Watson's understanding of Lewis's view of politics nicely mirrors my view of Lewis as a hedonist, and not a eudaemonist, about happiness.

4   In a manuscript now referred to as "Early Prose Joy," which is part of a notebook of Lewis from late 1930 or early 1931, Lewis discussed the influence of the plays of W. B. Yeats and the poems of William Morris on his idea of Joy. He explicitly noted that they thought of the object of this special desire as a place: "These plays and poems were all really written on the same theme: they told of men crazed with the desire for something out of reach, something here generally envisaged as a *place* ... beyond the world" (Lewis 2013a, 19).

morality

The morality of an action depends on the motive from which we act. If I fling half a crown to a beggar with intention to break his head, and he picks it up and buys victuals with it, the physical effect is good; but, with respect to me, the action is very wrong.

(Boswell 2008, 211)

"It might be well to give a thought to what the sin of Adam truly was. Augustine held it to be the fleshly act between man and woman, and considered it the root and origin of all sin ... "

"Neither the act nor abstention from the act is of itself either good or bad," said the bishop amiably, "but only in respect of its purpose ... "

(Peters 1990, 240)

I never see why we should do anything unless it is either a duty or a pleasure.

(Lewis 2007, 96)

4.1 More than Morality

When people hear or read about issues of value, about matters of good and evil, not infrequently their minds immediately turn to thinking about moral values and what is morally good or morally evil. Some, perhaps, even think that the purpose of life and that which makes life worth living are performing moral actions and being a morally good person. C. S. Lewis insisted that anyone who believes this is seriously mistaken. As we saw in Chapter 3, Lewis held that we are created for the purpose that we be perfectly happy, and he thought it is reasonable to maintain that were that purpose to be achieved, there would no longer be a need for morality.

Moreover, because Christianity affirms what is reasonable, it too acknowledges the transitory nature of morality:

> All right, Christianity will do you good—a great deal more good than you ever wanted or expected. And the first bit of good it will do you is to hammer into your head ... the fact that what you have hitherto called "good"—all that about "leading a decent life" and "being kind"—isn't quite the magnificent and all-important affair you supposed. It will teach you that in fact you can't be "good" (not for twenty-four hours) on your own moral efforts. And then it will teach you that even if you were, you still wouldn't have achieved the purpose for which you were created. Mere *morality* is not the end of life. You were made for something quite different from that ... The people who keep on asking if they can't lead a decent life without Christ, don't know what life is about; if they did they would know that a "decent life" is mere machinery compared with the thing we men are really made for. Morality is indispensable: but the Divine Life, which gives itself to us and which calls us to be gods, intends for us something in which morality will be swallowed up. (Lewis 1970, 112)

> [The moral realm] exists to be transcended ... [It is a] schoolmaster, as St. Paul says, to bring us to Christ. We must expect no more of it than of a schoolmaster; we must allow it no less. I must say my prayers today whether I feel devout or not; but that is only as I must learn my grammar if I am ever to read the poets.

> But the school-days, please God, are numbered. There is no morality in Heaven. The angels never knew (from within) the meaning of the word *ought*, and the blessed dead have long since gladly forgotten it. (Lewis 1992a, 115)

> You may ask, do I then think that moral value will have no place in the state of perfection? Well, it sounds a dreadful thing to say, but I'm almost inclined to answer No. It [the state of perfection] is never presented in Scripture in terms of service is it?—always in terms of suggesting fruition—a supper, a marriage, a drink. "I will give him the morning star." May not that be one of the divine jokes—to see people like Marcus Aurelius and [Matthew] Arnold & [John Stuart] Mill at last submitting to the fact that they can give up being *good* and start *receiving* good instead. (Lewis 2004b, 463–4)

Of course, on Lewis's view, the good that is received is perfect happiness. Reason plays a role analogous to that of a schoolteacher, and what it teaches is that we will never experience the perfect happiness for which we were created unless we take the moral life seriously. But successful students reach an endpoint after which they no longer need to go to classes, do their homework, and take exams. And Lewis maintained that when we experience perfect happiness, we will no longer need morality.

4.2   Morality, Pleasure, and Happiness

In what way, then, did Lewis believe morality is connected with happiness? The connection begins with practical reason, where by "practical reason" Lewis meant "judgement of good and evil" (Lewis 1967, 73), which is objective in nature. Given what he believed about what makes life worth living and the purpose of life, the judgment of practical reason about good and evil is first and foremost about the objective intrinsic goodness of pleasure and the objective intrinsic evilness of pain. Given our judgment about these values, morality involves our further judgment that we are sometimes required to give up, sacrifice, refrain from, or let pass a pursuit of the experiences of pleasure that we desire for ourselves:

> The ordinary idea which we all have before we become Christians is this. We take as our starting point our ordinary self with its various desires and interests. We then admit that something else—call it "morality" or "decent behaviour" ... —has claims on this self: claims which interfere with its own desires. What we mean by "being good" is giving in to those claims. Some of the things the ordinary self wanted to do turn out to be what we call "wrong": well, we must give them up. (Lewis 2001b, 195)

So while "every pleasure ... is ... a foretaste of ... the end for [which] we exist, the fruition of God ... [every pleasure] is ... not also, here [and] now, the *road* to that fruition for fallen creatures" (Lewis 2004b, 463). Sometimes we must forego pleasure. A logical question at this point is "But why should I sometimes, if not always, sacrifice satisfying my desire for pleasure? What is the purpose of my sacrifice? Is it something I should pursue for its own sake?" Lewis scoffed at the notion of pursuing the sacrifice of pleasure for its own sake. When one should give up satisfying one's desire for pleasure, the rationale for doing so should be respect for the *happiness* of others. Lewis expressed his view in comments about the concept of unselfishness:

> If you asked twenty good men today what they thought the highest of the virtues, nineteen would reply, Unselfishness. But if you had asked almost any of the great Christians of old, he would have replied, Love. You see what has happened? A negative term has been substituted for a positive, and this is of more than philological importance. The negative idea of Unselfishness carries with it the suggestion not primarily of securing good things for others, but of going without them ourselves, as if our abstinence and not their happiness was the important point. I do not think this is the Christian virtue of Love. The New Testament has lots to say about self-denial, but not about self-denial as an end in itself. (2001g, 25)

With not uncharacteristic terseness, Lewis wrote to Joan Lancaster that "*of course* you are quite right if you mean that giving up fun for no reason except that you think it's 'good' to give it up, is all nonsense" (2007, 871). Lewis was so convinced that unselfishness and/or sacrifice for its own sake is not the correct reason for being moral that he had the devilish Screwtape instruct his nephew Wormwood in *The Screwtape Letters* to "teach a man to surrender benefits not that others may be happy in having them [which is the right reason for the surrender] but that he may be unselfish in forgoing them [which is the wrong reason for the surrender]" (Lewis 1961b, 121). When a person is interested in rightly restraining himself, he is concerned that others fairly have an opportunity to experience the happiness for which they were created. Hence, Lewis wrote in *Mere Christianity* that "fair play ... between individuals" is the first concern "when we start thinking about morality ... " (2001b, 72).

For Lewis, the concept of happiness was also the key that unlocked the meaning of the word "Agapë" (love) in the New Testament. If love were an emotion or involuntary sentiment, reasoned Lewis, it would have made no sense to command it, because what is involuntary is not a matter of choice (the will). So Agapë must not have been used to refer to an emotion. Rather, "Agapë, is best seen ... in the words 'love your neighbour as yourself'. i.e. by an act of will, aim at your neighbour's good in the same way as you aim at your own" (Lewis 2004b, 408). And what is your good that makes intelligible the command to have regard for the good of your neighbor? "[Y]our own happiness" (Lewis 2004b, 408).

So Lewis believed happiness is the purpose of life and what makes life worth living, and when we are required to forego our happiness, it is because not foregoing it would unjustly and adversely impact the experiences of happiness of others. And Lewis understood that foregoing one's happiness is often displeasurable. In the letter to Joan Lancaster I quoted a moment ago, Lewis also penned:

> I don't think being good *always* goes with having fun: a martyr being tortured by Nero, or a resistance movement man refusing to give away his friends when tortured by the Germans, were being good but not having fun. And even in ordinary life there are things that [would] be fun to me but I mustn't do them because they [would] spoil other people's fun. (2007, 871)

Justin Dyer and Micah Watson capture Lewis's view concisely: "The propriety of pleasure is determined by its relationship to the moral law" (2016, 119).

But how do we know these moral truths about ways in which happiness should and should not be pursued? Lewis thought that all of us rationally just directly apprehend that the justification for basic moral principles like "Do not lie," "Do not steal," and "Do not commit adultery" is that we not wrongly pay for our happiness at the unjust expense of the sacrifice of the happiness of others:

> I myself … believe that the primary moral principles on which all others depend are rationally perceived. We "just see" that there is no reason why my neighbour's happiness should be sacrificed to my own, as we "just see" that things which are equal to the same thing are equal to one another. If we cannot prove either axiom, that is not because they are irrational but because they are self-evident and all proofs depend on them. Their intrinsic reasonableness shines by its own light. It is because all morality is based on such self-evident principles that we say to a man, when we would call him to right conduct, "Be reasonable." (Lewis 2001c, 54)[1]

So when people are tempted to sacrifice the happiness of others for their own happiness, they are tempted to act immorally for the sake of their own pleasure. For illustrative purposes, consider sexual pleasure. In his biography about Lewis's life, Chad Walsh writes about a time Lewis related a conversation he had had with some psychology-minded friends about sex:

> They had spent the entire evening discussing sex in the language of the clinic—"release for tensions," etc. Suddenly Lewis burst out, "If a visitor from Mars had overheard them he would never have suspected that sex has any connection with pleasure!" (1949, 13)

Lewis believed it is the goodness of the pleasure of sex that tempts one to wrest that pleasure from its proper context for an unacceptable reason and act immorally. And he thought the liberalizing use of contraceptives confirmed this point. While he wrote that he had "never propounded a general position about contraception" (Lewis 2004b, 798), and believed that its use is not intrinsically evil, he understood that those who had reservations about the commoditization of contraceptives were fighting an uphill battle. Indeed, he argued in *The Pilgrim's Regress* that "civilized man" would understandably cast a liberal use of contraceptives in a positive light. Thus, the character "Mr. Sensible," who Lewis, in a marginal note, stated represented "urbane heathen culture" (Lewis 2014, 77), maintained:

> To cut off pleasures from the consequences and conditions which they have by nature, detaching, as it were, the precious phrase from its irrelevant context, is what distinguishes the man from the brute and the citizen from the savage. I cannot join with those moralists who inveigh against the Roman emetics in their banquets: still less with those who would forbid the even more beneficent contraceptive devices of our later times. (Lewis 1992b, 78)

Contraceptives are designed to prevent what Lewis regarded as the obvious biological purpose of sex, namely, the conception of another life. But while he thought the biological purpose of sex is reproduction, he also believed that sex for pleasure between married persons was to be enjoyed. He wrote of his marital relationship with his wife, Joy Davidman, which occurred at a time in her life when she was in no condition to conceive or bear children, that

> [f]or those few years [she] and I feasted on love; every mode of it—solemn and merry, romantic and realistic, sometimes as dramatic as a thunderstorm, sometimes as comfortable and unemphatic as putting on your soft slippers. No cranny of heart or body remained unsatisfied. (Lewis 2001a, 7)

Thus, Lewis stressed that what one must not do is think the experience of sexual pleasure is in itself bad or evil:

> The biological purpose of sex is children … But if a healthy young man indulged his sexual appetite whenever he felt inclined, and if each act produced a baby, then in ten years he might easily populate a small village. This appetite is in ludicrous and preposterous excess of its function … Modern people are always saying, "Sex is nothing to be ashamed of." They may mean two things. They may mean "There is nothing to be ashamed of in the fact that the human race reproduces itself in a certain way, nor in the fact that it gives pleasure." If they mean that, they are right. Christianity says the same. It is not the thing, nor the pleasure, that is the trouble. The old Christian teachers said that if man had never fallen, sexual pleasure, instead of being less than it is now, would actually have been greater. I know some muddle-headed Christians have talked as if Christianity thought that sex, or the body, or pleasure, were bad in themselves. But they were wrong. (Lewis 2001b, 95–6, 98)

> The Christian attitude does not mean that there is anything wrong about sexual pleasure … It means that you must not isolate that pleasure and try to get it by itself … (Lewis 2001b, 105)

In sum, Lewis maintained that people who want sex without the result of offspring desire it for the purpose of experiencing pleasure, and what goes for sex goes for acts of other kinds. Thus, given his belief that an experience of pleasure is intrinsically good, Lewis insisted that the expression "bad pleasures" is just a common way of articulating the idea of

> "pleasures snatched by unlawful acts." It is the stealing of the apple that is bad, not the sweetness. The sweetness is still a beam from the glory. That does not palliate the stealing. It makes it worse. There is sacrilege in the theft. We have abused a holy thing … [and ignored] the smell of Deity that hangs about it. (1992a, 89, 90)

Pleasure itself, Lewis reiterated, is always good: "I think *all* pleasure simply good: what we call bad pleasures are pleasures produced by actions, or inactions, [which] break the moral law, and it is those actions or inactions [which] are bad, not the pleasures" (2004b, 462–3).

Lewis's belief that all experiences of pleasure are intrinsically good was the foundation of his view that we always in the end act under the guise or aspect of the good. Stated slightly differently, Lewis believed that we always act ultimately for the purpose of bringing into existence some state of affairs that is good. Thus, when in *The Abolition of Man* he criticized the two authors of what he referred to as *The Green Book* (the real title was *The Control of Language* by Alec King and Martin Ketley), he maintained that

> [t]hey write in order to produce certain states of mind in the rising generation, if not because they think those states of mind intrinsically just or good, yet certainly because they think them to be the means to some state of society which they regard as desirable ... The important point is not the precise nature of their end, but the fact that they have an end at all. They must have, or their book ... is written to no purpose. And this end must have real value in their eyes. To abstain from calling it good and to use, instead, such predicates as "necessary" or "progressive" or "efficient" would be a subterfuge. They could be forced by argument to answer the questions "necessary for what?", "progressing towards what?", "effecting what?"; in the last resort they would have to admit that some state of affairs was in their opinion good for its own sake. (Lewis 2001d, 28)

If we ultimately always act under the guise of the good, it follows that we ultimately never act for the sake of what is evil or bad in itself. And Lewis believed this is the case. In a comment about Christ's turning water into wine, Lewis stressed that the miracle, among other things, made clear that God is not a being who "loves tragedy and tears and fasting *for their own sake* (however He may permit or demand them for special purposes) ... " (Lewis 2001c, 221–2). In the midst of his grief over the death of his wife Joy Davidman, Lewis wrote "[b]ut we are not at all—if we understand ourselves—seeking the aches for their own sake" (2001a, 54). Lewis believed that the idea of someone pursuing evil for its own sake is most closely approximated in instances of cruelty. But he maintained that even in cases of cruelty, people are not pursuing evil for its own sake: "[C]ruelty does not come from desiring evil as such" (1970, 23), but from the desire for what is good, which is either pleasure or something that leads to pleasure. Thus, some people "take pleasure in making other people feel uncomfortable" (Lewis 2001b, 95), which is uncharitable, while the worst ways of getting the goodness of pleasure involve power over and hatred of others (Lewis 2001b, 102–3). Summing up, we have no experience of anyone liking badness just because it is bad. The nearest we can get to it is in cruelty. But in real life people are cruel for one of two reasons—either because they are sadists, that is, because they have a sexual perversion which makes cruelty a cause of sensual pleasure to them, or else for the sake of something they are going to get out of it—money, or power, or safety. But pleasure, money, power, and safety are all, as far as they go, good things. The badness consists in pursuing them by the wrong method, or in the wrong way, or too much. I do not mean, of course, that the people who do this are not desperately wicked. I do mean that wickedness, when you examine it, turns out to be the pursuit of some good in the wrong way. You can be good for the sake of goodness: you cannot be bad for the mere sake of badness ... [N]o one ever did a cruel action simply because cruelty is wrong—only because cruelty was pleasant or useful to him ... In order to be bad he must have good things to want and then to pursue in the wrong way ... (Lewis 2001b, 43–4)[2]

4.3 Pride

According to Lewis, in order for a person to be morally bad, there must be good things to want, and what is ultimately wanted is the experience of the intrinsic goodness of pleasure, where experiences of pleasure compose happiness. He also maintained that what all of us must face is one fundamental choice: will we choose to accept our creaturely status and ultimately depend upon God to provide the happiness for which He created us, or will we choose to reject our creaturely status and declare ourselves God with the prerogative of making ourselves happy as we see fit? Lewis regarded the latter choice as the essence of pride and, as Wesley Kort writes, pride in Lewis's mind connoted essentially "self-preoccupation, self-enhancement, and self-possession" (2016, 115). Lewis wrote that the "Fall [in Christian doctrine] is, in fact, Pride" (2004b, 585). He elaborated on his belief in the fundamental role of pride in explaining immoral action in the following way:

The moment you have a self at all, there is a possibility of putting yourself first—wanting to be the centre—wanting to be God, in fact ... What Satan put into the heads of our remote ancestors was the idea that they could "be like gods"—could set up on their own as if they had created themselves—be their own masters—invent some sort of happiness for themselves outside God, apart from God. And out of that hopeless attempt has come nearly all that we call human history—money, poverty, ambition, war, prostitution, classes, empires, slavery—the long terrible story of man trying to find something other than God [to provide him with the pleasure] which will make him happy. (2001b, 49)

Of course, Lewis believed the correct choice is the choice to admit one's creaturely status and the fact that it is wrong to pursue pleasure as one sees fit or on one's own terms. This, he often emphasized, is one of the central points that is made in Scripture: "This is the ultimate law—the seed dies to live, the bread must be cast upon the waters, he that loses his soul will save it" (Lewis 2001f, 154). Because the key to perfect happiness is death to self, Lewis wrote that "it is truly said of heaven 'in [it] there is no ownership'" (2001f, 154), not even ownership of oneself.

Not surprisingly, Lewis viewed the problem of pride as one that deeply involved pleasure. He conceded in personal correspondence that "Yes, I know one doesn't even *want* to be cured of one's pride because it gives pleasure" (2007, 429). One wants the pleasure that comes from knowing that one is getting pleasure on one's own terms. In *Perelandra*, which was his science fiction story about an encounter between fallen human beings from earth and an unfallen Lady on the planet Venus, Lewis depicted the either-or choice between dying or not dying to self with respect to experiencing pleasure in a couple of ways.

One way of not dying to self is to keep in mind a pleasure expected, instead of enjoying a given pleasure. Doing this will lead to a loss of the pleasure that one is actually experiencing:

> One goes into the forest to pick food and already the thought of one fruit rather than another has grown up in one's mind. Then, it may be, one finds a different fruit and not the fruit one thought of. One joy was expected and another is given ... The picture of the fruit you have *not* found is still, for a moment, before you. And if you wished—if it were possible to wish—you could keep it there. You could send your soul after the good you had expected, instead of turning it to the good you had got. You could refuse the real good; you could make the real fruit taste insipid by thinking of the other. (Lewis 2003b, 59)

A second way of not dying to self is to cling to a pleasure had and seek to repeat it, instead of relinquishing it for a new one to be given, "clinging to the old good instead of taking the good that came" (Lewis 2003b, 71). Lewis depicted this idea in terms of choosing to live on fixed land as opposed to floating islands:

> Early next morning ... [Ransom, a man from earth] was again seated on the shore looking out towards the Fixed Land ... [The unfallen Lady] came and stood on the edge of the floating island beside him and looked with him towards the Fixed Land.
>
> "I will go there," she said at last.
>
> "May I go with you?" asked Ransom.
>
> "If you will," said the Lady. "But you see it is the Fixed Land."

"That is why I wish to tread on it," said Ransom. "In my world all the lands are fixed, and it would give me pleasure to walk in such a land again."

She gave a sudden exclamation of surprise and stared at him.

"Where, then, do you live in your world?" she asked?

"On the lands."

"But you said they are all fixed."

"Yes, we live on the fixed lands." ...

"He has never bidden you not to," she said, less as a question than as a statement.

"No," said Ransom ...

"Is there a law in your world not to sleep in a Fixed Land?"

"Yes," said the Lady. "He does not wish us to dwell there. We may land on them and walk on them, for the world is ours. But to stay there—to sleep and awake there ... " she ended with a shudder.

"You couldn't have that law in our world," said Ransom. "There *are* no floating lands with us." (Lewis 2003b, 63–4)

In Lewis's mind, there are no floating lands on earth because we are fallen and seek to hold on to that which we should give up. We refuse to die to self. The Lewis scholar, Gilbert Meilaender, summarizes Lewis's point as follows:

What Lewis provides in *Perelandra* ... is his picture of the appropriate attitude toward created things. What we are to remember—and what is so easy to forget—is that they are ... gifts of the Creator meant to be received. This is the key to understanding the picture Lewis paints. The proper posture for the creature is one of receptivity. In *Perelandra* we see several ways in which this posture could be corrupted or destroyed. First it is always possible to seek ways to assure ourselves of repeating the pleasure. This is what makes money so suspect in Lewis' eyes—it is a means by which we assure ourselves that we can have the pleasure whenever we want it. It provides a measure of independence. One no longer has to throw oneself into the wave ...

This theme comes out most clearly in *Perelandra* in the symbolism of the Fixed Land. Perelandra is largely a world of floating islands, but it also has a Fixed Land. The Lady (and the King) are permitted to go onto the Fixed Land but not to dwell there or sleep there ... This sort of trust [of living on the floating islands] involves a willingness to receive what is given ... as well as a willingness to let it go again without grasping after repetition of the pleasure. Always, one must throw oneself into the wave. (1998, 17–19)

Elsewhere, Lewis made clear that it is only those who are willing to give up a thrill (a pleasure) to settle down to more sober interests are those who will find more thrills:

> What is more (and I can hardly find words to tell you how important I think this), it is just the people who are ready to submit to the loss of the thrill and settle down to the sober interest, who are then most likely to meet new thrills in some quite different direction. The man who has learned to fly and become a good pilot will suddenly discover music; the man who has settled down to live in the beauty spot will discover gardening.

> This is, I think, one little part of what Christ meant by saying that a thing will not really live unless it first dies. It is simply no good trying to keep any thrill: that is the very worst thing you can do. Let the thrill go—let it die away ... But if you decide to make thrills your regular diet and try to prolong them artificially, they will all get weaker and weaker, and fewer and fewer, and you will be a bored, disillusioned old man for the rest of your life. It is because so few people understand this that you find many middle-aged men and women maundering about their lost youth, at the very age when new horizons ought to be appearing and new doors opening all round them. (Lewis 2001b, 110–11)

The following encapsulates Lewis's position on the relationship between death to self and the experience of pleasure for which we were created: "When the sun is vertically above a man he casts no shadow: similarly when we have come to the Divine meridian our spiritual shadow (that is, our consciousness of self) will vanish" (Lewis 2007, 535). Ultimately, "humility [is] the road to pleasure" (Lewis 2001g, 167).

4.4 Moral Value and Purpose for Acting

Morality is concerned with actions. Lewis believed no action considered in itself is morally right or wrong. He used killing as an example: "I have no sympathy with the modern view that killing ... is simpliciter [independent of motive] a great evil" (Lewis 2004b, 327). Killing is a bodily action. Lewis thought that, strictly speaking, morality is concerned not with the bodily actions we choose to perform but "with the [mental] acts of choice themselves" (Lewis 2001b, 90), and ultimately, as we have seen, with the choice not to die or to die to self: "to put his own advantage first or to put it last ... [T]his free choice is the only thing that morality is concerned with" (Lewis 2001b, 90–1). Lewis maintained that what bestows status on a choice as morally right or wrong is the *reason* or *purpose* that explains the making of the choice. Thus, a "right" choice can be made for a wrong reason:

We might think that, provided you did the right thing, it did not matter how or why you did it ... But the truth is that right actions [and choices are mental actions] done for the wrong reason do not help to build the internal quality or character called a "virtue" ... (Lewis 2001b, 80)

And

[h]ow many of [my good actions] were done for the right motive? How many for fear of public opinion, or a desire to show off? How many from a sort of obstinacy or sense of superiority which, in different circumstances, might equally have led to some very bad act? (Lewis 2001b, 193)

Or consider vanity. Lewis pointed out that it is right not to be vain, but not for the purpose of attracting attention to oneself (which is pride) (Lewis 2001b, 126–7). Again,

it is very right ... not to care what people think of us, if we do so for the right reason; namely, because we care so incomparably more what God thinks. But the Proud man has a different reason for not caring. He says "Why should I care for the applause of that rabble as if their opinion were worth anything?" (Lewis 2001b, 126).

What about a "wrong" action (choice) for a right reason? Lewis believed in the obligatory lie: "The case I am clear about is where an impertinent question forces you *either* to lie *or* to betray a friend's secret" (2007, 1000). Here, it would be morally right to lie for the purpose that one not reveal the secret of a friend to a questioner who has no just cause to know it. And what about a right action that is done for a right reason? Lewis used as an example "a young man who has been going to church in a routine way [who] honestly realises that he does not believe in Christianity and stops going ... for honesty's sake and not just to annoy his parents ... " (2001b, 190). And "I do not think punishment inflicted by lawful authorities for the right motives is revenge: still less, violent action in the defence of innocent people" (2004b, 234). The following example explicitly linking the reason for acting with pleasure makes clear Lewis's view of the central role played by a motive, reason, or purpose for determining the moral status of a choice:

When people break the rule of propriety current in their time and place, if they do so in order to excite lust in themselves or others, then they are offending against chastity. But if they break it through ignorance or carelessness they are guilty only of bad manners. When ... they break it defiantly in order to shock or embarrass others, they are not necessarily being unchaste, but they are being uncharitable: for it is uncharitable to take pleasure in making other people uncomfortable. (2001b, 94–5)

Lewis's belief about the centrality of the reason why a choice is made and an action done for determining the moral status of the choice and action is also expressed in a manuscript of his referred to as "De Bono et Malo," which was written around the time of his conversion to theism:

> Whenever an act is done an attempt is made for certain motives to bring about a certain result, and certain consequences follow. Whether these consequences coincide with the result intended or not is morally irrelevant. Nor can they ever do so. For the consequences continue as long as time, but the intended result is definite. The moral quality of the act depends solely on the intention and motive. Thus A gives B a drug intending to save him, because B living is of use to him, and actually (because the bottle was wrongly labelled) kills him. A gives B a drug intending to save him, through charity, and actually kills him. A gives B a drug intending to save him, for charity, and does save him. A gives B a drug intending to kill him, because B stands between him and an estate, and actually saves him. A gives B a drug intending to kill him, because this is the only way to rid the world of a tyrant, and actually saves him. It will be seen that in all these cases the consequences make no difference (morally), but that every change in the intention and motive creates a new moral situation. (Feinendegen and Smilde 2015, 137)

Lewis believed that the acknowledged irrelevance of actual (as opposed to expected) consequences for the moral status of an action (choice) could actually provide comfort to the agent. There is solace in knowing that one chose and did as one should do, the results be what they may. In a letter to his friend Greeves in late 1935, Lewis wrote:

> There is always some peace having submitted to the right. Don't spoil it by worrying about the *results*, if you can help it. It is not your business to succeed (no one can be sure of that) but to do right: when you have done so, the rest lies with God … (2004b, 174)

With his stress on the idea that the moral status of an action is a function of the reason for which it is chosen, the actual results be whatever they will, Lewis believed that he was articulating commonsensical belief. In *The Problem of Pain*, he approvingly referred to Kant's notion of pure reverence for the moral law as what ordinary people think gives an action its moral worth. And he stressed that the choice to die to self is made strictly for the purpose of doing what is morally right to do:

> Kant thought that no action had moral value unless it were done out of pure reverence for the moral law, that is, without inclination … All popular opinion is, indeed, on Kant's side. The people never admire a man for doing something he likes: the very words "But he *likes* it" imply the corollary "And therefore it has no merit." Yet against Kant stands the obvious truth, noted by Aristotle, that the more virtuous a man becomes the more he enjoys virtuous actions …

We therefore agree with Aristotle that what is intrinsically right may well be agreeable, and that the better a man is the more he will like it; but we agree with Kant so far as to say that there is one right act—that of self-surrender—which cannot be willed to the height by fallen creatures unless it is unpleasant. (Lewis 2001f, 98, 100)

Lewis's insistence on the importance of a purpose to explain the distinction between moral and immoral choices was closely related to his rejection of naturalism. As I emphasized in Chapter 2, naturalists, as Lewis thought of them, are committed to the thesis that no event in this world can ultimately be explained in terms of what is mental in nature. Because a purpose or reason for acting is mental in nature (e.g., when I choose that I die to self I do so *for the purpose that I do what I morally ought to do*), naturalists hold that that reason cannot be what really explains the making of the choice, because no reason explains the choice. Here is what the naturalist David Armstrong says is the implication of naturalism for purposeful explanation:

Naturalism I define as the doctrine that reality consists of nothing but a single all-embracing spatio-temporal system ... [I]f the principles involved [in the spatio-temporal system] were completely different from the current principles of physics, in particular if they involve appeal to mental entities, such as purposes, we might then count the analysis as a falsification of Naturalism. But the Naturalist need make no more concession than this. (1978, 261, 262)

Some naturalists are *epiphenomenalists*—persons who believe the following: all mental events, which are themselves immaterial, are completely explained by material events, while themselves being explanatorily impotent in the sense of being thoroughly unable to produce any material events. This implies that our reasons for choosing cannot ultimately account for the occurrences of brain events that lead to the motions of our physical bodies. Lewis was well aware of this one-way form of naturalism. In the third book of his space trilogy, *That Hideous Strength*, Lewis made the character, Frost, an epiphenomenalist who maintained that "[w]hen you have attained real objectivity you will recognize, not *some* motives, but *all* motives are merely animal, subjective epiphenomena" (Lewis 2003c, 293). Frost believed that "all which appears in the mind as motive or intention is merely a by-product of what the body is doing" (Lewis 2003c, 354). And given a motive's lack of any explanatory power, Frost concluded that the mind can be eliminated: "the body and its movements [are] the only reality" and "the self which seem[s] to watch the body ... [is] a nonentity" (Lewis 2003c, 355). Lewis understood that the truth of naturalism would completely eliminate morality (and the reality of any action performed for a purpose, which amounts to just about all, if not all, actions). Given we know we act both morally and immorally, naturalism must be false. I will have a bit more to say about Lewis's thoughts regarding naturalism and morality at the end of this chapter.

4.5 Euthyphro's Dilemma

My treatment of Lewis's view of morality and its relationship to happiness, along with his views about the intrinsic goodness of pleasure and the intrinsic evilness of pain, raises the specter of what is known in philosophy as *Euthyphro's Dilemma*. A dilemma is a situation with two alternatives, neither of which is appealing to embrace. Euthyphro's Dilemma gets its name from the Platonic dialogue *Euthyphro*. In it, the major point of contention is the following dilemma: Do the gods say that something is pious because it is pious? Or is something pious because the gods say that it is pious? Through the millennia, piety for the most part has disappeared from the formulation of the Dilemma and has been replaced with the concept of the good, so that today we find the Dilemma most often expressed in something like the following form: Does God say that something is good because it is good? Or is something good because God says that it is good? Lewis made it very clear in several places that he sided with the former alternative:

> With Hooker, and against Dr Johnson, I emphatically embrace the first alternative. The second might lead to the abominable conclusion ... that charity is good only because God arbitrarily commanded it—that He might equally well have commanded us to hate Him and one another and that hatred would then have been right ... God's will is determined by His wisdom which always perceives, and His goodness which always embraces, the intrinsically good. (2001f, 99)

> If I had any hesitation in saying that God "made" the *Tao* [the moral law] it [would] only be because that might suggest that it was an arbitrary creation ... : whereas I believe it to be the necessary expression, in terms of temporal existence, of what God by His own righteous nature necessarily is. One [could] indeed say of it *genitum, non factum* [begotten, not made]: for is not the *Tao* the Word Himself, considered from a particular point of view? (2007, 1226–7)[3]

As applied to morality and happiness, Lewis's position on Euthyphro's Dilemma amounts to the following: Because moral principles like "Do not murder," "Do not steal," "Do not lie," and "Do not covet" are fundamentally about the happiness of others, moral principles cannot be a matter of what any being, including God, says or commands, because the value of happiness itself is not a matter of what any being says or commands.

Matters of value are in the nature of things. God created human nature out of which morality flows, but God created human nature in light of His own nature, which, Lewis believed, is the basis of all reality (see Dyer and Watson 2016, 90, 103, 107). Because pleasure is intrinsically good and pain is intrinsically evil, they are what they are independent of what God says or commands, but not of His nature. Lewis was convinced God could no more make pleasure not intrinsically good and pain not intrinsically evil than He could make Himself exist and not exist at the same time. And because something like hatred is productive of actions that aim to decrease pleasure and/or increase pain in the lives of others, God cannot decree that hatred is good. Were issues of value a function of what God (or anyone else) chose, then they would ultimately be arbitrary. And this is contrary to the nature of things.

At the beginning of *Mere Christianity*, Lewis set forth what is traditionally thought of as a moral argument for the existence of God, which, broadly considered, is an argument that the existence of morality is best explained by or makes best sense in terms of God's existence. He maintained that human beings everywhere have always acknowledged that certain forms of behavior are objectively right and others are objectively wrong, and he catalogued some of the moral principles that describe these kinds of behavior and constitute what he referred to in *The Abolition of Man* as the moral law or *Tao*. In Book One, Chapter 4 of *Mere Christianity*, Lewis asked "What lies behind the moral law?" and answered that God is the "somebody" who is behind it. A cursory reading of Lewis's argument might suggest that he believed God issued commands about what constitutes the moral law in a way that leads to the conclusion that he believed the moral law is the way that it is because God declares it to be that way, rather than God saying that it is that way because it is in the nature of things. And Lewis would then have denied what he elsewhere stated was his position concerning Euthyphro's Dilemma.

But in maintaining that God is behind the moral law, Lewis did not intend to convey the idea that the moral law is a function of what God decrees, where God could have said something else and fundamentally changed what is and is not good and evil. Rather, what Lewis was concerned with in the early chapters of *Mere Christianity* was the fact that God governs the moral system in such a way as to ensure the meaning of things in terms of their ultimately making sense. Thus, Book One of *Mere Christianity* is entitled "Right and Wrong as a Clue to the Meaning of the Universe." God is behind the moral law in the sense that Lewis stated in *The Problem of Pain*, which is that God is "the guardian of the morality to which [we] feel obligation" (2001f, 11–12). God is the guardian of morality insofar as He ultimately guarantees that those who choose to die to self (because that is the right thing to do) receive the perfect happiness for which they were created, while those who do not so choose do not receive this happiness. God guarantees this because it is part of His nature as just to ensure that those who choose rightly will ultimately experience the purpose for which they were created.

4.6 Natural Law

In a letter to Keith Masson, Lewis wrote that they took different approaches to morality: "You rather take the line that a traditional moral principle must produce a proof of its validity before it is accepted: I rather, that it must be accepted until someone produces a conclusive refutation of it" (Lewis 2007, 758). For the purposes of understanding why Lewis viewed the epistemic status of morality in this way, it is important to recognize that he was an advocate of natural law theory in the sense that he believed in the existence of moral principles that are grounded in the nature of human beings. As I indicated in Section 4.5, he referred to these moral principles as the *Tao*, which is a term that in Chinese thought means, among other things, the way, path, principle, or doctrine, and was likely chosen by Lewis "in order to de-emphasize Western categories and remind his readers that moral reality is universal" (Ward 2017, 10). According to Lewis, the *Tao* "is the doctrine of objective value, the belief that certain attitudes are really true, and others really false, to … the kind of things we are" (2001d, 18). And most definitive of the kind of things we are is the fact that we are beings whose good is that of being happy, so that the first moral principles of the *Tao* are like branches that have as their trunk the happiness of human beings. When a Confucian says: "Do not do to others what you would not like them to do to you" and the Christian affirms "Do as you would be done by" (Lewis 2001d, 46), each is affirming basic principles like "Do not act toward others in ways that would sacrifice their happiness, as you would not like them to act in those ways toward you at the expense of your happiness," and "Act toward others with respect for their happiness, as you would have them act toward you with respect to your happiness."

Just as Lewis believed that we begin with reason and cannot argue for or against it without conceding the soundness of reason, so also he believed that we begin with the *Tao* and can neither argue our way to it from valueless facts nor reasonably dismiss it. To clarify his position, he compared morality and reason with poetry. Lewis wrote that T. S. Eliot believed "the best contemporary practicing poets are the only 'jury of judgement' whose verdict on [Eliot's] own views of *Paradise Lost* [Eliot] will accept" (Lewis 1942, 9). In Lewis's estimation, Eliot's position amounted to the erroneous notion that the only legitimate judges of poetry are other poets. Lewis believed that while poets are qualified to tell us whether it is easy or difficult to write like Milton, they are not the only ones qualified to tell us whether reading Milton is a valuable (pleasurable) experience. Each of us is qualified to judge whether *Paradise Lost* is a good poem in this regard: "For who can endure a doctrine which would allow only dentists to say whether our teeth were aching [and] only cobblers to say whether our shoes hurt us … " (Lewis 1942, 11).

Lewis went on to suggest that Eliot might respond that the case with poetry is no different than cases concerned with morality and reason: "only a good man can judge goodness, or only a rational man can judge reasonings" (Lewis 1942, 10). Lewis answered that the claim that only a good man can judge goodness is false. While it is true that continued disobedience to the moral law can produce blindness toward it ("Now error and sin both have this property, that the deeper they are the less their victim suspects their existence; they are masked evil" (Lewis 2001f, 90)), even the bad man originally acts badly knowing full well what moral goodness and badness are. Indeed, it is only because he knows what nonmoral goodness is that he acts badly in pursuit of it. So the bad man, like any other man, is at least originally cognizant of nonmoral and moral goodness and badness. Thus, it is false that only good men are qualified to judge the good and the bad, just as it is false that only poets are qualified to judge good poetry. Poetry, concluded Lewis, can be judged by those outside the inner circle of poets.

But what about reason? Unlike poetry, it cannot be judged from the outside: "The critique of a chain of reasoning is itself a chain of reasoning: the critique of a tragedy is not itself a tragedy" (Lewis 1942, 11). And the idea of trying to argue our way to the *Tao*, of trying to get to it from the outside is as misguided as trying to argue our way to reason from the outside:

> Supposing we can enter the vacuum and view all Ethical Systems from the outside, what sort of motives can we then expect to find for entering any one of them?
>
> One thing is immediately clear. We can have no *ethical* motives for adopting any of these systems. It cannot, while we are in the vacuum, be our duty to emerge from it. An act of duty is an act of obedience to the moral law. But by definition we are standing outside all codes of moral law. A man with no ethical allegiance can have no ethical motive for adopting one. If he had, it would prove that he was not really in the vacuum at all. How then does it come about that men who talk as if we could stand outside all moralities and choose among them … nevertheless exhort us (and often in passionate tones) to make some one particular choice? They have a ready answer. Almost invariably they recommend some code of ethics on the ground that it, and it alone, will preserve civilization, or the human race. What they seldom tell us is whether the preservation of the human race is itself a duty or whether they expect us to aim at it on some other ground. (Lewis 1967, 48)

In philosophy, the attempt to stand initially outside the realm of the ethical and, more generally, the realm of value, and subsequently move into it is thought of as trying to move from a *fact* to a *value* or from an *is* to an *ought* (this is often referred to as the "is-ought" fallacy). Lewis maintained that such a move could not be made:

> From propositions about [valueless] fact alone no [moral] *practical* conclusions can ever be drawn. *This will preserve society* cannot lead to *do this* except by the mediation of *society ought to be preserved*. *This will cost you your life* cannot lead directly to *do not do this*: it can lead to it only through a felt desire or an acknowledged duty of self-preservation. (2001d, 31–2)

In sum, "[m]orality ... is a jump; ... [with morality] man goes beyond anything that can be 'given' in the [physical] facts of experience" (Lewis 2001f, 11). And Lewis held that "[u]nless the ethical is assumed from the outset, no argument will bring you to it" (1967, 56).

Of particular interest and concern to Lewis were persons who would debunk the *Tao*, while at the same time demanding that we respect the claims on us of peoples distant from us spatially (geographically) and/or temporally. He responded:

> All the practical principles behind [the critic of the *Tao*'s] case for posterity, or society, or the species, are there from time immemorial in the *Tao* ... [The critic] is really deriving our duty to posterity from the *Tao*; our duty to do good to all men is an axiom of Practical Reason, and our duty to do good to our descendants is a clear deduction from it. (2001d, 39–40, 42)

When all is said and done, what the critic of the *Tao* illegitimately does is pick and choose which principles of the *Tao* to reject on the basis of some other principle or principles within the *Tao*. But, asked Lewis,

> [b]y what right [does he] reject one and accept the other? ... This thing which I have called for convenience the *Tao*, and which others may call Natural Law ... is not one among a series of possible systems of value. It is the sole source of all value judgments. If it is rejected, all value is rejected. If any value is retained, it is retained. The effort to refute it and raise a new system of value in its place is self-contradictory. There has never been, and never will be, a radically new judgement of value in the history of the world. What purport to be new systems or ... "ideologies", all consist of fragments of the *Tao* itself, arbitrarily wrenched from their context in the whole and swollen to madness in their isolation, yet still owing to the *Tao* and to it alone such validity as they possess. If my duty to my parents is a superstition, then so is my duty to posterity. (2001d, 42–4)

The words just quoted were penned during World War II, by which time Lewis was a Christian. One of the reasons he believed it was important to defend the existence of the *Tao* was because certain persons at the time were claiming that England and the world must return to Christian ethics "in order to preserve civilization, or even in order to save the human species from destruction" (Lewis 1967, 44). Lewis thought this position was based on a serious misunderstanding of morality: "The whole debate between those who demand and those who deprecate a return to Christian ethics, seems to me to involve presuppositions which I cannot allow" (Lewis 1967, 44). What individuals in both camps presupposed was not only that one could somehow stand outside morality and argue one's way into it, but also that there is a Christian ethic that is at its core distinct from some other ethic, whether it be Aristotelian, Confucian, Buddhist, Egyptian, or whatever. Lewis maintained that there is no Christian ethic in this sense. There is only the *Tao* or "traditional morality, which is neither Christian nor Pagan, neither Eastern nor Western, neither ancient nor modern, but general" (Lewis 1967, 52):

> Men say "How are we to act, what are we to teach our children, now that we are no longer Christians?" You see ... how I would answer that question. You are deceived in thinking that the morality of your father was based on Christianity. On the contrary, Christianity presupposed it. That morality stands exactly where it did; its basis has not been withdrawn for, in a sense, it never had a basis [beyond that of human nature]. (Lewis 1967, 55)

Thus,

> [t]he idea ... that Christianity brought a new ethical code into the world is a grave error. If it had done so, then we should have to conclude that all who first preached it wholly misunderstood their own message: for all of them, its Founder, His precursor, His apostles, came demanding repentance and offering forgiveness, a demand and an offer both meaningless except on the assumption of a moral law already known and already broken ... Essentially, Christianity is not the promulgation of a moral discovery. It is addressed only to penitents, only to those who admit their disobedience to the known moral law ... A Christian who understands his own religion laughs when unbelievers expect to trouble him by the assertion that Jesus uttered no command which had not already been anticipated by the Rabbis—few, indeed, which cannot be paralleled in classical, ancient Egyptian, Ninevite, Babylonian, or Chinese texts. (Lewis 1967, 46–7)

Did Lewis, then, believe that there are no genuine moral differences between faiths, ideologies, or whatever? In the most general sense, yes. I must leave it to the reader to go to the appendix of *The Abolition of Man*, where Lewis compiled a list of similar moral injunctions from different times and places, to understand why I answer this question affirmatively. However, in a much narrower sense, Lewis did acknowledge ethical differences. For example, he recognized differences in sexual and religious practices (Lewis 1967, 54). Even here, however, he believed the differences were not as extreme as one might think. Take marriage. It is fairly common knowledge that monogamy is not the only recognized form of marriage. For example, some embrace polygamy. However, Lewis insisted no one condones the divorcing of spouses for no good reason. Even within the Christian community, where there are differences about grounds for divorce, it is still the case that "the Churches all agree with one another about marriage a great deal more than any of them agrees with the outside world. I mean, they all regard divorce as something like cutting up a living body, as a kind of surgical operation" (Lewis 2001b, 105).

In reading and rereading the works of Lewis, it is hard to avoid the conclusion that he held that matters concerning objective moral value are ultimately best expressed in terms of the idea of a person's conscience, which he considered to be a rational capacity for making moral judgments "as to what the content of right and wrong are" (Lewis 2001g, 65). As I pointed out earlier in this chapter, Lewis thought we directly apprehend truths about value. That he thought of this direct apprehension in terms of conscience is evident in the following comment:

> Two views have been held about moral judgements. Some people think that when we make them we are not using our Reason, but are employing some different power. Other people think that we make them by our Reason. I myself hold this second view …. If we are to continue to make moral judgements … then we must believe that the conscience of man is not a product of Nature … (2001c, 54, 60)

Lewis held that everyone has a conscience, even if, *per impossibile*, it turned out that the initial contents of one person's conscience were radically at odds with those of another. What each person is obligated to do is obey his or her conscience, which contains all the light about values (good and evil) that he or she has been given. Though Lewis wrote that "[w]hen I came first to the University I was as nearly without a moral conscience as a boy could be" (Lewis 2001f, 29), at the time of his conversion he was, as we have already seen, diligently seeking to obey his conscience as "the pressure a man feels upon his will to do what he thinks is right" (Lewis 2001g, 65). In accordance with what took place in his own conversion, he recommended to Rhona Bodle, who was wrestling with religious issues, that she should "go on steadily … attempting to obey the best light" (Lewis 2004b, 823) that God had given her.

One other noteworthy example of Lewis's belief in the importance of conscience comes from *The Last Battle*, which is the final book in the

Narnia series. The character Emeth had in good conscience served the evil god, Tash, but was still welcomed by the lion, Aslan, the true God. Emeth was welcomed because he had done what he did for the reason that it was what he was supposed to do:

> Then I fell at his feet and thought, Surely this is the hour of death, for the Lion (who is worthy of all honor) will know that I have served Tash all my days and not him ... But the Glorious One bent down his golden head and touched my forehead with his tongue and said, Son, thou art welcome. But I said, Alas, Lord, I am no son of thine but the servant of Tash. He answered, Child, all the service thou has done to Tash, I account as service done to me ... [I]f any man swear by Tash and keep his oath for the oath's sake, it is by me that he has truly sworn, though he know it not, and it is I who reward him ... But I said also (for the truth constrained me), Yet I have been seeking Tash all my days. Beloved, said the Glorious One, unless thy desire had been for me thou wouldst not have sought so long and so truly. For all find what they truly seek. (Lewis 1984, 204–6)

Finally, given Lewis's position on the objective nature of moral value, what did he think about the idea of moral progress? If, given the *Tao*, "[t]here has never been, and never will be, a radically new judgement of value in the history of the world" (Lewis 2001d, 43), does it follow that we can never improve our perception of value? Lewis believed that "the *Tao* admits development from within" (Lewis 2001d, 45), which is real moral progress: "From the Confucian 'Do not do to others what you would not like them to do to you' to the Christian 'Do as you would be done by' is a real advance" (Lewis 2001d, 46). But Lewis also believed that

> [f]rom within the *Tao* itself comes the only authority to modify the *Tao*. This is what Confucius meant when he said "With those who follow a different Way it is useless to take counsel". This is why Aristotle said that only those who have been well brought up can usefully study ethics ... Outside the *Tao* there is no ground for criticizing either the *Tao* or anything else. (2001d, 47–8)

So Lewis thought that moral improvements can be recognized and made only by those who acknowledge the *Tao*, because only it provides the principles in light of which the improvements are judged to be such.

4.7 Heaven without Morality

Lewis believed there is no morality in heaven, yet he was an objectivist about values. Given that he believed heaven is a real place in which people experience the nonmoral goodness of perfect happiness, why did Lewis think heaven did not also include morality?

In maintaining there is no morality in heaven, Lewis did not mean heaven is a place where moral principles cease to be true. They are just as true in heaven as they are on earth, because moral principles are grounded in the nature of persons as self-conscious potential experiencers of pleasure and pain, and that nature does not change with a change of place. However, given that those who occupy heaven do so only because of a choice to die to self, they ultimately become beings who no longer need such principles because they do what is right out of an acquired virtuous nature. The death to self produces the "tidying up or harmonizing [of] the things inside each individual," which Lewis regarded as the second concern of morality (Lewis 2001b, 72). The better a person becomes in terms of the degree of his acquired virtuous nature, the more he will enjoy performing virtuous actions. Lewis wrote to Mary van Deusen that she should not be sorry if she grew to like work originally undertaken in opposition to natural inclination:

> Surely that is what ought to happen? Isn't duty only a second-best to keep one going until one learns to *like* the thing, and then it is a duty no more? When love fulfills the Law, Law (as such) flies out of the window. Isn't that part of what St. Paul meant by being free from the Law? (2007, 685)

Lewis expressed the same idea in terms of paradisal man before the Fall:

> Now Paradisal man always chose to follow God's will. In following it he also gratified his own desire, both because all the actions demanded of him were, in fact, agreeable to his blameless inclination, and also because the service of God was itself his keenest pleasure ... Pleasure was then an acceptable offering to God because offering was a pleasure. (2001f, 97)

But once a person likes nothing other than doing that which is virtuous, he can no longer act morally: "[F]eeling a desire to help is quite different from feeling that you ought to help whether you want to or not" (Lewis 2001b, 9). "But he *likes* it," wrote Lewis, implies "And therefore it has no merit" (2001f, 98). Stated slightly differently, because the possibility of moral choice requires a reason to choose as one morally ought to do and a conflicting reason to choose to get pleasure in a way that one ought not to get it, and because this conflict of reasons does not exist in heaven, no one can choose to act morally or immorally in heaven. It is in this sense that Lewis believed "[t]here is no morality in heaven" (Lewis 1992a, 115). So, "though Christianity seems at the first to be all about morality, all about duties and rules ... yet it leads you on, out of all that, into something beyond ... where they do not talk of those things, except perhaps as a joke" (Lewis 2001b, 149).

Lewis's view of heaven as a place where thoroughly virtuous persons enjoy perfect happiness can be clarified by contrasting it with the philosopher Robert Nozick's thought experiment involving an experience machine (Nozick 1974). Nozick seeks to discredit the hedonistic conception of perfect happiness by envisioning an experience machine that, by hypothesis, provides a thoroughly passive subject connected to it with nothing but experiences of pleasure.

Would one want to connect to such a machine for eternity? Nozick answers "No," because he believes that upon reflection we will realize that we want to do things and be persons of a certain kind. What would Lewis have said about connecting to such a machine? I believe he would have maintained that the thought experiment wrongly disconnects the intrinsic good of experiencing nothing but pleasure from the intrinsic good of justice. On Lewis's view, it would be unjust for any and every person to ultimately experience perfect happiness, regardless of how they chose to live life. He believed only those who choose to die to self can justly experience the purpose for which they were created (he believed that justice trumps some ways of trying to experience pleasure). But justice equally requires that those who experience the goodness of that happiness respond with the appropriate actions. They should thank, praise, and worship the One who bestows it. However, because they have died to self and become virtuous, they enjoy doing what they ought to do (see my treatment of Lewis's appreciative pleasures in Chapter 3). While they understand what they ought to do, they no longer need do what they ought for the reason that that is what they ought to do. They no longer need act for that reason because they desire to do what is required of them (and they have no conflicting desire which might get in the way of their doing what they ought). The actions of giving thanks to and praising and worshipping God for His goodness are now sources of pleasure. Thus, Lewis would have answered Nozick that the intrinsic goodness of justice is itself an attractive force that binds together the passion of pleasure and the appropriate action which it accompanies. Lewis would have insisted that while an experience machine can be conceptualized, it cannot be actualized in a world that ultimately makes sense in terms of justice.

4.8 Naturalism and Morality

In light of Lewis's interest in naturalism, it is appropriate to consider what he thought about it in relationship to the *Tao*. Did he believe a naturalist can consistently embrace the *Tao*, or did he think that a naturalist must renounce it and always remain on the outside? All the evidence points in the direction that Lewis thought the naturalist, if consistent, must renounce the *Tao* and the objective values on which it rests, for two principal reasons.

First, Lewis believed that to espouse the *Tao* is to believe in its truth. But given naturalism, there is no reason to believe in its truth. Indeed, there is good reason to believe that its truth would be an incredible fluke. The following are two ways in which Lewis stated his position:

> My reason is either a product of Nature or it is not. If it is, then it is a by-product of natural selection, "selected", not because its logic yields truth but because its mental habits have "survival value" for mating and food hunting ... On *its own premises*, therefore, there is no reason to believe it true ... "This is unjust" is a moral judgement (M.J.). Now my M.J. is itself either a product of Nature or not. If it is how can I at the same moment trust my M.J. and condemn that Nature which, on this assumption, has doled my M.J. out to me? Seeing the *source* to be senseless and detestable I ought of course equally to despise the M.J. which comes from it. In which case my condemnation ["This is unjust"] must be abandoned. (Fetherston 1988, 88–9)

> If the fact that men have such ideas as *ought* and *ought not* at all can be fully explained by irrational and non-moral causes, then those ideas are an illusion [not true]. The Naturalist is ready to explain how the illusion arose. Chemical conditions produce life. Life, under the influence of natural selection, produces consciousness. Conscious organisms which behave in one way live longer than those which behave in another. Living longer, they are more likely to have offspring. Inheritance, and sometimes teaching as well, pass on their mode of behaviour to their young. Thus in every species a pattern of behaviour is built up ...

> This account may (or may not) explain why men do in fact make moral judgements. It does not explain how they could be right in making them. It excludes, indeed, the very possibility of their being right. For when men say "I ought" they certainly think they are saying something, and something true, about the nature of the proposed action, and not merely about their own feelings. But if Naturalism is true, "I ought" is the same sort of statement as "I itch" or "I'm going to be sick." ... But in a world of Naturalists (if Naturalists really remembered their philosophy out of school) the only sensible reply would be, "Oh, are you?" All moral judgements would be statements about the speaker's feelings, mistaken by him for statements about something else (the real moral quality of actions), which does not exist. (Lewis 2001c, 55–7)

Lewis's position can be summarized as follows: the naturalistic explanation for our holding moral beliefs is that they are adaptive in the sense that they promote survival and reproduction. But to promote these things, the beliefs need not be true. All that is required is that people believe they are true. Thus, given naturalism, moral beliefs, like other non-inferred beliefs, are caused by processes which are blind to the truth of the beliefs.

There are naturalists who disagree with the position defended by Lewis regarding naturalism and the *Tao*. For example, Walter Sinnott-Armstrong (Sinnott-Armstrong 2009) and Erik Wielenberg (Wielenberg 2014) have recently written in defense of objective moral truth. But other naturalists agree with what Lewis argued about the implications of naturalism for the truth of and a belief in the *Tao*. Thus, Michael Ruse argues that the pressures of natural selection through the interaction of human genetics and culture have hardwired into us widely distributed dispositions to believe and act in certain ways. These dispositions have had adaptive value (they tend toward reproductive success and survival) and include ones that have given us a sense of moral obligation (beliefs about moral obligations). According to Ruse, moral beliefs exist not because they are true but because they are adaptive:

> The Darwinian argues that morality simply does not work (from a biological perspective), unless we believe that it is objective. Darwinian theory shows that, in fact, morality is a function of (subjective) feelings; but it shows also that we have (and must have) the illusion of objectivity. (Ruse 1998, 253)

In short, Ruse maintains that the belief in moral objectivity (that our moral beliefs are true) is a fiction that is useful for survival purposes: "In a sense, therefore, morality is a collective illusion foisted upon us by our genes" (1998, 253). What explains the survival and reproduction of human beings is the belief in the *Tao*, not its truth. One can believe in it without that belief being true, because the truth of the belief does no explanatory work in accounting for the adaptive power of the belief.

At this juncture, naturalists like Sinnott-Armstrong and Wielenberg might insist that belief in the *Tao* will promote survival only if it is true (there really are moral obligations). What might justify this response? The most plausible answer is that if the *Tao* were not objective, then people would cease to believe in its truth and cease to act morally. The survival of the species would then be undermined. However, even if it is true that both the *Tao* and survival would be undermined if people ceased to believe in the *Tao*'s objectivity, Lewis's (and Ruse's) point was that belief in its objectivity does not require its objectivity. Someone might now ask "But why think the *Tao* is not objective, given that so many people believe that it is? After all, is not the fact that so many people believe it is objective, evidence of its objectivity?" Lewis thought that there is no reason to think that the *Tao* is objective in a naturalistic evolutionary world, even though so many people believe that it is, because its objectivity has no survival value. It has no survival value because its objectivity does no explanatory work to promote survival. The belief that it is objective (regardless of its truth) does this explanatory work.

But might belief in the *Tao* nevertheless be true, even if Lewis's argument is sound? I think Lewis would have conceded that it might be true, but add that its truth would be a fluke. Moreover, he would have attempted to make clear that even if belief in the *Tao* just happened to be true, the naturalist would still not be able to reason his way to a belief in its truth, because naturalism excludes anything mental *as mental* from the explanatory story.

The second reason Lewis believed the naturalist must renounce the *Tao* is because he (Lewis) thought there was no plausible explanation for the existence of something that is objectively good in a naturalistic universe. The experience of pleasure is an instance of what contemporary philosophers refer to as a *quale* (plural *qualia*). What is especially interesting in the present context is how they have sought to explain away the reality of *qualia*; how they have attempted to reduce them to material things configured in certain ways. The following extensive comments by the naturalist Jaegwon Kim highlight the naturalist attitude toward a *quale* like pleasure:

> For most of us, there is no need to belabor the centrality of consciousness to our conception of ourselves as creatures with minds. But I want to point to the ambivalent, almost paradoxical, attitude that philosophers [read "naturalists"] have displayed toward consciousness … [C]onsciousness had been virtually banished from the philosophical and scientific scene for much of the last century, and consciousness-bashing still goes on in some quarters, with some reputable philosophers arguing that phenomenal consciousness, or "qualia," is a fiction of bad philosophy. And there are philosophers … who, while they recognize phenomenal consciousness as something real, do not believe that a complete science of human behavior, including cognitive psychology and neuroscience, has a place for consciousness … in an explanatory/predictive theory of cognition and behavior [read "there is no place for mental-to-physical explanation"] …
>
> Contrast this lowly status of consciousness in science and metaphysics with its lofty standing in moral philosophy and value theory. When philosophers discuss the nature of the intrinsic good, or what is worthy of our desire and volition for its own sake, the most prominently mentioned candidates are things like pleasure, absence of pain, enjoyment, and happiness … To most of us, a fulfilling life, a life worth living, is one that is rich and full in qualitative consciousness. We would regard life as impoverished and not fully satisfying if it never included experiences of things like the smell of the sea in a cool morning breeze, the lambent play of sunlight on brilliant autumn foliage, the fragrance of a field of lavender in bloom, and the vibrant, layered soundscape projected by a string quartet … It is an ironic fact that the felt qualities of conscious experience, perhaps the only things that ultimately matter to us, are often relegated in the rest of

philosophy to the status of "secondary qualities," in the shadowy zone between the real and the unreal, or even jettisoned outright as artifacts of confused minds. (Kim 2005, 10–12)

In other words, naturalists are intent on denying real and primary status to pleasures because *qualia* in general are not "at home" in a naturalistic world. They do not "fit" in it. Lewis held that they are bearers of real, objective value, but, as we have just seen, on the naturalistic evolutionary view of things all the explanatory work concerning reproduction and survival is done by what is material in nature. Hence, the existence of such value in the world would be explanatorily superfluous (epiphenomenal) and mysterious. Its existence would be a fluke. Better to explain it away, if possible, than admit its "weirdness." This is the position of the naturalist Kim. And Lewis, had he been a naturalist, would have agreed.[4]

4.9 Naturalism and Making Sense of Things

If naturalism has the implications for morality that Lewis believed it has, why do naturalists even bother to attempt to explain morality's existence? Here, Lewis thought it was necessary to return to the idea of making sense of things. All of us, he wrote, "are influenced by some innate sense of the fitness of things" (2001c, 166). Hence, the idea that we might have moral beliefs for which there is no explanation as to how they fit with everything else strikes us as utterly incongruous. Lewis argued that scientists push ahead in explaining things by focusing on apparent irregularities and seeking to find hypotheses under which they can be subsumed as regularities and, thereby, made sense of (Lewis 2001c, 166–7). So naturalists, who craft their philosophy with the belief that only it is scientifically respectable, seek, no less than theists, to fit things together in a way that makes sense of them.

To illustrate what Lewis had in mind, it is helpful to consider briefly the modern evolutionary biologist Edward O. Wilson's explanation of how there can be meaning in life in a naturalistic universe. Wilson, in his book, *The Meaning of Human Existence*, acknowledges that "[i]n ordinary usage the word 'meaning' implies intention, intention implies design, and design implies a designer ... This is the heart of the philosophical worldview of organized religions ... Individuals have a purpose in being on Earth" (2014, 12). However, he insists there is a

> broader way the word "meaning" is used and a very different worldview [naturalism] implied. It is that the accidents of history, not the intentions of a designer, are the source of meaning ... Humanity arose as an accident of evolution, a product of random mutation and natural selection. (2014, 13, 174)

Now, one might ask, how is there meaning to an individual's life, if that life is through and through an accident? According to Wilson, "[t]o explain the human condition ... [is] thereby to give meaning to the human existence ... " (2014, 15). From this comment, one might think that Wilson believes *any* explanation of a person's existence, regardless of the nature of that explanation, provides that existence with meaning just in virtue of its being an explanation. Even an explanation that implies that every person exists for no purpose, has no significance, and has nothing in his or her life that makes it worth continuing would count as one that gave each individual's life a meaning. At this point, one can easily understand why Susan Wolf, in a review of Wilson's book, writes that "the title [of Wilson's book] is misleading ... " (2015, 137).

However, while Wolf is justified in saying what she does about the title of Wilson's book, I think Lewis would have insisted that there is more substance to Wilson's position than initially meets the eye. Lewis would have pointed out that even without incorporating the notion of purpose, Wilson is proposing that the meaning of life (human existence) is a matter of making sense of things. Not surprisingly, Wilson takes up our belief in morality and the idea that certain actions are morally right and others morally wrong. He acknowledges that this belief seems to indicate the existence of objective values that ground ways in which we ought and ought not to behave, where these values and our belief in them are important parts of the explanation of human existence. How do such values fit into the naturalist account of our lives? His answer is that they do not fit because they do not exist. While we believe that such values are real, our belief in their reality is false. According to Wilson (and his co-author, Ruse), "our belief in morality ... is merely an adaptation put in place to further our reproductive ends ... [E]thics as we understand it is an illusion fobbed off on us by our genes to get us to cooperate. It is without external grounding" (Ruse and Wilson 1993, 310). In short, according to Wilson's explanation of human existence, we believe in objective values as the result of blind causal processes that have no room for such values. Although our belief is false, it nevertheless "makes sense" within the evolutionary naturalist's account because the accidental development of it proved to be adaptive for the beings who had it.

Of course, we know by now that Lewis would have responded that Wilson's attempt to make sense of things is one that makes use of reasoning. It is one that involves conceding the existence of beliefs with their aboutness and the making of inferences. However, any reasoned attempt to make sense of things in terms of a metaphysic that excludes these things must be false. Hence, naturalism must be false. But setting aside this issue, Lewis would have made clear that the fact that Wilson attempts to explain how there is meaning in life in a naturalistic universe confirms that he and we are beings who are committed to making sense of things. We find the idea that things do not make sense repugnant.

So even those who argue for the ultimate absurdity of things in terms of beliefs about values which are false and desires for perfect happiness which cannot be satisfied must make clear that this absurdity makes sense in terms of fitting into a naturalistic philosophical framework. Given the importance of this issue in Lewis's thought, I will return to it at the end of Chapter 7.

4.10 Naturalism, Science, and Certitude

Throughout this and the previous two chapters, it has become clear that Lewis believed naturalism is a philosophy which holds that science is our only source of acceptable explanations and knowledge. In addition to believing that naturalism undercuts any justification for believing it by making reasoning itself impossible, Lewis also thought the certitude of naturalists regarding naturalism's truth was unjustified in light of the hypothetical nature of the scientific methodology on which it is supposedly based. For example, in contrasting the geocentric medieval model of the universe with our own heliocentric Copernican view, Lewis wrote the following:

> In every age it will be apparent to accurate thinkers that scientific theories, being arrived at [as hypotheses to save the appearances], are never statements of fact. That stars appear to move in such and such ways, or that substances behaved thus and thus in the laboratory—these are statements of fact. The astronomical or chemical theory can never be more than provisional. It will have to be abandoned if a more ingenious person thinks up a supposal which would "save" the observed phenomena with still fewer assumptions, or if we discover new phenomena which it cannot save at all.

> This would, I believe, be recognised by all thoughtful scientists today. It was recognised by Newton if, as I am told, he wrote not "the attraction varies inversely as the square of the distance", but "all happens as if" it so varied. It was certainly recognised in the Middle Ages ...

> On the highest level, then, the [medieval] Model [of the universe] was recognised as provisional. What we should like to know is how far down the intellectual scale this cautious view extended. In our age I think it would be fair to say that the ease with which a scientific theory assumes the dignity and rigidity of fact varies inversely with the individual's scientific education ... The mass media which have in our time created a popular scientism, a caricature of the true sciences, did not [in the medieval ages] exist. The ignorant were more aware of their ignorance then than now. (Lewis 1964, 15–16, 16, 16–17)

Lewis believed that a careful consideration of the methodology of science would reveal that it is a discipline which is through and through hypothetical or conjectural in nature. In science, no theory is a fact, but is rather a hypothesis waiting to be overturned. How odd, then, thought Lewis, that naturalism, which supposedly takes its inspiration from science, is adhered to with a certitude not found in science itself. What is also interesting is that Lewis used the hypothetical nature of science in his response to those who insisted miracles are not possible. I turn to this topic in Chapter 5, which I begin with a discussion of Lewis's view of free will.

notes

1   Gilbert Meilaender (2010) points to what he believes is an inconsistency in Lewis's position about our knowledge of basic moral principles. In *Mere Christianity*, Lewis wrote:

> This law was called the Law of Nature because people thought that everyone knew it by nature and did not need to be taught it ... [T]hey thought that the human idea of decent behaviour was obvious to everyone. And I believe they were right. (2001b, 5)

Meilaender believes this is a different formulation of Lewis's position regarding knowledge of the *Tao* than that stated by Lewis in *The Abolition of Man*. There, claims Meilaender, Lewis held that

> The precepts of the Tao constitute a kind of natural law not because everyone knows them without being taught but because they express fundamental truths—which we may or may not learn—about human nature. Those of us who do learn them will, to be sure, just "see" them ... [B]ut, at the same time, there is no reason to assume we all can or will easily discern these first principles of natural law ... Indeed, if Lewis really held that the precepts of the Tao were "obvious", the central theme of *The Abolition of Man* could make little sense; for it is a book about our need for moral education. (2010, 123–4)

I believe there is no tension in Lewis's view. Lewis believed both that the principles of the *Tao* expressed fundamental truths about human nature and that they did not need to be taught because they were obvious to everyone. A careful reading of *The Abolition of Man* makes clear that Lewis thought moral education was needed to train the *emotions* so that when the basic rational principles of the *Tao* were just seen to be true, the emotions would not conflict with what was believed about the principles and make following them more difficult:

> [E]motional states can be in harmony with reason (when we feel liking for what ought to be approved) or out of harmony with reason (when we perceive that liking is due but cannot feel it) ... The heart never takes the place of the head: but it can, and should, obey it. (Lewis 2001d, 19)

Moreover, Lewis regarded the authors of what he calls *The Green Book* as debunkers, as people trying to undermine the belief that there are objective values at which the emotions, when properly ordered through education, are rightly directed. But this debunking presupposes a belief in objective values, values which Lewis thought we just see.

Meilaender adds that he not only finds Lewis's account of knowledge of the *Tao* in *Mere Christianity* to be different from but also "less satisfactory" than that found in *The Abolition of Man*, "because human reason and desire are disordered by what Christians have called sin" (Meilaender 2010, 124). Lewis, however, believed the problem of sin was not a problem of the intellect but a problem of the will (choice).

2 Erik Wielenberg claims that "from the fact that we have no experience of beings who love evil for its own sake it hardly follows that such beings are impossible" (2008, 72). He goes on to point out that Augustine wrote in his *Confessions* that as a youth he stole pears for no other reason than that it was wrong (Augustine 1961, 49–52; Book II: 6–8), and that even Lewis in a diary entry at age 24 agreed that "most of us could find positive Satanic badness down there somewhere [in one's mind], the desire for evil not because it was pleasant but because it was evil" (Lewis 1991, 191).

It seems to me that Lewis in the end embraced the view that it is an *a priori* truth that no one pursues evil for its own sake. It is true that Lewis wrote in *Mere Christianity* that we have no experience of anyone liking badness just because it is bad. And it is also true (as Wielenberg claims) that it does not follow from our lack of experience of anyone liking badness for its own sake that it is impossible to do so. But Lewis probably believed by the time he gave the radio talks that became *Mere Christianity* that we have no experience of people liking badness for its own sake because it is *a priori* impossible.

On a related but different matter, Milton Walsh writes that Lewis believed "goodness can be sought for its own sake, whereas evil can be sought only because it is perceived (wrongly) to be good" (2008, 184). He then immediately quotes Lewis: "In order to be bad [a man] must have good things to want and then to pursue them in the wrong way" (Walsh 2008, 184–5; the quote comes from Lewis 2001b, 44). But Lewis did not say in this sentence that evil can be sought only because it is perceived wrongly to be good. What Lewis believed is that people (at least initially) knowingly act immorally (no wrong perception here); they seek in impermissible ways what they know to be good.

3 Cf. Lewis (1967, 79–80) and Lewis (1992b, 129–30). In "Early Prose Joy," Lewis wrote "[n]o one could argue more hotly than I that a morality which depended on divine command was no morality at all" (2013a, 37).

4 Interestingly, Kim believes that *qualia* are the biggest bug-a-boo for naturalism and he concedes that no naturalistic account of their non-existence as irreducible features of the world has succeeded (Kim 2005).

free choice and miracles

A miracle is a violation of the laws of nature; and as a firm and unalterable experience has established these laws, the proof against a miracle, from the very nature of the fact, is as entire as any argument from experience can possibly be imagined.

(Hume 1962, 119)

If the laws of Nature are necessary truths, no miracle can break them: but then no miracle needs to break them. It is with them as with the laws of arithmetic. If I put six pennies into a drawer on Monday and six more on Tuesday, the laws decree that—*other things being equal*—I shall find twelve pennies there on Wednesday. But if the drawer has been robbed I may ... find only two. Something will have been broken (the lock of the drawer or the laws of England) but the laws of arithmetic will not have been broken.

(Lewis 2001c, 92)

5.1   Lewis the Supernaturalist

Though C. S. Lewis was not a trained theologian, he was familiar with the works of scholars like Albert Schweitzer, Rudolf Bultmann, and Paul Tillich. He regarded them as "liberal" theologians, because they shared "a constant use of the principle that the miraculous does not occur" (Lewis 1967, 158), and maintained that the standard "'if miraculous, [then] unhistorical'" was one they unjustifiably brought "to their study of the [biblical] texts, not one they ... learned from it" (Lewis 1967, 158). Lewis, as an avowed supernaturalist, explained that "[t]he real reason why I can accept as historical a story in which a miracle occurs is that I have never found any philosophical grounds for the universal negative proposition that miracles do not happen" (1986b, 109–10).

C. S. Lewis, First Edition. Stewart Goetz.
© 2018 John Wiley & Sons, Inc. Published 2018 by John Wiley & Sons, Inc.

As we will see in Chapter 6, Lewis's belief in the supernatural allowed him to affirm that events like the resurrection of Jesus Christ from the dead actually occurred. What made his affirmation of supernaturalism particularly interesting philosophically was that he defended the reality of divine miracles on the basis of the supernatural nature of human reasoning. In Chapter 2, I made clear how Lewis believed the process of reasoning not only involves mental-to-mental causation but also leads to mental-to-physical causation. To requote Lewis concerning the latter, "whenever we think rationally we are, by direct spiritual power, forcing certain atoms in our brain ... to do what they would never have done if left to Nature" (2001c, 205). In light of the nature of our thought, it is right to maintain that "[h]uman minds ... are ... supernatural entities ... [and, therefore, that] a supernatural element is present in every rational man" (2001c, 43, 67). And because a miracle is no more, but no less, than "an interference with Nature by supernatural power" (2001c, 5), Lewis concluded that our thinking produces material events that are miraculous in the sense that they would not have occurred had nature proceeded on her own.

Lewis believed that in addition to being reasoners, we are also choosers. But while reasoning and choosing are both mental in nature, they are different. Inference (reasoning) is an event with respect to which we are directly passive, while a choice is an event with respect to which we are directly active. An inferred belief is causally determined by other mental events. Thus, we do not, strictly speaking, "do" it. A choice, however, is a mental event that is not causally determined by the occurrence of other mental events. Indeed, Lewis maintained a choice is not causally determined by any events. He believed a choice is "undetermined" or "self-determined" (Lewis seems to have regarded the concepts as synonymous[1]). Lewis stressed the undetermined nature of a choice in a letter to Mr. Beimer:

> [T]he particular events we call moral choices can be sufficiently free from the [cause and effect] nexus to be determined by some different kind of nexus—i.e. to be *self-determined*. Hence the absolutely universal conviction that we are free to choose need not be an illusion. (2007, 1356)

And just as Lewis made clear how our reasoning posed philosophical problems for naturalists, so also he stressed how our making choices was equally problematic for them. Thus, just as no thoroughgoing naturalist can acknowledge that we reason, so also "no thoroughgoing Naturalist believes in free will: for free will would mean that human beings have the power of independent action, the power of doing something more or other than what was involved by the total series of [natural] events" (Lewis 2001c, 8). The nature of choice and its relation to events in the material world are the subjects of this chapter.

5.2   Choice

In a letter to Jonathan Goodridge, Lewis emphasized a real distinction between passion and action, between "what *happens in [and] to me* ... and what I *do* ... " (Lewis 2007, 1581). In addition to stressing the difference between passion and action, Lewis also commented on the frequency of occurrence of the different kind of events. While our lives are filled with passions (e.g., experiences of pleasures and pains), they are for the most part bereft of choices. In the letter to Mr. Beimer mentioned a moment ago, Lewis wrote that "[a]s logical thinking occupies a comparatively small part of our mental activity ... so free action occupies a small part of our active life. Nine times out of ten we *do* behave in obedience to our conditioning, like animals" (2007, 1357).

Lewis's conviction about the relative infrequency of our choices merits a bit of conjectural elaboration. I discussed in Chapter 4 how Lewis thought there would be no morality in heaven. So, by implication, he believed that the need for the relatively few choices we make in this life would be completely eliminated (at least, moral choices would be totally eliminated) upon fulfillment of the purpose of our existence in the afterlife. What else might plausibly be said at this point about how Lewis understood the relationship between choice and morality? I think Lewis's experience with his brother Warnie's alcoholism can prove helpful here. A close read of Lewis's letters reveals that Warnie would often remain sober for substantial periods of time, only to relapse and then retreat to a nunnery in Ireland to "dry out." I have a good friend who has also struggled with alcohol. On more than one occasion, he has stressed to me how he *chose* to renounce drinking, which involved his refusing to frequent various establishments and associate with certain people, emptying his home of all alcoholic beverages, joining Alcoholics Anonymous, etc. In short, the choice to lead a certain kind of life, one free of alcohol, essentially amounted to a commitment to a way of life in which he sought to reduce to the best of his ability situations in which he would need to make a choice to resist the temptation to drink. His initial choice had the practical effect of reducing the need to make choices of a certain kind in the future. The initial choice reduced his subsequent freedom. But as he well knew, his best-laid plans might not succeed. Through no fault of his own, he might accidentally find himself in a situation with the opportunity to drink. And then the choice he had sought to avoid having to make would have to be faced. I can imagine Warnie's struggles through my friend's account of his own battles. It seems Warnie would choose to renounce alcohol and successfully do so for extended periods of time. But then perhaps, through no fault of his own, he would find himself in the kind of situation he had aimed to avoid. The dreaded choice had to be made and Warnie sometimes made the wrong choice.

In pointing out the relative infrequency of the need to make choices, Lewis seems to have understood how the making of them now reduces the need for them in the future. His writings are interspersed with comments about how choices build character and the determined behavior which issues from it. But given the world in which we live, Lewis also understood that the future course of events is ultimately outside of our control. What we plan not to happen by means of our choices might come to be. Lewis was attracted to the idea of heaven in part because he understood it as a place where there would no longer be the need to make moral choices. I quote again what Lewis wrote to Canon Oliver Chase Quick, but this time with a footnote of his that I previously had omitted:

> May not that be one of the divine jokes—to see people like Marcus Aurelius and [Matthew] Arnold [and John Stuart] Mill at last submitting to the fact that they can give up being *good** and start *receiving* good instead.
>
> *I don't mean, of course, "can begin being bad", but that when the *beata necessitas non peccandi* [the blessed necessity of not sinning] is attained, the will—the perilous bridge by [which] we get home—will cease to be the important thing or to exist, as we now know it, at all. The sword will be beaten into a ploughshare. The supreme volition of self-surrender is thus a *good suicide* of will: we will thus once, in order to will no more. (Lewis 2004b, 463–4)

Of course, the good to be received along with the cessation of the need for being morally good is that of perfect happiness. And Lewis believed that the suicide of will, which is the choice to die to self that was discussed in Chapter 4, and to which I will return at length in Chapter 6, was the overall governing choice of one's life that ultimately led to the final cessation of the need to make moral choices. But while Lewis saw the choice to die to self as leading to a final perfect state where morality was a thing of the past, he never wavered from his view that the perfect happiness which would be that final perfect state itself required the existence of free will in order to be achieved. In theological terms,

> [t]he sin ... of men ... was rendered possible by the fact that God gave them free will ... because He saw that from a world of free creatures, even though they fell, He could work out ... a deeper happiness ... than any world of automata would admit. (Lewis 2001c, 196–7)

And "Evil begins ... from free will, which was permitted because it makes possible the greatest good of all" (Lewis 2004b, 585).

5.3 The Nature of Freedom

At its heart, Lewis believed "the freedom of a creature must mean freedom to choose: and choice implies the existence of things to choose between" (2001f, 20). Were he alive today, Lewis would have been classified as an *incompatibilist*, where an incompatibilist is someone who believes that one and the same event, which for present purposes is a choice, cannot be both free and determined. There are two kinds of incompatibilists. *Hard determinists*—those who believe that human beings do not perform free acts because even their choices, if they make choices, are determined, and *libertarians*—those who believe that human beings make undetermined choices.

Lewis was a libertarian. As such, he highlighted two features of human freedom. First, when agents make choices they are free to choose otherwise. Thus, if an agent chose one way at a certain time, he was at that time free, relative to the past up until that time and the laws of nature, to have chosen another way (for simplicity of presentation, I assume going forward the qualifications in terms of time and the laws of nature). Lewis thought that without the freedom to choose otherwise, the idea of praise for an action made and encouragement to do what one ought made no sense. Thus, in *The Abolition of Man*, he wrote the following in response to the idea that we are determined to obey instinct: "Is it maintained that we *must* obey Instinct, that we cannot do [choose] otherwise? But if so ... [w]hy this stream of exhortation to drive us where we cannot help going? Why such praise for those who have submitted to the inevitable?" (Lewis 2001d, 34). In contemporary philosophy, the idea that if we are free we must be free to choose otherwise, is termed *leeway* incompatibilism.

Second, Lewis believed that we are the ultimate originators of our choices:

> Determinism does not deny the existence of human behaviour. It rejects as an illusion our spontaneous conviction that our behaviour has its ultimate origin in ourselves. What I call "my act" is the conduit-pipe through which the torrent of the universal process passes, and was bound to pass, at a particular time and place. The distinction between what we call the "voluntary" and the "involuntary" movements of our bodies is not obliterated, but turns out (on this view) to be not exactly the sort of difference we supposed. What I call the "involuntary" movements necessarily ... result from mechanical causes outside my body or from pathological or organic processes within it. The "voluntary" ones result from conscious psychological factors which themselves result from unconscious psychological factors dependent on my economic situation, my infantile and pre-natal experience, my heredity ... and so on back to the beginnings of organic life and beyond. I am a conductor, not a source. I never make an original contribution to the world-process. (Lewis 1992a, 36–7)

In contemporary philosophy, the idea that freedom requires that we be the sources of our choices, not mere conduits of a deterministic chain of events, is known as *source* incompatibilism. There is much philosophical discussion today about whether leeway or source incompatibilism captures the core notion of libertarian freedom. Lewis affirmed the inseparability of the two. He believed they are two sides of one coin, where being the source of a choice entails being able to choose otherwise, and being able to choose otherwise entails being the source of a choice.[2]

As I stressed in Chapter 4, Lewis maintained that choices are explained by the reasons for which they are made, where reasons are purposes. Given a human choice requires that at the time of its making the agent could have chosen otherwise under the exact same conditions, the agent must not only have had a reason for choosing as he did but also must have had a reason to choose otherwise. And given this kind of freedom, the future must have been genuinely open and not predetermined. Theologically, Lewis believed the problem with predestinarians and universalists (those who hold, in theological language, that all will be saved) alike is that they view agents atemporally and without a future to be made real in part by the agents' undetermined choices. Both views "are trying to leap on into eternity ... trying to see the final state of all things as it *will* be ... when there are no more possibilities left but only the Real ... " (Lewis 2001e, 140). Both views step outside the reality of lived, temporal experience into a future whose realization is in fact dependent in part on choices which at an earlier time of making were not determined.

5.4 The "Iffyness" of Nature

Lewis believed not only that each of us makes moral choices, but also that none of us is an isolated or singular chooser. We share a public space within which our choices are made. Indeed, he argued that without such a shared framework, the exercise of free will would be impossible:

> A creature with no environment would have no choices to make: so that freedom ... demands the presence to the self of something other than the self ... [And as] soon as we attempt to introduce the mutual knowledge of fellow-creatures we run up against the necessity of "Nature" ... I see no possibility of [two immaterial minds becoming aware of each other] except in a common medium which forms their "external world" or environment ... What we need for human society is exactly what we have—a neutral something, neither you nor I, which we can both manipulate so as to make signs to each other ... Society, then, implies a common field or "world" in which its members meet ...

But if [something] is to serve as a neutral field it must have a fixed nature of its own ... [I]f you were introduced into a world which thus varied at my every whim, you would be quite unable to act in it and would thus lose the exercise of your free will. (Lewis 2001f, 20–2)

So to be one "I" or self among others which are capable of indeterministically interacting with each other, there must be a neutral playing field that "has a fixed nature and obeys constant laws ... " (Lewis 2001f, 23). Lewis believed that for us the neutral playing field is the material world with its objects that behave in accordance with laws of nature. But what is a law of nature? Lewis thought of it as something that, for lack of a better expression, is inherently *iffy* in nature:

[Y]ou know what will happen to the two billiard balls—provided nothing interferes. If one ball encounters a roughness in the cloth [interference] which the other does not, their motion will not illustrate the law in the way you had expected. Of course what happens as a result of the roughness in the cloth will illustrate the law in some other way ... All interferences leave the law [of colliding billiard balls] perfectly true. But every prediction of what will happen in a given instance is made under the proviso "other things being equal" or "if there are no interferences". Whether other things *are equal* in a given case and whether interferences may occur is another matter ... The laws of motion do not set billiard balls moving: they analyse the motion after something else (say, a man with a cue ...) has provided it. They produce no events: they state the pattern to which every event—if only it can be induced to happen—must conform .... If I knock out my pipe I alter the position of a great many atoms ... Every law can be reduced to the form "If A, then B." (Lewis 2001c, 90–1, 93, 94, 138)

If I strike ball A in a certain way, and it collides with ball B, then ball B will move in a particular way, provided nothing interferes. If I knock out my pipe, then the ashes will fall a certain way, all other things being equal. If A, then B. In terms of human freedom, I must have beliefs about what would happen in the material world *if* I were to choose in such-and-such a way. I must believe that if I choose in such-and-such a way, then so-and-so will follow. Lewis made it clear that all of us are inveterate "supposers," where supposing takes the form "If this were to happen, then that would follow":

Such supposing appears to us the ... inveterate habit of the human mind. We do it all day long ...

Every supposal is an ideal experiment: an experiment done with ideas because you can't do it any other way. And the function of an experiment is to teach us more about the things we experiment on. When we suppose the world of daily life to be invaded by something other, we are subjecting either our conception of daily life or our conception of that other, or both, to a new test. We put them together to see how they will react. (Lewis 1982, 23)

As I pointed out in Chapter 2, Lewis believed we are souls. Because we are, our choices are mental events that produce effects in the physical world. Lewis understood all too well that naturalists find this notion deeply problematic. In Section 5.5, I set forth an important naturalistic argument against libertarian freedom and explain how Lewis would have responded to it.

5.5 Arguments against Mental-to-Physical Causation

Lewis believed the regularity of nature is required for the making of undetermined choices that directly or indirectly cause events in the material world. The naturalist Ted Honderich argues that this regularity of nature excludes the making of such choices(Honderich 1993). Honderich begins his argument by asking us to consider a scenario in which a woman, Juliet, sees her boyfriend, Toby, and subsequently chooses to tell Toby that they should have a child. Honderich then queries how we are to view the neurological events in Juliet that correlate with what may be called the relevant teleological (purposeful) events (Table 5.1):

What, asks Honderich, is the relationship between the neurological events that have been labeled $N1$ and $N2$? In order for Juliet to have libertarian free will (and for the purpose for which she chooses to be explanatorily efficacious), $N2$ cannot be the unavoidable (determined) effect of $N1$ or anything else because its unavoidability will make its correlate teleological event (Juliet's choice) equally unavoidable. According to Honderich, however, it is nothing less than unreasonable to think that $N2$ can be anything other than unavoidable in relationship to $N1$ and the physical series of events that precedes $N1$. To see why it is supposedly unreasonable to think anything other than this, let $N3$ and subsequent neural events be those that lead to and include the movements of Juliet's lips when she tells Toby that they should have a child. Is there or is there not an unavoidable connection between $N2$ and what causally results from it, namely, $N3$ and the neural and other physical events that follow $N3$ and yield the movements of Juliet's lips?

Table 5.1

Teleological events	Juliet sees Toby	Juliet chooses to tell Toby about wanting a child	Further teleological events
Neurological events	$N1$	$N2$	$N3\rightarrow$

If there is not a very high probability that items like [N2] will be followed by other neural events, then actions [e.g., speaking with our lips] we fully and absolutely intend [or choose] will on too many occasions mysteriously not happen. So the links *after* [N2] have to be pretty tight. But then in consistency so do the neural links *before* [N2]. That is unfortunate, since the theory [of libertarian free will] needs these earlier links to be pretty loose in order for Juliet to be held really responsible for what is tied to [correlated with] [N2], her [choice] to speak up [to Toby]. (Honderich 1993, 37)

Can this alleged problem of inconsistency be dealt with? Honderich believes that the answer to this question is "No." Lewis, however, would have responded that there is no problem of inconsistency, and this is because of the iffy nature of an object's propensity (capacity) to be causally triggered, where the triggering in this instance is the actualization of the capacity of a neuron (N2) to fire. Lewis would have argued that Honderich's own treatment of the concept of causation supports the nonexistence of the alleged inconsistency and the possible existence of explanatory gaps (openness to invasion by souls) in the physical story. In the course of discussing the nature of causation, Honderich asks the reader to consider the lighting of a match here and now. I quote Honderich at some length:

> When we assume that this event was the effect of the match's being struck, what are we assuming? One good reply is likely to be that it was an event that wouldn't have happened if the match hadn't been struck. On the assumption that the striking was cause and the lighting effect, what is true is that *if the striking hadn't happened, neither would the lighting* ... We are inclined to think ... that something else isn't true of an ordinary striking and lighting. We are reluctant to say that *if or since the match was struck, it lit*. The explanation of our reluctance is that even if the match was struck, had it been wet, it wouldn't have lit ... [N]ot only the striking was required for the lighting, but also the match's being dry. That was not all that was required. There had to be oxygen present, and the surface on which the match was struck had to be of a certain kind ... An event which caused a certain effect is not necessarily such that all like events are followed by like effects. Not all strikings are followed by lightings. A causal circumstance for a certain effect, on the other hand, really is such that all like circumstances *are* followed by like effects ... [G]iven a causal circumstance, whatever else had been the case [e.g., the match's color had been different], the effect would still have occurred. A necessitated event just is one for which there was a circumstance which was such that since it occurred, whatever else had been true, the event would still have occurred. (1993, 7, 8, 9, 11)

Lewis would have conceded that *given* a causal circumstance, the effect had to occur (provided there was no interference), and *since* the circumstance occurred, the effect was necessitated to occur. But did the circumstance—in the case of the match, the presence of oxygen, the dryness of the match, the match's being struck, etc.—have to occur? Was it unavoidable? Lewis would have answered that there is no reason to think so, *unless one has presupposed the truth of determinism*. Honderich says that "the causal circumstance for an effect will typically be made up of parts which were also effects themselves ... This fact about effects—the fact of what you might call causal chains—is very important to determinism" (1993, 11). While Lewis would have conceded that causal circumstances for effects are often made up of parts which were also effects themselves, he would have added that this fact about causal circumstances is not sufficient for (does not guarantee) the truth of determinism. This is because what is often the case is not necessarily always so. In the case of the causal circumstance involving the match, he would have had us ask whether we think it was unavoidable that the match be struck. And he would have answered that we believe it was not unavoidable. After all, a person might strike a match in virtue of having *chosen* to have a fire in the fireplace for the purpose that he stay warm. He need not, however, have *chosen* to have the fire. He might have chosen to turn up the thermostat instead for the same purpose.

What, then, about the causal circumstance that includes the neural event (*N2*), which is correlated with the teleological event of Juliet choosing to tell Toby that they should have a child, subsequent neural events (*N3*—>), and the movement of Juliet's lips? Was that causal circumstance unavoidable? Did it have to occur? Lewis would have pointed out that the answer to this question depends upon what one says about the relationship between Juliet choosing to tell Toby about having a child and *N2*. If one believes that this teleological event alone causes *N2* (there is no physical cause of *N2*), then there is no reason to think that *N2*, absent Juliet's choice, had to occur, because there is no reason to think that the choice had to occur, *unless one assumes the truth of determinism*. Honderich might respond that it is reasonable to believe that there must be a neural event such as *N1*, which is correlated with Juliet seeing Toby and produces *N2*. However, Lewis would have wondered why one should think this is the case. After all, *N1* could be the cause of Juliet's seeing Toby without also being the cause of *N2*. Moreover, one could concede that a neuroscientist might experimentally discover that triggerings of a neural propensity to fire (neural events like *N2*) can be produced by stimulation with an electrode or by causal events involving other neurons. But Lewis would have wanted to know why we should think that every actualization of a neural capacity can only be produced in these ways. Why could not an actualization of a neural capacity (e.g., *N2*) be caused by a mental event (e.g., a choice) alone which is made for a purpose, so that there is a soul causing certain neurons in its brain to fire in ways they would never have fired on their own? Lewis would have emphasized that there is no reason to think this cannot be the case, unless one begs the question at hand and assumes the naturalist's view that the physical world is causally closed to any event that is not physical in nature. The philosopher Keith Campbell writes "[a] material thing can, without ceasing to be a material thing, respond to forces other than physical ones. The brain, without ceasing to be material, can act under the influence of an immaterial mind" (1980, 17). And Lewis concurred: "The brain does not become less a brain by being used for rational thought" (2001c, 205–6). In other words, mental-to-physical causation does not undermine the integrity of the brain.

Honderich's argument against the making of undetermined choices begins with the regularity of events in the material world. If such-and-such occurs, then so-and-so will follow. Lewis believed that an agent must believe in this regularity in order to make a choice, but maintained, against someone like Honderich, that this regularity itself in no way threatens the freedom to make choices. A different argument which, if successful, would exclude the production of physical effects by undetermined mental choices, appeals to a methodological consideration that is necessary for the pursuit of science. A consideration of it will further elucidate why Lewis believed there is nothing unscientific or otherwise intellectually suspect about supernaturalism in the form of undetermined choices made for purposes causally producing material effects.

To begin constructing this argument, consider the following comments by the philosopher Richard Taylor:

> Consider some clear and simple case of what would ... constitute the action of the mind upon the body. Suppose, for example, that I am dwelling in my thought upon high and precarious places, all the while knowing that I am really safely ensconced in my armchair. I imagine, perhaps, that I am picking my way along a precipice and visualize the destruction that awaits me far below in case I make the smallest slip. Soon, simply as the result of these thoughts and images ... perspiration appears on the palms of my hands. Now here is surely a case, if there is any, of something purely mental ... and wholly outside the realm of physical nature bringing about observable physical changes ... Here ... one wants to say, the mind acts upon the body, producing perspiration. (1992, 20)

However, Taylor cautions us against such a simple supposition:

> But what actually happens, alas, is not nearly so simple as this. To say that thoughts in the mind produce sweat on the hands is to simplify the situation so grossly as hardly to approximate any truth at all of what actually happens ... The perspiration ... is secreted by tiny, complex glands in the skin. They are caused to secrete this substance, not by any mind acting on them, but by the contraction of little unstriated muscles. These tiny muscles are composed of numerous minute cells, wherein

occur chemical reactions of the most baffling complexity ... These ... connect eventually, and in the most dreadfully complicated way, with the hypothalamus, a delicate part of the brain that is centrally involved in the emotional reactions of the organism ... [B]ut it is not seriously considered by those who do know something about it that mental events must be included in the description of its operations. The hypothalamus, in turn, is closely connected with the cortex and subcortical areas of the brain, so that physical and chemical changes within these areas produce corresponding physical effects within the hypothalamus, which in turn, by a series of physical processes whose complexity has only barely been suggested, produces such remote effects as the secretion of perspiration on the surface of the hands. (1992, 20–1)

Taylor wraps up his overview of the goings-on in emotional perspiration with the following:

Such, in the barest outline, is something of the chemistry and physics of emotional perspiration ... The important point, however, is that in describing it as best we can, there is no need, at any stage, to introduce mental or nonphysical substances or reactions. (1992, 21–2)

According to Taylor, while we are inclined to believe that certain physical events in our bodies are ultimately explained by mental events of nonphysical substances (human souls/minds), as a matter of fact there is no need at any point to step outside the physical causal story to explain the occurrences of those physical events. Jaegwon Kim uses an example of a neuroscientist to make the same point:

You want [or choose] to raise your arm, and your arm goes up. Presumably, nerve impulses reaching appropriate muscles in your arm made those muscles contract, and that's how the arm went up. And these nerve signals presumably originated in the activation of certain neurons in your brain. What caused these neurons to fire? We now have a quite detailed understanding of the process that leads to the firing of a neuron, in terms of complex electrochemical processes involving ions in the fluid inside and outside a neuron, differences in voltage across cell membranes, and so forth. All in all we seem to have a pretty good picture of the processes at this microlevel on the basis of the known laws of physics, chemistry, and biology. (1996, 131–2)

According to Kim, the physical explanatory story is unproblematic until one introduces an immaterial mind (a soul) to explain the raising of one's arm:

If the immaterial mind is going to cause a neuron to emit a signal (or prevent it from doing so), it must somehow intervene in these electrochemical processes. But how could that happen? At the very interface between the mental and the physical where direct and unmediated mind-body interaction takes place, the nonphysical mind must somehow influence the state of some molecules, perhaps by electrically charging them or nudging them this way or that way. Is this really conceivable? Surely the working neuroscientist does not believe that to have a complete understanding of these complex processes she needs to include in her account the workings of immaterial souls and how they influence the molecular processes involved ... Even if the idea of a soul's influencing the motion of a molecule ... were coherent, the postulation of such a causal agent would seem neither necessary nor helpful in understanding why and how our limbs move ... Most physicalists ... accept the causal closure of the physical not only as a fundamental metaphysical doctrine but as an indispensable methodological presupposition of the physical sciences ... If the causal closure of the physical domain is to be respected, it seems prima facie that mental causation must be ruled out ... (1996, 132, 147–8)

While Kim agrees with Taylor about the lack of a need on the part of a scientist to go outside the physical explanatory story, he introduces the stronger idea that to be successful, the physical sciences need to make the methodological assumption of the causal closure of the physical world. Is he right about this? To ensure clarity about what is at issue, consider one more example of movements of our bodies.

It is well known that Lewis took the time to respond personally in writing to the many individuals who wrote to him. It is only reasonable to assume that he wrote letters quite purposefully so that reference to his mental activity was not only helpful but also necessary to explain the movements of his hand when he wrote. If, for the sake of discussion, we take Lewis's view that "there must be some point (probably the brain) at which created spirit [a human soul] ... can produce effects on matter ... simply by the wish to do so" (Lewis 2001c, 245), then when he moved his hand for the purpose of writing a letter he must have directly caused initial neural events in his brain that ultimately led to the movements of his hand. In other words, in order to explain adequately (teleologically) the movements of his hand, there must have been causal openness or a causal gap in his brain.[3]

While Kim recognizes, like Lewis, that the causal interaction between a soul and its brain requires causal openness in the latter, he also believes it is because such interaction implies this openness that it must be mistaken. Kim maintains that because the neuroscientist must methodologically assume the causal closure of the physical world, what she discovers as the explanation for what occurs in our brains and limbs must not and need not include reference to the mental causal activity of souls and the ultimate and irreducible explanatory purpose of their choices to act. Lewis, in response, would have maintained that there is good reason to hold that the argument from causal closure is unsound. We will do justice to his view by distinguishing between a neuroscientist as an *ordinary human being* and a neuroscientist as a *physical scientist*. A neuroscientist as an ordinary human being who is trying to understand how and why Lewis moved his hand in writing letters would refer to Lewis's reasons (purposes) for corresponding by letter in a complete account of why he moved his hand. Must the neuroscientist, however, as a physical scientist, avoid making such a reference? Kim claims that she must avoid such a reference, because as a physical scientist she must make a methodological assumption about the causal closure of the physical world. Is Kim right about this and, if he is, is such a commitment compatible with a commitment on the part of a physical scientist as an ordinary human being to causal openness? Or must a neuroscientist, who as a physical scientist assumes causal closure, also assume, if she is consistent, that, as an ordinary human being, her mention of choices and their teleological explanations is no more than an explanatory heuristic device that is necessary because of an epistemic gap in her knowledge concerning the physical causes of human behavior?

In order to understand what Lewis would have said in answer to these questions, let us first consider some comments he made about a physicist observing the interactions and motions of the previously mentioned billiard balls. The physicist, he held, studies these things *as a physicist*, which means that he considers the motions and interactions of the billiard balls under the assumption that they are closed off to interference by outside causal influences. In other words, the physicist assumes the principle of causal closure in his study of the billiard balls. However, wrote Lewis:

> The physicist, as a physicist, does not know how likely I am to catch up a cue and "spoil" his experiment with the billiard balls: you had better ask someone who knows *me*. In the same way the physicist, as such, does not know how likely it is that some supernatural power is going to interfere with them: you had better ask a metaphysician. But the physicist does know, just because he is a physicist, that if the billiard balls are tampered with by any agency, natural or supernatural, which he has not taken into account, then their behaviour must differ from what he expected. Not because the law [describing their behavior] is false, but because it is true. The more certain we are of the law the more clearly we know that if new factors have been introduced the result will vary accordingly. What we do not know, as physicists, is whether Supernatural power might be one of the new factors. (2001c, 91–2)

A few sentences later, Lewis added the following:

> Miracle [which is an interference with nature by a supernatural power] is, from the point of view of the scientist, a form of doctoring, tampering, (if you like) cheating. It introduces a new factor into the

situation, namely supernatural force, which the scientist had not reckoned on. He calculates what will happen, or what must have happened on a past occasion, in the belief that the situation, at that point in space and time, is or was A. But if supernatural force has been added, then the situation really is or was AB … The necessary truth of the laws, far from making it impossible that miracles should occur, makes it certain that if the Supernatural is operating they must occur. (2001c, 92–3)

In discussing the physicist *as a physicist*, Lewis meant to distinguish between the physicist as a working scientist and the physicist in his non-scientific garb as an ordinary human being.[4] In his capacity as the former, the physicist purposefully assumes that what he studies is closed off to outside influences. But this is perfectly appropriate, because physics is "engaged on those specialised inquiries for which truncated thought [the assumption of causal closure] is the correct method" (Lewis 2001c, 66). But *as an ordinary human being*, the physicist knows perfectly well that there are influences in the form of personal supernatural agents who have the power to interfere in what, for his work as a scientist, he assumes is a closed system. What, then, would Lewis have said about Kim's argument from causal closure that involves the neuroscientist?

First and foremost, Lewis would have had us remember what it is about physical entities that a physical scientist is often trying to discover in her experimental work: "Experiment finds out what regularly happens in Nature: the norm or rule to which she works" (Lewis 2001c, 72). Lewis, as we now know, believed the experimental enterprise is inherently iffy in character. The Nobel laureate physicist Richard Feynman agreed: "[Scientific questions are those] that you can put this way: 'if I do this, what will happen?' … And so the question 'If I do it what will happen?' is a typically scientific question" (1998, 16, 45). Lewis would have gone on to insist that what a neuroscientist is trying to discover as a physical scientist are the propensities of neurons to be causally affected by other physical entities, including other neurons. For example, a neuroscientist might stimulate the cortical motor areas in patients' brains with an electrode and observe neural impulses that result. Lewis believed that during such experimental work, a neuroscientist must assume that the areas of the brains in which she is doing her investigative work are closed to other causal influences. Without this methodological assumption, he thought the neuroscientist could not conclude that it was her electrical probing, as opposed to a non-physical and supernatural soul "behind the scenes," which was causally affecting the capacities of the neurons to conduct electrical impulses and produce the movements of the patients' limbs.

However, Lewis would have insisted that, while a neuroscientist's investigation of the brain requires the methodological assumption of causal closure of the areas of the brains she is studying during her experiments, there is no reason to think that she also has to be committed as a physical scientist to the assumption that the physical world is *universally* (in *every* context) causally closed, where universal causal closure entails that the relevant brain (neural) events can *only* be causally produced by events involving other physical entities and not instead by mental events of immaterial souls alone when they indeterministically choose to act for purposes. All that the neuroscientist as a physical scientist must assume is that, during her experiments, souls (of either the patients themselves or others) are not causally producing the relevant events in the micro-physical entities in the areas of the brain that she is studying. Lewis would have added that if the neuroscientist makes the universal assumption that in *any* context events in micro-physical entities can only have other physical events as causes and can never be causally explained by mental events of souls and their purposes, then she does so, not as a scientist, but as a *naturalist*.

Lewis was convinced that when considering the idea of the mental invading the physical, which is a miracle in his way of thinking, "it is mere confusion of thought to suppose that advancing science has made it harder for us to accept miracles. We always knew they were contrary to the natural course of events" (Lewis 2001c, 76), where by "the natural course of events" Lewis meant the course of events that nature takes without any intervention by the mental. Thus,

> [a] belief in miracles, far from depending on an ignorance of the laws of nature, is only possible in so far as those laws are known. We have already seen that if you begin by ruling out the supernatural you will perceive no miracles. We must now add that you will equally perceive no miracles until you believe that nature works according to regular laws. (Lewis 2001c, 75)

Lewis believed that it is the business of science to help specify in greater detail the laws of nature. And, as I already mentioned earlier in this chapter, he thought the additional details are no more than descriptions of how physical entities behave. The laws described are themselves causally impotent:

> The laws of motion do not set billiard balls moving: they analyse the motion after something else … has provided it. They produce no events: they state the pattern to which every event—if only it can be induced to happen—must conform … Thus in one sense the laws of Nature cover the whole field of space and time; in another, what they leave out is precisely the whole real universe—the incessant torrent of actual events which makes up true history. That must come from somewhere else … For every law, in the last resort, says "If you have A, then you will get B". But first catch your A: the laws won't do it for you. (Lewis 2001c, 93–4)

So on Lewis's view, laws of nature are descriptions with an iffy character: If such-and-such occurs, so-and-so will follow. But what happens when the such-and-such does not happen because a mental cause intervenes to produce the so-and-so? According to Lewis,

> Nature digests or assimilates this [so-and-so] event with perfect ease and harmonises it in a twinkling with all other events. It is one more bit of raw material for the laws to apply to ... We see every day that physical nature is not in the least incommoded by the daily inrush of events from biological nature or from psychological nature. (2001c, 94–5)

In other words, once a miracle occurs, nature absorbs it and things go on as normal. So miracles are not "contradictions or outrages; we mean [by the term 'miracles'] that, left to her own resources, [nature] could never produce [the events that occur]" (Lewis 2001c, 98). By herself, nature could never have produced the purposeful, planned motions of Lewis's hand that occurred in the writing of his letters. Neither, he believed, could nature produce on her own the motions of certain atoms in our brains on the occasions when we think. The material motions that result from such mental events falsify the idea that nature is a causally closed or, in his terms, an "interlocked system":

> If Naturalism is true, every finite thing or event must be (in principle) explicable in terms of the Total System. I say "explicable *in principle*" because of course we are not going to demand that naturalists, at any given moment, should have found the detailed explanation of every phenomenon. Obviously many things will only be explained when the sciences have made further progress ... If any one thing exists which is of such a kind that we see in advance the impossibility of ever giving it [an explanation in terms of the Total System], then Naturalism would be in ruins. (Lewis 2001c, 17–18)

5.6   The Relevance of the Subnatural

According to Lewis, we understand that brain events resulting from our thoughts, reasonings, and choices could never be explained by nature left to herself. There is supernatural causation. Miracles do occur. While thinking and writing about the topic of miracles, Lewis was aware that physicists themselves were challenging the dogma that nature is a closed system: "They seem to think that the individual unit of matter (it would be rash to call it any longer a 'particle') moves in an indeterminate or random fashion; moves, in fact, 'on its own' or 'of its own accord'" (Lewis 2001c, 18-19). Lewis believed that the assertion of the causally indeterminate character of such movements at the micro-level amounted to an admission that naturalism is false, because those movements would explain some of the behaviors of the material objects which constitute nature at the macro-level (the world of rocks, trees, animals, etc.). There would be interference with nature from a subnatural level:

> Indeed, if we define nature as the system of events in space-time governed by interlocking laws, then the new physics has really admitted that something other than nature exists. For if nature means the interlocking system, then the behaviour of the individual unit is outside nature [and interferes with it]. (Lewis 1970, 133)

If the effects of these indeterminate subnatural events can be absorbed by macro-level nature as a lawful order of events with no ill effects, then why could not she also absorb the effect of indeterminate supernatural events with no ill effects? "[C]learly if [nature] thus has a back door opening on the Subnatural, it is quite on the cards that she may also have a front door opening on the Supernatural—and events might be fed into her at that door too" (Lewis 2001c, 19).

Lewis went on to make clear that because of his philosophical education, he found it almost impossible to believe that physicists—at least some of them—really meant what they seemed to be saying, which was that events occur at the subnatural level for which there is neither a causal nor a teleological explanation: "I cannot help thinking they mean no more than that the movements of individual units are permanently incalculable *to us*, not that they are in themselves random and lawless" (Lewis 2001c, 20). But if physicists were to be taken at their word, then Lewis believed that none of them could have a principled reason to doubt the reality of invasions of nature from the supernatural.

5.7 Lewis as a Causal Interactionist

Lewis affirmed what I have termed "mere dualism" (see Chapter 2). Everything said in Chapter 2 about his view of the relationship between the mental and the physical indicates that he also affirmed causal interactionism, which, though it is almost universally identified with mere dualism is, strictly speaking, a supplementation of it. When we reason and choose, we causally produce effects in our brains. How do we do this? Lewis thought the soul-body relation was shrouded in mystery: "We cannot conceive how the [soul] ... of any man ... dwells within his natural organism" (2001c, 178). Part of what I quoted in Chapter 2 warrants requoting here: "[W]aves ... of air ... reach my eardrum and travel up a nerve and tickle my brain. All this is behind the scenes ... Then somehow (I've never seen it explained) they step on to the stage [the soul] (no one can tell me *where* this stage is) and become, say, a friend's voice or the *Ninth Symphony*" (Lewis 1970, 247–8). Elsewhere, Lewis stressed that "[n]o Model yet devised has made a satisfactory unity between our actual experience of sensation or thought or emotion and any available account of ... corporeal processes ... " (1964, 165).

Lewis's comments about the mysteriousness of the soul-body causal interaction echo Descartes's thoughts about the issue. In response to a query from Princess Elizabeth of Bohemia about how a soul moves its body, Descartes wrote that concerning the idea of the "soul and body [operating] together we have no notion save that of their union [in the form of a human being]" (1958, 252). And Descartes penned the following in a letter to the philosopher Arnauld:

> [T]hough we are not in a position to understand, either by reasoning or by any comparison drawn from other things, how the mind, which is incorporeal, can move the body, none the less we cannot doubt that it can, since experiences the most certain and the most evident make us at all times immediately aware of its doing so. This is one of those things which are known in and by themselves and which we obscure if we seek to explain them by way of other things. (1958, 262)

Lewis was well aware that medieval philosophers also could not elucidate the mystery of the soul-body causal relationship. In one attempt to explain it, they drew upon an ancient maxim from Plato that it is not possible to pass from one extreme to another except through a mean. Lewis regarded this "solution" to the problem as woefully inadequate because it did not really explain anything:

> This deep-seated principle would probably have moved the medievals to put something in between soul and body even if the psycho-physical question did not in all periods offer the raw edge [of causal interaction] that I have indicated. And this principle made it certain in advance that their method of coping with the raw edge would be to supply a *tertium quid*.
>
> This *tertium quid*, this phantom liaison-officer between body and soul, was called *Spirit* or (more often) the *spirits*. It must be understood that this sense does not at all overlap with the sense which enables us to speak of angels or devils or ghosts as "spirits" ...
>
> The spirits were supposed to be just sufficiently material for them to act upon the body, but so very fine and attenuated that they could be acted upon by the wholly immaterial soul ... This doctrine of the spirits seems to me the least reputable feature of the Medieval Model. If the *tertium quid* is matter at all ... both ends of the bridge rest on one side of the chasm; if not, both rest on the other. (Lewis 1964, 166–7)

The causal interaction between soul and body is typically taken by causal interactionists to explain why one thinks of a particular body as "my" body: my body is that material entity which, when causally modified directly produces psychological events in me, and when I choose directly has movements produced in it. I know of no evidence that suggests Lewis would have disagreed with this view. However, he was cognizant of different senses of "my" and pointed out how it is not uncommon to think that "my body" expresses the idea of ownership.

> Much of the modern resistance to chastity comes from men's belief that they "own" their bodies—those vast and perilous estates, pulsating with the energy that made the worlds, in which they find themselves without their consent and from which they are ejected at the pleasure of Another! It is as if a royal child whom his father has placed, for love's sake, in titular command of some great province, under the real rule of wise counsellors, should come to fancy he really owns the cities, the forests, and the corn, in the same way as he owns the bricks on the nursery floor ... [There are] different senses of the possessive pronoun—the finely graded differences that run from "my boots" through "my dog," "my servant," "my wife," "my father," "my master," and "my country," to "my God." They can be taught to reduce all these senses to that of "my boots," the "my" of ownership. (Lewis 1961b, 97–8)

Lewis recognized the silliness of thinking of "my body" as expressing ownership, as if one buys one's body to own it as one buys a pair of boots to own them. He believed that, strictly speaking, none of us owns one's body, and that "all the time the joke is that the word 'mine' in its fully possessive sense cannot be uttered by a human being about anything" (1961b, 98). Ultimately, Lewis thought that, if we are honest, we will recognize that God is the owner of all things, on the "ground that He made [them]" (1961b, 99).

As I pointed out in Chapter 3, during Lewis's lifetime the philosophy of language was dominant in Oxford. Adherents to the linguistic school of thought typically believed one arrived at the truth about things by considering what is said in language. Hence, Lewis would have likely been aware that, when one says things like "I weigh 190 pounds" and "I am 6′3″ tall," many of his contemporaries concluded that one is identical with one's body and, therefore, that dualism is false. But Lewis was at odds with the linguistic approach to philosophy. While he would have readily acknowledged that we often say things in ordinary language which, if taken literally, imply we are our bodies, he also made clear that "language is not an infallible guide" (Lewis 1988, 2). While I am not aware of any place where he specifically addressed this kind of linguistic argument against dualism, it is easy to imagine that he would have said something like the following in response to it: Not infrequently, we hear people say "I am down the road out of gas" or "I was hit by that other vehicle." Strictly speaking, we all know that I am not down the road out of gas. My car is. Similarly, I was not hit by the other vehicle. My car was. What explains our talking in this way? Most plausibly, we extend the scope of "I" to include things with which we are closely causally associated. Thus, because I am closely causally associated with my car, I ascribe features of it (e.g., its being hit and its being down the road) to me. Similarly, with my body. Because I am so closely causally linked with it, I naturally ascribe features of it (e.g., its weight and height) to me. What we must not do is draw philosophical conclusions about the nature of the world directly from things that we say.

5.8　"Miracles" and Miracles

Lewis believed our reasonings and choices produce effects in our brains, and he held that both of these occurrences are miracles: "The presence of human rationality in the world is therefore a Miracle [it is something mental producing an effect in nature from the outside] ... " (Lewis 2001c, 67–8). Lewis realized that a reader might understandably rejoin "'Oh, if *that's* all he means by a Miracle ... ' and fling the book away" (2001c, 68). He asked for patience and did so because of the importance of the issue at stake. He well understood that what most people have in mind when they think of miracles are events like physical healings, incarnations, virgin births, and resurrections from the dead. Being the rationalist that he was, Lewis wanted the ordinary person to understand that what he or she typically thinks of as a miracle is in reality no different in kind from everyday mental-to-physical causation. Reasoning, choosing, and rising from the dead are all invasions by the mental into the physical: "Whether you choose to call the regular and familiar invasion by human Reason a Miracle or not is largely a matter of words. Its regularity ... may incline you not to do so" (Lewis 2001c, 68). But, for Lewis, each invasion by the mental is, strictly speaking, a miracle. And he believed this is no small matter. In his estimation, whether or not one is open to the possibility of a divine miracle is in the end a function of whether one believes miracles occur as a result of one's own mental events. If one denies the latter, then one will surely deny the former. If one affirms the latter, then "the [philosophical] difficulty which we [feel] in the mere idea of the Supernatural descending into the Natural is apparently non-existent, or is at least overcome in the person of every man" (Lewis 2001c, 177).

Lewis concluded that someone who grasps what the topic of miracles is really about understands that there is nothing *per se* problematic with divine miracles. They differ most noticeably from miracles produced by human thought in terms of the infrequency of their occurrence. Assuming that there are one-off miraculous events, Lewis maintained that the singularity of such events made them unsuitable for study by science: "What cannot be trusted to recur is not material for science: that is why history is not one of the sciences" (Lewis 1970, 134). It seems, however, that Lewis might be mistaken at this point. After all, the idea of the Big Bang can plausibly be accepted as a singular occurrence in the sense that it is something that occurred only once in our universe, yet at the same time rightly regarded as subject matter for the science of astronomical physics. As the philosopher Alvin Plantinga has asked, if science by definition only deals with events of a kind that are repeatable, then "would we be obliged to conclude that contemporary cosmological inquiries into the nature of the Big Bang and into the early development of the universe are not really a part of science?" (1997, 146). The answer is obviously, "Yes." So it seems something is wrong with Lewis's position. Plausibly, what he should have said is that certain singular events are not suitable for study by the sciences, not in virtue of their singularity but because they are ultimately explicable only in terms of irreducible purposes. This is the explanation why history is not one of the sciences.[5]

Histories of human behavior are teleological accounts of particular events in space and time. They are explanations of the bodily doings of human beings that most likely have their initial causal effects in human brains. But, as Lewis acknowledged, most people wonder whether "Supernature ever produce[s] particular results in space and time *except* through the instrumentality of human brains acting on human nerves and muscles" (2001c, 68). To state it differently, most people wonder whether God occasionally gets involved in our world once it exists.

Lewis was aware that even if his argument for the supernatural nature of human activity was sound, many people might still have problems with the idea that God invades this world every now and then. For example, they might wonder whether such invasions, though philosophically non-problematic, are problematic for a different reason, that reason being that they would occur for no rhyme or reason. In short, the occurrence of such invasions would make no sense. Lewis conceded that "a great deal of the modern objection to miracles is based on the suspicion that they are marvels of the wrong sort" (Lewis 2001c, 156). In response, he claimed that with Christianity

> [t]here is no question ... of arbitrary interferences just scattered about. It relates not a series of disconnected raids on Nature but the various steps of a strategically coherent invasion ... The fitness, and therefore credibility, of the particular miracles depends on their relation to the Grand Miracle; all discussion of them in isolation from it is futile. (Lewis 2001c, 173–4)

What Lewis believed was the Grand Miracle and how it played the central role in making sense of other miracles is the subject of Chapter 6.

notes

1   Those who are familiar with contemporary philosophical literature about human freedom might think Lewis is making two points about choices: (1) that they are causally undetermined by events of any kind (they are not produced by event causation); and (2) that they are causally determined

by the self or agent (they are produced by agent causation). It seems to me that Lewis never conceptualized the issue of human freedom by distinguishing between event and agent causation. Hence, it is impossible to answer a question about his belief in human freedom that is framed in terms of these types of causation (e.g., did he believe choices are not caused at all or did he think choices are uncaused by other events but caused by the agents who make them?).

2 For more on this issue, see Goetz (2005) and Timpe (2013, 141–61).

3 Neil Levy (2014, 70–4) describes instances of what he terms "global automatisms" in which subjects engage in complex and seemingly teleological behavior, while supposedly not being conscious of what they are doing. Levy summarizes a case of a man, Kenneth Parks, who walked to his car, drove 23 kilometers to his in-laws' home, strangled his father-in-law into unconsciousness and repeatedly stabbed his mother-in-law, who later died. Parks subsequently drove to a police station, where he notified police of what he thought he might have done and first noticed severed tendons in his severely injured arms. He pleaded not guilty and was acquitted on the grounds that his behavior was caused by a serious sleep disorder. Levy also mentions a case of sleep emailing in which a subject was caused by a sleep disorder to type an intelligible email, without being conscious of what she was doing.

   If subjects can be unconsciously and blindly caused to perform these seemingly purposeful behaviors, might it be plausible to maintain that *all* of our behavior, even Lewis's writing of letters and books, is ultimately explicable in terms of purposeless causes, so that there is no need for causal openness in our brains? Lewis would have responded that such a position is thoroughly implausible. Borrowing a term from Levy, he would have claimed that one can plausibly hold that subjects originally engage in conscious, purposeful activity that programs their brains with "*action scripts*," which are sets of motor representations that can subsequently be non-consciously causally activated to produce forms of behavior that could only have had their causal origins in conscious purposefully held intentions and choices. Thus, Lewis would have concluded, there can be instances of global automatisms only because there is conscious, purposeful activity at the outset.

   The following words of the English mathematician Alfred North Whitehead, a contemporary of Lewis, accurately capture Lewis's view: "Scientists [and philosophers] animated by the purpose of proving that they [and their behaviors] are purposeless constitute an interesting subject for study" (Whitehead 1958, 16).

4 Richard Purtill (2004, 88) also picks up on the importance of the distinction between "the scientist … *as* a scientist" and the scientist as a human being for Lewis's treatment of miracles.

5 One might retort at this point that while the Big Bang is not part of human history, it might be part of divine history because it was caused by God for a purpose. Even if this is true, it seems that the Big Bang is still a proper subject for scientific explanation, despite its singularity.

the grand miracle, death to self, and myth

> I heard a voice that cried,
> Balder the beautiful
> Is dead, is dead—
> (Lewis 1955, 17)

IN ANCIENT EGYPT the god whose death and resurrection were annually celebrated with alternate sorrow and joy was Osiris ... and there are good grounds for classing him in one of his aspects with Adonis and Attis as a personification of the great yearly vicissitudes of nature, especially of the corn.

(Frazer 2006, 201)

6.1 Incarnation

Conceptually at least, it is possible to distinguish between Christian and non-Christian (what Lewis called "pagan") miracles. But what about the actual occurrence of one or the other? If there are Christian miracles, does it follow that nothing miraculous of a non-Christian nature occurs? Lewis thought not:

> I do not think that it is the duty of a Christian apologist ... to disprove all stories of the miraculous which fall outside Christian records, nor of a Christian man to disbelieve them. I am in no way committed to the assertion that God has never worked miracles through and for Pagans or never permitted created supernatural beings to do so ... If it can be shown that one particular Roman emperor ... once was empowered to do a miracle, we must of course put up with the fact ... [However, the] idiotic interferences attributed to gods in Pagan stories, even if they had a trace of historical evidence, could be accepted only on the condition of our accepting a wholly meaningless universe. (2001c, 216–17)

C. S. Lewis, First Edition. Stewart Goetz.
© 2018 John Wiley & Sons, Inc. Published 2018 by John Wiley & Sons, Inc.

But what about the acceptance of Christian miracles? Lewis maintained that their occurrence is plausible only if they make sense. How, then, might one go about trying to show that Christian miracles make sense? Lewis thought that one way of doing this would be to consider the multiplicity of miracles performed by Jesus (e.g., healings, feedings, raising individuals from the dead) and ask how they were related to each other. And to answer this question he suggested we consider what he termed the "Grand Miracle" and query how to make sense of all other miracles in light of their relationship to it (they would be related in the appropriate way to each other by being related to it). To illustrate his idea, Lewis asked his readers to suppose they had in their possession parts of a novel or symphony of which they were having difficulty making sense, only to have someone come along and provide them with what he said was the missing part of the musical composition or book: "Our business would be to see whether the new [part], if admitted to the central place which the discoverer claimed for it, did actually illuminate all the parts we had already seen and 'pull them together'" (Lewis 2001c, 175). If upon every new hearing and reading of the new part we were able to make more sense of the other parts, then the new part's credibility would be enhanced.

So what did Lewis think is the Grand Miracle? He held it is the Incarnation, God becoming man in the person of Jesus of Nazareth (Lewis 2001c, 173), whose capacity to illumine other miracles Lewis likened to the illuminative power of the sun: "We believe that the sun is in the sky at midday in summer not because we can clearly see the sun (in fact we cannot) but because we can see everything else [by it]" (2001c, 176). But if other miracles acquire their intelligibility to each other through the light shed upon them by the Grand Miracle (in simplest terms, Lewis thought the Incarnation encapsulates the idea that God came down to "bring the whole ruined world up with Him" (2001c, 179) totally remade), it seems the Grand Miracle could not acquire its intelligibility as a miracle by illuminating itself. Hence, assuming it is not intrinsically intelligible, it would have to get its intelligibility in some other way.

Lewis believed our self-knowledge is the primary illuminative lens through which we are able to make sense of the Incarnation. Thus, when asked "What can be meant by 'God becoming man'? In what sense is it conceivable that eternal self-existent Spirit ... should be so combined with a natural human organism as to make one person?" (2001c, 176), Lewis responded that we can understand the Incarnation because we already understand that human beings are soul-body composites, where the soul is a supernatural entity that is able to engage in "the act of reasoning" (2001c, 177). In essence, Lewis appealed to his argument from reason and soul-body dualism to help make sense of the Incarnation, with the result that "the difficulty which we felt in the mere idea of the Supernatural descending into the Natural is apparently non-existent, or is at least overcome in the person of every man" (2001c, 177):

> If we did not know by experience what it feels like to be a rational animal ... we could not conceive, much less imagine, the [Incarnation] happening. The discrepancy between a movement of atoms in an astronomer's cortex and his understanding that there must be a still unobserved planet beyond Uranus, is already so immense that the Incarnation of God Himself is, in one sense, scarcely more startling. (2001c, 177–8)

Lewis regarded his argument from reason and soul-body dualism as the primary principle for illuminating the Incarnation. However, he believed there is an additional illuminative principle, what he termed "the pattern of descent and reascension" (2001c, 191–2), which Lewis believed is exemplified in various aspects of nature:

> In this descent and reascent everyone will recognise a familiar pattern: a thing written all over the world. It is the pattern of all vegetable life. It must belittle itself into something hard, small and deathlike, it must fall into the ground: then the new life reascends. It is the pattern of all animal generation too. There is descent from the full and perfect organisms into the spermatozoon and ovum, and in the dark womb a life at first inferior in kind to that of the species which is being reproduced: then the slow ascent to the perfect embryo, to the living, conscious baby, and finally to the adult. (2001c, 180)

According to Lewis, then, the Incarnation is illuminated for us in a second way by the descent and reascent pattern found in nature. However, I think it is reasonable to hold that he believed the descent and reascent motif observed in nature is in turn illuminated for us by the same pattern as it is found in our own lives. Thus, Lewis followed the sentences just quoted above with the words "[so the descent and reascent pattern] is also in our moral and emotional life. The first innocent and spontaneous desires have to submit to the deathlike process of control and total denial ... " (2001c, 180). Given Lewis's backdrop belief that we know ourselves better than anything else, he thought that one of the things evident to us concerning ourselves is that we must die to self in order ultimately to experience the perfect happiness for which we were created. Furthermore, as I will make clear in Chapter 7, Lewis thought that belief in God's existence is not inferred from beliefs about the external world but from beliefs about the self. The combined implication of these points is that it is not the least implausible to hold that Lewis believed the descent and reascent pattern found in the Incarnation is illuminated through that pattern found in nature only because that pattern in nature is itself illuminated in terms of that motif as it is found in the self. Given the centrality of the idea of descent and reascent in Lewis's thought about the meaning of life and its importance for understanding the Grand Miracle that is the Incarnation, I devote the next two sections to an extended discussion of it.

6.2 The Seed Must Die

I made clear in Chapter 3 that Lewis believed experiences of pleasure make life worth living and compose happiness, where perfect happiness is the meaning of life in the sense of being the purpose for which we were created. But it is one thing to have a purpose and another to fulfill or achieve it. So if we were created for perfect happiness, how do we attain it?

In answer to this question, Lewis insisted that we must not become preoccupied with achieving happiness in this world and forget or refuse to acknowledge that the complete experience of that for which we were created can only be had beyond this world. It is worth requoting Lewis on this point:

> If there lurks in most modern minds the notion that to desire our own good and earnestly to hope for the enjoyment of it is a bad thing, I submit that this notion … is no part of the Christian faith. Indeed, if we consider the unblushing promises of reward and the staggering nature of the rewards promised in the Gospels, it would seem that Our Lord finds our desires not too strong, but too weak. We are half-hearted creatures, fooling about with drink and sex and ambition when infinite joy is offered us, like an ignorant child who wants to go on making mud pies in a slum because he cannot imagine what is meant by the offer of a holiday at the sea. (2001g, 26)

But why do we fool around with things like drink, sex, and ambition? We know Lewis did not think that these things are intrinsically evil, and he affirmed that the pleasure that comes from them is intrinsically good. What he believed is problematic is that our desire for the intrinsic goodness of pleasure entices us to pursue it in illicit ways. In other words, because we are selves who want to have what is good for us, we choose to pursue that good on our own terms. We choose to try to make ourselves as happy as we can in ways that *we* deem fit. We choose to arrogate to ourselves to do as *we* please, even at the expense of the happiness of others. This is the problem of pride and Lewis maintained that God cannot allow people who insist on trying to experience happiness on their own terms to experience the perfect happiness for which He created them. It is only by dying to self that they will experience that happiness, where the experience of it will be had by the resurrected self that gave it up. Lewis tried to impress this point upon Phyllis Sandeman in personal correspondence in terms of her desire for a house:

> I think that about Houses the answer is this. Nothing rises again which has not died. The natural and possessive love for a house *if* it has been crucified, if it has become disinterested, if it has submitted to sacrifice, will rise again: i.e. the love for a house *you were willing to give up* will rise again. The wilful, grasping love will not—or only rise as a horror ...

> But the whole point is that you can *keep* forever only what you *give up*: beginning with the thing it is hardest to give up—one's self. What you grab you lose: what you offer freely and patiently to God or your neighbor, you will have. (Your heavenly library will contain only the books you have given or lent! ... I'm joking of course, but to illustrate a serious principle.) (2004b, 788)

Lewis expressed the "death to self/resurrection of self" principle in many other places and ways. As a literary critic, he stressed that "[t]he first demand any work of any art makes upon us is surrender. Look. Listen. Receive. Get yourself out of the way" (Lewis 1961a, 19). The "true reader ... makes himself as receptive as he can" (Lewis 1961a, 11). When discussing medieval courtly oral poetry, Lewis emphasized that the feasts which were the occasions for oral poetry were the proper occasions of pomp. For us, wrote Lewis, pomp has negative connotations, so to recover the original sense of the term,

> you must think of a court ball, or a coronation, or a victory march, as these things appear to people who *enjoy* them ... Above all, you must be rid of the hideous idea ... that pomp, on the proper occasions, has any connexion with vanity or self-conceit. A celebrant approaching the altar, a princess led out by a king to dance a minuet, a general officer on a ceremonial parade ... —all these wear unusual clothes and move with calculated dignity. This does not mean that they are vain, but that they are obedient ... The modern habit of doing ceremonial things unceremoniously is no proof of humility; rather it proves the offender's inability to forget himself in the rite, and his readiness to spoil for every one else the proper pleasure of ritual. (1942, 17)

Lewis insisted that what is the case with reading and pomp is true of life overall and the way to the fulfillment of its purpose: "This is the ultimate law—the seed dies to live, the bread must be cast upon the waters, he that loses his soul will save it" (Lewis 2001f, 154); and "a crucifixion of the natural self is the passport to everlasting life" (Lewis 2001g, 172). In terms of happiness, "the proper good of a creature is to surrender itself to its Creator ... When it does so, it is good and happy" (Lewis 2001f, 88) because "God designed the human machine to run on Himself ... That is why it is just no good asking God to make us happy in our own way without bothering about religion" (Lewis 2001b, 50). Lewis asked, "[w]as [not] ... "the great 19th century heresy—that 'pure' or 'noble' passions didn't need to be crucified & reborn but [would] of themselves lead to happiness?" (2004b, 530).

6.3 The Paradox of Hedonism

At this juncture, it is important to clarify two explanatory matters concerned with the pursuit of happiness. One is sometimes referred to as the "paradox of hedonism." Alister McGrath has written that this paradox is "the simple yet stultifying fact that pleasure cannot satisfy ... " (1988, 111). If McGrath means that pleasure, even at its height in this life, does not satisfy because it ceases and leaves us yearning for more, then Lewis would have agreed. However, if he means that pleasure does not satisfy, period, then Lewis would have disagreed. Indeed, Lewis thought other things satisfy us only if and to the extent that they in the end lead to pleasure. In contrast to McGrath's construal of the paradox of hedonism, one typically finds the idea that to find happiness, one must not make it the object of one's pursuit, the reason for one's actions. For example, the hedonist John Stuart Mill wrote in his autobiography that

> I now thought that this end [happiness] was only to be attained by not making it the direct end. Those only are happy (I thought) who have their minds fixed on some object other than their own happiness ... Aiming thus at something else, they find happiness by the way. (1964, 112)

And the philosopher Henry Sidgwick, following Mill, acknowledged as the "fundamental paradox of Hedonism, that the impulse towards pleasure, if too predominant, defeats its own aim" (1966, 48). Echoing Mill and Sidgwick, Lewis wrote:

> How right you are: the great thing is to stop thinking about happiness. Indeed the best thing about happiness itself is that it liberates you from thinking about happiness—as the greatest pleasure that money can give us is to make it unnecessary to think about money. (2007, 93)

And similarly, "there is no use trying to keep the first thrill. It will come to life again and again only on *one* condition: that we turn our backs on it and get to work and go through all the dullness" (Lewis 2007, 698). In the terminology of Samuel Alexander's *Space, Time and Deity*, which, as we saw in Chapter 2 was influential in Lewis's understanding of thought and reasoning, the more one *contemplates* happiness, the less one is able to *enjoy* it. Or in words taken from Lewis's "Meditation in a Toolshed" (Lewis 1970), the more one *looks at* happiness, the less one is able to *look along* it.

We saw in Chapter 4 that Lewis was a Kantian about the importance of reason as a determinant of the moral status of a choice. It is therefore plausible to suppose that Lewis was also familiar with Kant's hedonistic understanding of happiness (Irwin 1996) and recognition of the paradox of hedonism. Regarding the latter, Kant believed that if the purpose of an individual's existence were that he be happy, then it would be a very bad arrangement if reason were provided as the tool for fulfilling this purpose (Kant 1956, 63). Why so? Because it is impossible for even the most intelligent person to have any certainty about what will bring him happiness:

> Is it riches he wants? How much anxiety, envy, and pestering might he not bring in this way on his own head! Is it knowledge and insight? This might perhaps merely give him an eye so sharp that it would make evils at present hidden from him and yet unavoidable seem all the more frightful, or would add a load of still further needs to the desires which already give him trouble enough. Is it long life? Who will guarantee that it would not be a long misery? Is it at least health? How often has infirmity of body kept a man from excesses into which perfect health would have let him fall!—and so on. In short, he has no principle by which he is able to decide with complete certainty what will make him truly happy, since for this he would require omniscience. (Kant 1956, 85–6)

Samuel Johnson, the subject of James Boswell's *The Life of Samuel Johnson*, which Lewis cited as one among the ten most influential books in shaping his philosophy of life (Lewis 1962), wrote words much like Kant's:

> Life is not long, and too much of it must not pass in idle deliberation how it shall be spent; deliberation, which those who begin it by prudence, and continue it with subtilty, must, after long expence of thought, conclude by chance. To prefer one future mode of life to another, upon just reasons, requires faculties which it has not pleased our Creator to give us. (Boswell 2008, 273)

Lewis agreed with Kant and Johnson, and used education in his own Kantian/Johnsonian-like examples:

> The good results which I think I can trace to my first school would not have come about if its vile procedure had been intended to produce them. They were all by-products thrown off by a wicked old man's desire to make as much as he could out of deluded parents and to give as little as he could in return. That is the point. While we are planning the education of the future we can be rid of the illusion that we shall

ever replace destiny. Make the plans as good as you can, of course. But be sure that the deep and final effect on every single boy will be something you never envisaged and will spring from little free movements in your machine which neither your blueprint nor your working model gave any hint of. (Lewis 1986a, 26)

[R]emember how much religious education has exactly the opposite effect to that [which] was intended, how many hard atheists come from pious homes. (Lewis 2007, 507)

In places, Lewis expressed his belief in the paradox of hedonism in terms of our preoccupation with the future: constantly trying to ascertain how to be happy requires us to live in the future, where this preoccupation with what is temporally ahead prevents us from being happy in the present. So convinced was Lewis of this point that he had the devil Screwtape advise his nephew Wormwood to aim at getting human beings to live in the future:

It is far better to make them live in the Future. Biological necessity makes all their passions point in that direction already, so that thought about the Future inflames hope and fear ... In a word, the Future is, of all things, the thing *least like* eternity. It is the most completely temporal part of time—for the Past is frozen and no longer flows, and the Present is all lit up with eternal rays ... He [God] does not want men to give the Future their hearts, to place their treasure in it ... We [Screwtape, Wormwood and the legion of devils] want a whole race perpetually in pursuit of the rainbow's end, never ... happy *now* ... [A] man may be untroubled about the Future, not because he is concerned with the Present, but because he has persuaded himself that the Future is going to be agreeable. As long as that is the real course of his tranquility, his tranquility will do us good, because it is only piling up more disappointment ... for him when his false hopes are dashed ... [W]ith the present ... all pleasure dwell[s] ... (Lewis 1961b, 68, 69, 70)

Also of interest at this point is that Lewis seems to have regarded the paradox of hedonism as an instance of a more general "curious and unhappy psychological law" that

[our psychological] attitudes often inhibit the very thing they are intended to facilitate ... [For example], a couple never felt less in love than on their wedding day, many a man never felt less merry than at Christmas dinner, and when at a lecture we say "I must attend", attention instantly vanishes. (Lewis 2007, 1023)

And again, "[t]he dutiful effort prevents the spontaneous feeling; just as if you say to an old friend during a brief reunion 'Now let's have a good talk', both suddenly find themselves with nothing to say" (Lewis 2007, 1075).

"Even in social life, you will never make a good impression on other people until you stop thinking about what sort of impression you are making" (Lewis 2001b, 226). As a final example of this psychological law, Lewis wrote about Lord Berners that "his taste [in books] was excellent as long as he did not think about it. To the present day one meets men, great readers, who write admirably until the fatal moment when they remember that they are writing" (1954, 151).

The second of the two explanatory matters concerned with the pursuit of happiness is the issue of the reason for which one acts when one chooses to die to self. In Lewis's mind, in order to receive the heavenly reward of perfect happiness for which one was created, one cannot act for the purpose that one receive that heavenly reward. Choosing for that reason would amount to no more than a pursuit of self-interest. Instead, the choice to die to self and trust God for perfect happiness must be made for the reason that it is the morally right thing to do. Thus, not only is it the case, as Erik Wielenberg has pointed out, that "from the fact that action A had a particular *consequence* C, it does not follow that the agent who performed A did so *for the sake of* C" (2008, 73), but also the agent can *believe* that C will be the result of his performing A yet not perform A for the sake of C.

Lewis addressed the issue of the relationship between motivation and eternal reward in terms of a bribe:

> [We] are afraid that heaven is a bribe, and that if we make it our goal [purpose] we shall no longer be disinterested. It is not so. Heaven offers nothing that a mercenary soul can desire. It is safe to tell the pure in heart that they shall see God, for only the pure in heart want to. (2001f, 149)

Choosing to die to self and trust God for the perfect happiness for which one was created is not a mercenary act when done for the reason that is what one ought to do (from a pure heart). While the reward of heaven is found in the content of the choice (I choose to trust God to provide me with perfect happiness), it is not found in the content of the purpose for which the choice is made (the content of the purpose is that I do what I ought to do). Were the reward of heaven found in the content of the purpose for making the choice, the choice would end up being explained in terms of self-interest. Lewis believed that because the choice of death to self implies a willingness to give up any attempt to maximize one's happiness on one's own terms here and now for the reason that that is what one ought to do, the mercenary soul refuses to make it. The mercenary soul does not want to "see" God because seeing God would require the making of the choice to die to self and forfeiting opportunities for pleasure on one's own terms in the present moment. When God requires humans to lose "their selves, He means only abandoning the clamour of self-will" (Lewis 1961b, 59). Death to self is a choice "to bring your picture of yourself down to something nearer life-size" (Lewis 1967, 169). Lewis wrote that what one finds in that picture is not all that pleasant: "[P]resently you begin to wonder whether you are yet, in any full sense, a person at all; whether you are entitled to call yourself 'I' (it is a sacred name)" (Lewis 1967, 169).

The requisite death to self, which is necessary for receiving the happiness for which one was created, was in Lewis's own case noticeable and recounted by his lifelong friend, Owen Barfield:

> I first met him [Lewis] in 1919, and the puzzlement [about Lewis] has had to do above all with the great change that took place in him between the years 1930 and 1940—a change which roughly coincided with his conversion to Theism and then to Christianity ... [A]t a certain stage in his life he deliberately ceased to take any interest in himself except as a kind of spiritual alumnus taking his moral finals ... [What] began as a deliberate choice became at length (as he had no doubt always intended it should) an ingrained and effortless habit of soul. (Barfield 1989, 17–18, 24–5)

Lewis pointedly recalled that learning to dive into water was especially significant for him because it had "important (religious) connections" (2004a, 915) in terms of death to self. In *The Pilgrim's Regress*, the main character John says "'Alas ... I have never learned to dive.' 'There is nothing to learn,' said she [Mother Kirk, who represented the Christian church]. 'The art of diving is not to do anything new but simply to cease doing something. You have only to let yourself go'" (Lewis 1992b, 166–7).

One further point is worth making about Lewis's view of the death to self. He stressed that the death-to-self motif is not a Christian notion in the sense that it is only found within the Christian religion. Just as Lewis believed that Jesus did not teach a new morality (see Chapter 4), so also he believed that neither Jesus nor St. Paul introduced a new idea with their stress on the need to lose one's life in order to find it, and the seed's having to be buried in order to live:

> The doctrine of death which I describe is not peculiar to Christianity. Nature herself has written it large across the world in the repeated drama of the buried seed and the re-arising corn ... The Indian ascetic, mortifying his body on a bed of spikes, preaches the same lesson; the Greek philosopher tells us that the life of wisdom is "a practice of death". The sensitive and noble heathen of modern times makes his imagined gods "die into life". Mr Huxley expounds "non-attachment". We cannot escape the doctrine by ceasing to be Christians. It is an "eternal gospel" revealed to men wherever men have sought, or endured, the truth: it is the very nerve of redemption, which anatomising wisdom at all times and in all places lays bare; the unescapable knowledge which

the Light that lighteneth every man presses down upon the minds of all who seriously question what the universe is "about". The peculiarity of the Christian faith is not to teach this doctrine but to render it, in various ways, more tolerable. (Lewis 2001f, 102–3)

Lewis went on to emphasize that what is peculiar to Christianity is not the die-to-live doctrine, but its commonsensical understanding of it. Whereas Buddhism tries to convince us that death to self requires a realization of the anti-commonsensical idea that the self (soul/atman) does not even exist as a substance or entity that endures through time (see Lewis's letter to Leo Baker, quoted in Chapter 1), Jesus and Christianity affirm the reality of the self but teach the need for a choice to reject the pursuit of the maximization of happiness on one's own terms so as to receive it from one's Creator.

6.4   Pleasure and Passion

Lewis was a hedonist about happiness, and his understanding of happiness provided the backdrop for his acceptance of the paradox of hedonism and the need to die to self. What is also a significant part of this hedonistic backdrop is the fact that an experience of pleasure is an event with respect to which a person is directly a patient, not an agent; directly passive, not active. An experience of pleasure happens to a person.

Aristotle, a eudaemonist philosopher whose work Lewis knew well, understood our relationship to pleasure. According to him, happiness is an activity of the soul in accordance with virtue (Aristotle 1962, 17 [1098a16-17]; 22 [1099b26]) and pleasure accompanies this activity and perfects or completes it: "[P]leasure is intimately connected with the activity which it completes" (Aristotle 1962, 283 [1175a29-30]). Indeed, because pleasure is so intimately connected with the activity it perfects, Aristotle claimed it is tempting to think that the two are identical: "[P]leasure is so closely linked to activity and so little distinguished from it that one may dispute whether < or not > activity is identical with pleasure" (Aristotle 1962, 284 [1175b33-4]). And "because [pleasure and activity] are never found apart, some people get the impression that they are identical" (Aristotle 1962, 284 [1175b35]). However, it is a mistake to think that they are identical.

If an experience of pleasure is not an activity but an event that accompanies an activity and with respect to which we are immediately passive, then whether or not we experience pleasure is something that is ultimately beyond our control. The Aristotelian scholar Gerd van Riel puts the point as follows:

[W]e never know for sure what to do in order to attain pleasure: it is never guaranteed. As an additional element, pleasure can occur, but it is just as likely to fail to appear. [Consider] Beethoven's fourth piano concerto. It is not certain that I will experience pleasure in attending a performance of this work. Even if all the circumstances are in an optimal state, I cannot be sure that I will enjoy the concert ... If this is true, it should be possible that an activity is perfectly performed even without yielding pleasure. But this dismisses the immediate link between pleasure and a perfect activity, and moreover, it implies that the perfection of an activity is not enough to secure our pleasure. Even if all circumstances are perfectly arranged, and the activity perfectly performed, pleasure is not guaranteed. This "escape from our control" is not an accidental quality of pleasure, dependent on circumstances, but a characteristic of the very essence of pleasure. (1999, 219–20)

Because happiness, on a hedonistic understanding of it, consists of nothing but experiences of pleasure, one would expect to find van Riel affirming that happiness is also something with respect to which we have no absolute control. And this is exactly what he claims. Pleasure is like happiness insofar as "it is something which we may hope to attain, without ever being sure how to behave in order to guarantee its appearance" (van Riel 1999, 219). Given that pleasure and the happiness it composes are ultimately not under our control, Lewis concluded that, in terms of the success of our own efforts, happiness is a matter of luck: "'[A] right to happiness' ... sounds to me as odd as a right to good luck. For I believe ... that we depend for a very great deal of our happiness ... on circumstances outside all human control" (Lewis 1970, 318).

In light of our lack of ultimate control over our pleasure and happiness, Lewis's affirmations of the paradox of hedonism and the need to die to self are even more readily understandable: That over which one lacks ultimate control is something it is prudentially wise not to invest one's effort in obtaining, because there is no guarantee that one will obtain it. And no matter what degree of imperfect happiness one is lucky enough to obtain in this life, it remains the case that the perfect happiness for which one was created is most certainly beyond one's reach. Hence, the need to die to self in order finally to experience that happiness in the afterlife.

6.5 Myth

Lewis was a lover of myth and came to the conclusion that Christianity is a true myth. In this section, I briefly explain how the descent-reascent/dying-rising motif was important in leading him to this conclusion.

Lewis believed a myth is a story that supplies a narrative by which to make sense of things. He wrote to his friend Greeves that what had proven especially difficult for him to make sense of in the Christian myth was the idea of redemption:

> What has been holding me back ... has not been so much a difficulty in believing as a difficulty in knowing what the doctrine [of redemption] *meant*: you can't believe a thing while you are ignorant *what* the thing is. My puzzle was the whole doctrine of Redemption: in what sense the life and death of Christ "saved" or "opened salvation to" the world. (2004a, 976)

The extended walk with Hugo Dyson and J. R. R. Tolkien in 1931 (see Chapter 1) helped him to understand the concept of redemption rooted in the death and resurrection of Jesus of Nazareth in terms of the philosophical importance of dying and rising set forth in Section 6.2:

> Now the story of Christ is simply a true myth: a myth working on us in the same way as the others, but with this tremendous difference that *it really happened*: and one must be content to accept it in the same way, remembering that it is God's myth where the others are men's myths: i.e. the Pagan stories are God expressing Himself through the minds of poets, using such images as He found there, while Christianity is God expressing Himself through what we call "real things". Therefore it is *true*, not in the sense of being a "description" of God ... but in the sense of being the way in which God chooses to (or can) appear to our faculties. The "doctrines" we get *out* of the true myth are of course *less* true: they are translations into our *concepts* and *ideas* of that [which] God has already expressed in a language more adequate, namely the actual incarnation, crucifixion, and resurrection. (Lewis 2004a, 977)

But why should God choose to appear to our faculties in this way? Alistair McGrath writes that in Lewis's thought

> a myth is a story which evokes awe, enchantment, and inspiration, and which conveys or embodies an imaginative expression of the deepest meanings of life—meanings that prove totally elusive in the face of any attempt to express them abstractly or conceptually. (2014, 63)

Lewis, however, believed that the deepest meanings of life do not completely elude conceptualization. He thought pleasure (happiness) is what makes life worth living, and the experience of it is the purpose for which God created us. In order to ultimately make sense of things, Lewis concluded that those who choose to die to self will ultimately rise up perfectly happy in heaven. And it was his non-elusive convictions about this and the paradox of hedonism which, at a fundamental level, provided the framework for his belief that the story of Christ is the true myth.

Lewis encapsulated everything, including his anti-naturalism, in the following thoughts:

> For the essence of religion, in my view, is the thirst for an end higher than natural ends; the finite self's desire for, and acquiescence in, and self-rejection in favour of, an object wholly good [God] and wholly good for it [perfect happiness]. That the self-rejection will turn out to be also a self-finding, that bread cast upon the waters will be found after many days, that to die is to live—these are sacred paradoxes ... Myths have been accepted as literally true, then as allegorically true (by the Stoics), as confused history (by Euhemerus), as priestly lies (by the philosophers of the enlightenment), as imitative agricultural ritual mistaken for propositions (in the days of Frazer). If you start from a naturalistic philosophy, then something like the view of Euhemerus or the view of Frazer is likely to result. But I am not a naturalist. I believe that in the huge mass of mythology which has come down to us a good many different sources are mixed—true history, allegory, ritual, the human delight in story telling, etc. But among these sources I include the supernatural, both diabolical and divine ... If my religion is erroneous then occurrences of similar motifs in pagan stories are, of course, instances of the same, or a similar error. But if my religion is true, then these stories may well be a *preparatio evangelica*, a divine hinting in poetic and ritual form at the same central truth which was later focussed and (so to speak) historicised in the Incarnation. (Lewis 1970, 131–2)

Pagan stories also captured the dying-and-rising motif. Lewis believed we should not be surprised by this, given that all people desire perfect happiness and one must die to self in order to experience it. Thus, in contrast with the atheist, who must "believe that the main point in all the religions of the whole world is simply one huge mistake ... [the] Christian ... [is] free to think that all those religions, even the queerest ones, contain at least some hint of the truth" (Lewis 2001b, 35). But while Lewis believed we should not be the least bit surprised by the commonalities between pagan myths and Christianity, he recognized that in and of itself the shared descent-reascent idea is consistent with either the truth or falsity of Christianity:

> The truth is that the resemblances tell nothing either for or against the truth of Christian Theology. If you start from the assumption that the Theology is false, the resemblances are quite consistent with that assumption. One would expect creatures of the same sort, faced with the same universe, to make the same false guess more than once. But if you start with the assumption that the Theology is true, the resemblances fit in equally well. Theology, while saying that a special illumination has been vouchsafed to Christians and (earlier) to Jews, also says that there is some divine illumination vouchsafed to all men.

The Divine light, we are told, "lighteneth every man." We should, therefore, expect to find in the imagination of great Pagan teachers and myth makers some glimpse of that theme which we believe to be the very plot of the whole cosmic story—the theme of incarnation, death, and rebirth. (Lewis 2001g, 128)

But if things can go either way in terms of the truth or falsity of a myth, what finally led Lewis to conclude that it is the Christian story that is the true myth? Against the backdrop of everything else discussed in this chapter, he became convinced that the accounts of Jesus in the gospels were true. Lewis had read both pagan myths and the gospels, and he believed he knew the difference between false and true myths. He wrote that those who regarded the death and resurrection of Christ as just one more false myth (here, Lewis had in mind people like the New Testament scholar and theologian, Rudolf Bultmann) perhaps had never given serious attention to anything other than the gospels:

[W]hatever these men may be as Biblical critics, I distrust them as critics. They seem to me to lack literary judgement, to be imperceptive about the very quality of the texts they are reading. It sounds a strange charge to bring against men who have been steeped in those books all their lives. But that might be just the trouble. A man who has spent his youth and manhood in the minute study of New Testament texts and of other people's studies of them, whose literary experiences of those texts lacks any standard of comparison such as can only grow from a wide and deep and genial experience of literature in general, is, I should think, very likely to miss the obvious things about them. If he tells me that something in a Gospel is legend ... I want to know how many legends ... he has read, how well his palate is trained in detecting them by the flavour; not how many years he has spent on that Gospel. (Lewis 1967, 154)

After briefly examining the gospel of John and its regard for fine detail in the account of Jesus with the Samaritan woman at the well, Lewis wrote "I have been reading ... legends [and] myths all my life. I know what they are like. I know that not one of them is like this" (1967, 155). Lewis recounted how even one of his atheist colleagues knew the difference:

The real clue had been put into my hand by that hard-boiled Atheist [a philosophy colleague T. D. Weldon] when he said, "Rum thing, all that about the Dying God. Seems to have really happened once"; by him and by Barfield's encouragement of a more respectful, if not more delighted, attitude to Pagan myth. The question was no longer to find the one simply true religion among a thousand religions simply false. It was rather, "Where has religion reached its true maturity? Where, if anywhere, have the hints of all Paganism been fulfilled?" (1955, 235)[1]

In the end, Lewis concluded that religion had reached its maturity in Christianity. He became intellectually convinced that Christianity was the true myth because it made sense in light of what he already knew about the meaning of life and what makes life worth living. Lewis understood the meaning of life as experiences of pleasure which compose the perfect happiness that is the purpose for which we were created. While morality (action) is necessary to determine who will justly experience this happiness (passion), it is not needed for the actual experience of it. Morality is something that will be done away with in the end. Such was the teaching of Christianity and to Lewis it all seemed so reasonable. But Lewis came to Christianity after he had come to theism. Why, then, did he first believe that God exists? The answer to this question is the subject of Chapter 7.

note

1   Lewis also mentioned the conversation in his personal diary. The entry is from April 27, 1926, in which Lewis wrote "We somehow got on the historical truth of the Gospels, and agreed that there was a lot that could not be explained away" (1991, 379).

belief in god

It was a remark of Harwood's … [that] first suggested to me that God might be defined as "a Being who spends his time having his existence proved and disproved."

(Lewis 2004b, 7)

Nobody can imagine how nothing could turn into something. Nobody can get an inch nearer to it by explaining how something could turn into something else. It is really far more logical to start by saying "In the beginning God created … "

(Chesterton 2007, 19)

7.1 Reason and Religion

Much has been written since Lewis's day about belief that God exists (belief in the existence of God). One of the most interesting and influential writers on the topic has been the philosopher Alvin Plantinga. To oversimplify his thoughts, Plantinga argues that for too long people have worked with the wrong paradigm about belief in the existence of God. According to that paradigm, belief that God exists is irrational, unreasonable, or unjustified, if it is not inferred from other beliefs. Plantinga maintains that belief that God exists is properly basic, by which he means that belief that God exists, when it is properly held, is not arrived at on the basis of reasoning (argument). A good way of getting a sense of Plantinga's view is to compare belief that God exists with belief in one's own existence. Just as one non-inferentially believes in one's own existence (it would be extremely odd to think that one had, or needed to have, an argument to believe that one exists), so also one non-inferentially believes that God exists.

What would Lewis have thought about Plantinga's position? If we focus on the idea of basicality, there is good reason to think Lewis's view was that belief that God exists is not basic. For example, in a letter to Arthur Greeves, he stated: "I have no rational ground for going back on the arguments that convinced me of God's existence ... " (2004a, 944). And Lewis's interactions with others convinced him that they, too, believed in God's existence on the basis of arguments:

> Nearly everyone I know who has embraced Christianity in adult life has been influenced by what seemed to him to be at least probable arguments for Theism. I have known some who were completely convinced by Descartes' Ontological Proof ... Even quite uneducated people who have been Christians all their lives not infrequently appeal to some simplified form of the Argument from Design. Even acceptance of tradition implies an argument which sometimes becomes explicit in the form "I reckon all those wise men wouldn't have believed in it if it weren't true." (1970, 173)

So what arguments convinced Lewis that God exists? As best as I know, he never fully explained his position on the matter. Nevertheless, I think it is possible to piece together a fairly coherent account of his view of the issue. And while I wrote a moment ago that it seems Lewis would have regarded the view that belief that God exists is basic as mistaken, I also think he would have insisted that the view is close to the truth, because the arguments for God's existence that he found convincing do not themselves involve complicated inferences, though criticisms and defenses of those arguments involve complicated reasoning.

7.2 Supernaturalism versus Theistic Supernaturalism

For Lewis, the question of God's existence was not a stand-alone matter. That is, for him belief that God exists could only be philosophically addressed after having addressed the issues that have been the subject matter of the earlier chapters of this book. Most importantly, as Erik Wielenberg writes, "Lewis [thought] that we can understand God by first understanding ourselves" (2008, 4), and what Lewis believed we first understand about ourselves is that we are supernatural beings. As early as 1918, Lewis wrote to Arthur Greeves:

> I believe in no God ... but I do believe that I have in me a spirit, a chip, shall we say, of universal spirit; and that, since all good & joyful things are spiritual & non-material, I must be careful not to let matter ... get too great a hold on me ... " (2004a, 379)

It would be many years before Lewis became a theist. But what he thought in 1918 indicates that he would first resolve the issue of supernaturalism as opposed to naturalism in terms of his own self, before becoming a theistic supernaturalist. The distinctions between naturalism, supernaturalism, and theistic supernaturalism are reflected in Lewis's frequent references to those who believed England and Europe were reverting to paganism. Lewis disputed this view on the grounds that contemporary Englishmen and Europeans increasingly disbelieved in souls and psychological events that transcended nature and, thereby, were post-Christian anti-supernaturalists (naturalists), while pagans were sub- or pre-Christian supernaturalists:

> It is hard to have patience with those Jeremiahs, in Press or pulpit, who warn us that we are "relapsing into Paganism". It might be rather fun if we were. It would be pleasant to see some future Prime Minister trying to kill a large and lively milk-white bull in Westminster Hall. But we shan't. What lurks behind such idle prophecies, if they are anything but careless language, is the false idea that the historical process allows mere reversal; that Europe can come out of Christianity "by the same door as in she went" and find herself back where she was. It is not what happens. A post-Christian man is not a Pagan; you might as well think that a married woman recovers her virginity by divorce. The post-Christian is cut off from the Christian past and therefore doubly from the Pagan past. (Lewis 1969, 10; cf. Lewis 1970, 172)

So for the purposes of this chapter, I will take for granted that in Lewis's mind the question of the existence of God was in the end not a question about being a supernaturalist *per se* but a question about being a theistic supernaturalist, the question about the truth of supernaturalism having already been resolved.

7.3   From Self to God

In thinking about the question of God's existence, Lewis maintained it is helpful to distinguish between two senses of the word "faith" (1970, 172–4). In one sense, what Lewis termed Faith-A, faith is settled intellectual assent. For example, Faith-A is what a person has when he has faith in the uniformity of nature or in the consciousness of other people (what philosophers call belief in the existence of other minds). In a second sense, what Lewis termed Faith-B, faith is a trust or confidence that requires "an alteration of the will" (Lewis 1970, 221) or choice. Lewis impressed upon his readers that a person can have Faith-A without having Faith-B. For illustrative purposes, he sometimes referred to a verse in the biblical book of James (2:19), which states that even the demons believe that God is one, yet tremble. Faith-A is consistent with cursing or ignoring God, which manifests a lack of Faith-B. But a person cannot have Faith-B without having Faith-A.

An example from everyday life of Lewis's distinction between the two faiths is a man's Faith-A in his wife's existence, and his Faith-B in her ability to drive their car safely to get them to their destination. Faith-A is a necessary condition of Faith-B. The husband could not have Faith-B in his wife as a driver if he did not have Faith-A in her existence. Lewis believed becoming a Christian involves a choice to renounce the pursuit of one's own happiness on one's own terms. One then puts one's trust (Faith-B) in someone else, God, to provide the happiness one so deeply desires and for which one was created. However, one could not make this choice unless one already had Faith-A in God's existence.

So what explains Faith-A? Lewis maintained one does not "find" God in the world, and he likened not finding God in the world to not finding Shakespeare in his plays:

> If there were an idiot who [said] ..., quite truly, that he had studied all the plays and never found Shakespeare in them ... [it would not be incongruous for the] rest of us ... [to say we] "found Shakespeare" in the plays. But it [would be] a quite different sort of "finding" from anything our poor friend [had] in mind ... He lacked the necessary apparatus for detecting Shakespeare. (Lewis 1967, 168)

Lewis summarized his point by insisting that if God does exist, then

> He is related to the universe more as an author is related to a play than as one object in the universe is related to another ... If God ... exists, mere movement in space will never bring you any nearer to Him or any farther from Him than you are at this very moment. (1967, 168)

Having claimed that God is like the author of a play rather than a character in it, Lewis acknowledged that some would raise the following objection:

> When I said ... it was nonsensical to look for God as one item within His own work, the universe, some readers may have wanted to protest. They wanted to say, "But surely, according to Christianity, that is just what did once happen? Surely the central doctrine is that God became man and walked about among other men in Palestine? If that is not appearing as an item in His own work, what is it?" (1967, 171)

Lewis responded that most of those who had contact with Jesus had no inkling that he was the maker of the whole world in which they existed. Perhaps Peter understood that Jesus was God, but even he seemed to have only glimpsed the identity and for a very limited period of time. So while Lewis made clear that "[i]f you do not at all know God, of course you will not recognize Him … " (1967, 172), he thought it also evident that even those who knew both God and Jesus did not recognize them as one and the same "item" in the world.

So Lewis thought that if one is to believe that God exists, it will be a belief in His existence as Creator, as the author of, and not an actor in, the *created* order. Here is what Lewis had to say about the notion of "creation": "I take it to mean 'to cause to be, without pre-existing material … *something pre-conceived in the Causer's thought [which], after creation, is other than the Cause'*" (Lewis 2004b, 870). Thus, Lewis was convinced a belief in God's existence includes belief in the idea that He creates *ex nihilo* or *out of nothing.*

What inference, then, might have led Lewis to believe in the existence of God as Creator? A classical argument for the existence of God is the cosmological argument, which typically moves from the existence of the world as a dependent or contingent being (i.e., a being that exists but might not exist, so that both its existence and its non-existence are causally possible) to the existence of God as an independent or necessary being (i.e., a being that must exist, so that its non-existence is not causally possible). But Lewis wrote to Dom Bede Griffiths that "[t]he Cosmological argument is, for some people at some times, ineffective. It always has been for me" (2007, 195).[1]

Another argument for the existence of God is the teleological or design argument. Probably the most well-known version of this argument was put forth by William Paley, who argued from the organized complexity of the human eye to the conclusion that it was designed. While the design argument, strictly speaking, is an argument for a designer, as opposed to a Creator, Lewis seems to have thought even less of it than he did the cosmological argument: "I still think the argument from design the weakest possible ground for Theism, and what may be called the argument from un-design the strongest for Atheism" (Lewis 2004b, 747).

Both the cosmological and teleological arguments concern inferences based on observational beliefs about the nature of the external world. In *The Problem of Pain*, Lewis was emphatic about his conviction that a belief in theism is not inferred from such beliefs: "The spectacle of the universe as revealed by experience can never have been the ground of religion: it must always have been something in spite of which religion, acquired from a different source, was held" (2001f, 3–4). Lewis thought that this different source was the internal world of the supernatural self or soul. Of what did he think one is aware in self-awareness that causes one to believe in the existence of a Creator who is God?

One thing that was obvious to Lewis about himself was that he was a being that lacked much. For example, he wrote in response to a letter from Joan Lancaster that "I think you are exaggerating a bit … Everything I need is in my soul? The Heck it is!" (Lewis 2007, 1039). Lewis went on to describe to Lancaster how his soul lacked much needed wisdom and virtue.

He thought his lack of virtue (his acting immorally) in particular revealed "that somebody or something wants me to behave in a certain way" (2001b, 25). In keeping with his framework belief that we know ourselves better than anything else, Lewis also thought that if there is "a controlling power outside the universe ... [t]he only way in which we could expect it to show itself would be inside ourselves as an influence or a command trying to get us to behave in a certain way" (2001b, 24). Thus, Lewis regarded our experience of and failure to fulfill moral obligation, our experience of being "haunted by the idea of a sort of behavior [we] ought to practise" (2001b, 16), as information about the ultimate nature of reality. What we know is that there is "a Something which is directing the universe, and which appears in me as a law urging me to do right and making me feel responsible and uncomfortable when I do wrong" (Lewis 2001b, 25). Lewis added,

> I think we have to assume [this Something] is more like a mind than it is like anything else we know—because after all the only other thing we know is matter and you can hardly imagine a bit of matter giving instructions. (2001b, 25)

Though his reasoning here is extremely condensed, it is not implausible to think Lewis believed "a law urging me to do right and making me feel responsible and uncomfortable when I do wrong" is conscience as "the pressure a man feels upon his will to do what he thinks is right" (Lewis 2001g, 65), where conscience is an inner voice of a mind expressing thoughts with aboutness (see Chapter 2). Lewis, then, not only regarded the moral law as rooted in the nature of things (see Chapter 4), but also thought the urge and unease caused by the failure to keep it reveal, in virtue of their aboutness, that ultimate reality is something resembling a mind.

Lewis believed that what we know from morality provides some inside information about the ultimate nature of the universe. Not surprisingly, he thought there is additional inside information relevant to belief in God's existence. He maintained not only that we know we lack virtue, but also that it is obvious to us that the soul lacks self-existence; it is contingent or dependent in nature. That is, while the soul exists, it does not exist on its own, and Lewis believed that because the soul does not exist on its own, it must be caused to exist by a Creator.

An early terse statement of Lewis's argument for God's existence from the soul's lack of self-existence is found in minutes from a meeting of the Oxford Socratic Club which contain a summary of a talk he gave on the importance of reason in argumentation. The relevant words are these: "Neither Will nor Reason is the product of Nature. Therefore either I am self-existent (a belief which no one can accept) *or* I am a colony of some Thought and Will that are self-existent" (Lewis 1970, 276). The following is a later and more developed form of Lewis's argument, which begins with his belief that reasoning falsifies naturalism because it is independent of the causal nexus of the material world and causally interferes with it:

> Within each man there must be an area ... of activity which is outside or independent of her [Nature]. In relation to Nature, rational thought goes on "of its own accord" or exists "on its own". It does not follow that rational thought exists *absolutely* on its own. It might be independent of Nature by being dependent on something else. For it is not dependence simply but dependence on the non-rational which undermines the credentials of thought ... It is thus still an open question whether each man's reason exists absolutely on its own or whether it is the result of some (rational) cause—in fact, of some other Reason. That other Reason might conceivably be found to depend on a third, and so on; it would not matter how far this process was carried provided you found Reason coming from Reason at each stage. It is only when you are asked to believe in Reason coming from non-reason that you must cry Halt, for, if you don't, all thought is discredited. It is therefore obvious that sooner or later you must admit a Reason which exists absolutely on its own. The problem is whether you or I can be such a self-existent Reason. (Lewis 2001c, 41–2)

Lewis thought it obvious that none of us is a *self-existent* Reason. In philosophical terms, he seems to have held that we are directly (non-inferentially) aware of not being a necessary being:

> This question [whether you are or I am a self-existent Reason] almost answers itself the moment we remember what existence "on one's own" means. It means that kind of existence which Naturalists attribute to "the whole show" and Supernaturalists attribute to God. For instance, what exists on its own must have existed from all eternity ... It must also exist incessantly: that is, it cannot cease to exist and then begin again ... Now it is clear that my Reason has grown up gradually since my birth and is interrupted for several hours each night. I therefore cannot be that eternal self-existent Reason which neither slumbers nor sleeps. Yet if any thought is valid, such a Reason must exist and must be the source of my own imperfect and intermittent rationality. Human minds, then, are not the only supernatural entities that exist. They do not come from nowhere. Each has come into Nature from Supernature: each has its tap-root in an eternal, self-existent, rational Being, whom we call God. (2001c, 42–3)

A few paragraphs later, Lewis added the following:

> In a pond whose surface was completely covered with scum and floating vegetation, there might be a few water-lilies. And you might of course be interested in them for their beauty. But you might also be interested

in them because from their structure you could deduce that they had stalks underneath which went down to roots in the bottom. The Naturalist thinks that the pond (Nature—the great event in space and time) is of an indefinite depth—that there is nothing but water however far you go down. My claim is that some of the things on the surface (i.e. in our experience) show the contrary. These things (rational minds [souls]) reveal, on inspection, that they at least are not floating but attached by stalks to the bottom. Therefore the pond has a bottom. It is not pond, pond for ever. Go deep enough and you will come to something that is not pond—to mud and earth and then to rock and finally the whole bulk of Earth and the subterranean fire. (2001c, 45)[2]

The philosopher and Lewis scholar, Richard Purtill, has written about this argument that Lewis maintained "it is overwhelmingly more probable that mind will be produced by a previously existing mind than by a process such as evolution, which only selects characteristics favorable to survival under the conditions prevailing at a given time" (2004, 44). But I think a close reading of the argument makes clear that Lewis believed it is not merely overwhelmingly more probable that a dependent mind is ultimately produced by an independent mind; he believed this *must* causally be the case. Why, then, did he believe this has to be the case?

To answer this question, it is helpful to understand why Lewis believed one must cry "Halt" at the proposal that the existence of a dependent reasoner, a self or "I," comes from non-reason. The answer seems to be as follows: Whenever Lewis insisted that natural processes could not explain the existence of a dependent, reasoning being, he was, for the sake of argument, supposing the self is a material entity and asking whether it could reason. As mentioned previously in Chapter 2, Lewis was fond of quoting J. B. S. Haldane's statement that "[i]f my mental processes are determined wholly by the motions of atoms in my brain, I have no reason to suppose that my beliefs are true … and hence I have no reason for supposing my brain to be composed of atoms" (Lewis 2001c, 22). Lewis took Haldane's point to imply that if my reasoning were material in nature, that is, if it were identical with material events occurring in a material self, then it could be explained in terms of material, nonmental causation. However, given our reasoning cannot be explained in terms of such causation (it is only explicable in terms of mental-to-mental causation), it is not material in nature. Therefore, he believed it must occur in an immaterial soul. And because this soul is a contingent being, it must be caused to exist by a necessary being, which makes this necessary being the soul's Creator.[3]

At this juncture, one might ask of Lewis why one's reasoning could not occur in a material substance that has two kinds of properties, material and mental, where reasoning involves only mental causation between the mental properties. In other words, why not embrace a form of what philosophers call "dual-aspect theory" or "property dualism," instead of soul-body substance dualism? The answer seems to be that Lewis never considered dual-aspect theory a commonsense metaphysical view. Rather, it appears he believed that given an awareness of the reality of the aboutness of thought and the nature of reasoning, one is directly aware that what is mental in nature occurs in a soul.

Lewis maintained *reasoning* cannot be explained by, in Haldane's terms, the motions of atoms, and, therefore, it must occur in souls, but why did he think the existence of the *soul* in which reasoning occurs cannot be explained by arrangements among atoms? Lewis held that no material objects standing in relations to each other could cause the existence of a soul *ex nihilo*. Because he thought a soul is a simple entity that has no separable parts (see Chapter 2; and cf. Goetz and Taliaferro, 2011), there is no other way than *ex nihilo* for a soul to come into existence. Lewis thought that an evolutionary explanatory story of the soul's origin is in principle impossible, because such a story would have to be a *compositional* story about a whole and its separable parts. And in accord with his view that events at what he called the subnatural level could not occur uncaused (see Chapter 5), Lewis seems to have believed that no event of coming into existence could happen without a cause. Thus, he wrote that "[i]t is clear that there never was a time when nothing existed; otherwise nothing would exist now [because there would be nothing to cause its coming into existence]" (Lewis 2001c, 141). So given that the soul, which is not made up of any separable parts, exists and is dependent for its existence on something else (it came into existence), Lewis concluded its existence must ultimately be caused by an independent, uncaused soul or Reason, the being we call "God."

Lewis well understood that no naturalist would agree with him that God, at a certain point in the history of the material world, brought into existence a new kind of entity, an immaterial soul that is rational in nature. Even some non-naturalists, though not directly addressing Lewis, have expressed concern over a belief like his. For example, Timothy O'Connor, a theistic property dualist who denies the existence of the soul, writes:

> The fundamental problem [with a view like Lewis's] is that our sciences point to highly continuous processes of increasing complexity, but the two-substance account [which includes a view like Lewis's] requires the supposition of abrupt discontinuity. The coming to be at a particular point in time of *a new substance* with a suite of novel psychological capacities ... would be a highly discontinuous development ... (O'Connor 2013)

So what does O'Connor suggest as an alternative? He proposes that at some point in the continuous biological story, psychological/conscious properties "different in kind" *emerged* from the hierarchically-structured physico-chemical properties of the brain: "[T]hese conscious states have distinctive intrinsic features, immediately apprehended by their subject, that in no way resemble the sorts of features science attributes to complex neural states" (O'Connor 2013). Lewis likely would have answered O'Connor that if substance dualism is objectionable on the grounds that it introduces discontinuity into the developmental processes in the natural world, then O'Connor's view is no less objectionable. After all, O'Connor's view appeals to emergent psychological/conscious properties which, in virtue of their being different in kind from physico-chemical properties, are just as discontinuous, strange, and magical as a specially created soul. And Lewis would likely have stressed that he was merely claiming that the distinctive intrinsic psychological features to which O'Connor rightly draws our attention are properties of a soul.

7.4   Further Considerations

The foregoing is Lewis's argument for the existence of a Creator, whom we call "God." But there are three additional points to note with regard to the argument.

First, although Lewis explicitly wrote that the cosmological argument for God's existence was ineffective for him, the argument that he did find effective was, like the cosmological argument, an argument from effect to cause. So while the cosmological argument seeks to prove the existence of God from the dependent character of the cosmos as a whole, what Lewis found persuasive was an argument that began with awareness of the dependent nature of a particular object within the cosmos, namely, his own self, soul, or "I," and inferred from its causally contingent existence the existence of a causally independent, rational Creator. The argument was simple: I am aware that I exist and am a contingent being. Therefore, I depend for my existence on a Creator.

Second, there are different forms of the argument for God's existence from the dependent nature of the self which Lewis endorsed, and it is not absolutely clear which he espoused. For example, consider the issue of temporality as it relates to the soul's dependent nature. On the one hand, one might think that Lewis was arguing that he was initially caused to exist *ex nihilo* at some finite temporal distance in the past. On the other hand, one might think he believed the issue of when he came into existence was completely irrelevant to his argument.

Someone who understood the argument from dependency in the latter way was the philosopher Richard Taylor:

> [T]he concept of creation ... is often misunderstood, particularly by those whose thinking has been influenced by Christian ideas. People tend to think that creation—for example, the creation of the world by

God—*means* creation *in time*, from which it of course logically follows that if the world had no beginning in time, then it cannot be the creation of God. This, however, is erroneous, for creation means essentially *dependence*, even in Christian theology. If one thing is the creation of another, then it depends for its existence on that other, and this is perfectly consistent with saying that both are eternal, that neither ever came into being, and hence, that neither was ever created at any point of time. (1992, 103–4)

Lewis's argument, with its example of the water-lilies (a dependent entity) attached *right now* by stalks to the bottom of the pond (the independent entity), is naturally read as conveying the idea that the soul is at every point in time at which it exists, no matter how long that time might be, ultimately dependent for its existence on God's creative and sustaining activity. That Lewis believed in the reality of this kind of simultaneous sustaining causality is evident from the following quotation about the supportive relationship between books:

Imagine two books lying on a table one on top of the other. Obviously the bottom book is keeping the other one up—supporting it. It is because of the underneath book that the top one is resting, say, two inches from the surface of the table instead of touching the table. Let us call the underneath book A and the top one B. The position of A is causing the position of B ... Now let us imagine ... that both books have been in that position for ever and ever. In that case B's position would always have been resulting from A's position. But all the same, A's position would not have existed before B's position. In other words the result does not come *after* the cause. (Lewis 2001b, 172)

Lewis thought it is clear that this simultaneous causation of book A supporting book B cannot be one link in a causal chain of books supporting books that goes back *ad infinitum*. That is, there must be a table on which book A directly or indirectly sits, where the table is analogous to God, the necessarily existing being. Were there no table, book A could not be supporting book B (book A could not itself be supported by book Z, which is supported by book Y, and on and on with no table, because, in that case, book A could never support book B). Elsewhere, Lewis wrote that "[o]ur life is, at every moment, supplied by Him" (2001f, 33), and "[a] man can neither make, nor retain, one moment of time; it all comes to him by pure gift ... " (1961b, 96). In other words, Lewis believed that every moment at which a created person exists is a gift in the sense that he or she is being causally kept in existence and can do nothing but receive that continued existence as a gift. Such is the nature of a dependent being.

So when Lewis considered the dependent existence of the soul, it is plausible to hold that he had in mind God's continuous simultaneous causation of its existence. But even if Lewis thought that a soul must have been created a finite time ago, in addition to its being caused to exist at every subsequent point in time that it exists, he believed it is the soul's awareness of its contingent nature that leads to a belief in a Creator God:

> When we are considering Man as evidence for the fact that this spatio-temporal Nature is not the only thing in existence, the important distinction is between that part of Man which belongs to this spatio-temporal Nature and that part which does not: or, if you prefer, between those phenomena of humanity which are rigidly interlocked with all other events in this space and time and those which have a certain independence. These two parts of a man may rightly be called Natural and Supernatural: in calling the second "Super-natural" we mean that it is something which invades, or is added to, the great interlocked event in space and time, instead of merely arising from it. On the other hand this "Supernatural" part is itself a created being—a thing called into existence by the Absolute Being ... (Lewis 2001c, 275–6)

And:

> We must go back to a much earlier view. We must simply accept it that we are spirits ... at present inhabiting an irrational universe, and must draw the conclusion that we are *not derived from it*. We are strangers here. We come from somewhere else. Nature is not the only thing that exists. There is "another world", and that is where we come from. And that explains why we do not feel at home here. (Lewis 1986a, 78)

In sum, Lewis believed the soul's awareness of itself *here and now* reveals both the falsity of naturalism and the dependent nature of its existence. Because of the reality of mental-to-mental causation, this awareness by the soul of its contingent existence causes a belief in the existence *here and now* of the necessarily existing Being on which it *here and now* depends for its existence. This Being, thought Lewis, is God: "I presume that only God's attention keeps me (or anything else) in existence at all" (1992a, 20).

A third point to make about Lewis's argument is that he believed that proving the existence of God as Creator from the existence of the soul left unanswered the question whether God is the only independent being (excluding from consideration the issue of whether or not he thought there are necessarily existing abstract objects like numbers, propositions, etc.). Might not the material world also be an independent being? "Might God and Nature both be self-existent and totally independent of each other?" (Lewis 2001c, 47). Lewis responded that there is a huge problem with trying to conceive two things which simply co-exist and are unrelated in any other way, which amounts to conceiving an ultimate disunity of things. This is a problem, Lewis held, because we are beings who have "some innate sense of the fitness of things"

(2001c, 166), where this sense expresses itself in the ordinary person's imagination as a "natural appetite for an impressive unity" (Lewis 1967, 83), and among scientists as a "belief in [the] Uniformity [of nature]" (Lewis 2001c, 166). In terms of science, the belief in uniformity is a belief that things do and will go on as they are, as long as there are no interferences from outside the system. As we know all too well by now, Lewis was convinced that this belief in uniformity was consistent with a belief in (and the reality of) outside interference by us through our reasoning and choices, and with divine miracles like that of the resurrection of Jesus from the dead. Our innate sense of the fitness of things does not presuppose or require a naturalistic philosophy in which our reasoning and choices are reduced to material events in a closed causally deterministic system and divine miracles are impossible.

In the end, Lewis believed that our innate sense of the fitness of things, the sense that things ultimately fit together in the right way, is satisfied by a universe in which the only necessary being is God and there is an immortality of perfect happiness available to created souls. He thought that one would only invoke the existence of an additional necessary being if one needed to do so to make better sense of things. Similarly, he reminded his readers in his discussion of the origins of courtly love that, in literary theory, the regulative principle of simplicity, "Occam's razor" (the simplest explanation is the preferred explanation), is operative: "[N]o hypothesis is permissible except that which covers the facts with the fewest possible assumptions ... " (Lewis 2013b, 60). And elsewhere he pointed out that scientists like evolutionary biologists invoke the regulative principle of simplicity in support of their theory:

> To the biologist Evolution is a hypothesis. It covers more of the facts than any other hypothesis at present on the market and is therefore to be accepted unless, or until, some new supposal can be shown to cover still more facts with even fewer assumptions. (Lewis 1967, 85)

So while Lewis thought that belief in God's existence as Creator was the result of an argument from a factual premise about his own dependent existence, as opposed to a hypothesis to explain that datum, he believed there was no reason to supplement that belief with a hypothesis about the existence of an additional necessary being or beings. So long as God's existence as Creator could account for the existence of any other contingent being, such a hypothesis would be superfluous. Given Lewis's views about the preference for explanatory simplicity, the following words penned by him make perfect sense: "Monotheism should not be regarded as the rival of polytheism, but rather as its maturity. Where you find polytheism, combined with any speculative power and any leisure for speculation, monotheism will sooner or later arise as a natural development" (Lewis 1936, 57).

I close this section with a brief comment about Purtill's exposition of Lewis's view about reasons to believe that God exists. Purtill devotes an entire chapter to what Lewis supposedly said about the matter and never once mentions the argument from the soul's contingency that I have discussed (for the record, he is not alone in terms of his silence about this argument). Then, in the immediately succeeding chapter, he states the following:

> The modern person sometimes asks, "Why should I care about God?" The first step in answering is to point out that if the traditional idea of God is true, we would cease to exist if God did not think of us and will to keep us in existence. (2004, 48)

The *first* step is to draw the person's attention to the traditional idea that he would cease to exist if God did not keep him in existence. First, make the person attentive to the idea that *his* existence depends upon the causal activity of God. First, appeal to the person's self-knowledge. This is exactly what Lewis did in explaining his belief in the existence of God. Lewis believed we have inside knowledge about our own selves. With regard to ourselves, we are in the know. Hence, it makes perfect sense to conclude he believed that what we know about ourselves provides the best evidence we have for belief in the existence of God. Because we are in the know about ourselves, we are also in the know about God.

7.5   The Argument from Desire

As we saw in Chapter 3, Lewis believed that we are created for the purpose of experiencing perfect happiness. There, I discussed Lewis's idea of Joy or *Sehnsucht*, which, given Lewis's stress on happiness and pleasure, is plausibly understood as a desire for a place beyond this world where perfect happiness will be experienced in relationship with God. In addition to describing Joy, some believe Lewis thought the idea of Joy itself could be used to develop an argument for the existence of the afterlife and God. The sources of their belief are passages like the following from the Lewis corpus:

> [W]e remain conscious of a desire which no natural happiness will satisfy. But is there any reason to suppose that reality offers any satisfaction to it? "Nor does the being hungry prove that we have bread." But I think it may be urged that this misses the point. A man's physical hunger does not prove that man will get any bread; he may die of starvation on a raft in the Atlantic. But surely a man's hunger does prove that he comes of a race which repairs its body by eating and inhabits a world where eatable substances exist. In the same way, though I do not believe ... that my desire for Paradise proves that I shall

enjoy it, I think it a pretty good indication that such a thing exists and that some men will. A man may love a woman and not win her; but it would be very odd if the phenomenon called "falling in love" occurred in a sexless world. (2001g, 32–3)

And:

Creatures are not born with desires unless satisfaction for those desires exists. A baby feels hunger: well, there is such a thing as food. A duckling wants to swim: well, there is such a thing as water. Men feel sexual desire: well, there is such a thing as sex. If I find in myself a desire which no experience in this world can satisfy, the most probable explanation is that I was made for another world. If none of my earthly pleasures satisfy it, that does not prove that the universe is a fraud. Probably earthly pleasures were never meant to satisfy it, but only to arouse it, to suggest the real thing. (2001b, 136–7)

It is now common to refer to this supposed "argument" as Lewis's "Argument from Desire" (e.g., Beversluis 1985, 8–31; McGrath 2014, 105–28). There are other statements of it by Lewis (e.g., Lewis 1992b, 202–5), but the versions I have just quoted will suffice for our discussion.

If we assume that there is an argument for the existence of God and paradisal life after death, just what is it? Certainly, many familiar ideas are present: desire, pleasure, happiness, etc., and the argument (from here on, I assume there is one) seems to be concerned with a desire for perfect hedonistic happiness that cannot be fulfilled in this life. An additional idea appears to be that no natural desire is in vain, and because none is and the desire for perfect happiness is such a desire, then there must be an afterlife in which the desire for perfect happiness can be fulfilled.

The Argument from Desire has been subjected to various criticisms. For example, John Beversluis responds that

[t]he phenomenon of hunger simply does not prove that man inhabits a world in which food exists. One might just as well claim that the fear that grips us when we walk through a dark graveyard proves that we have something to be afraid of. What proves that we inhabit a world in which food exists is the discovery that certain things are in fact "eatable" and that they nourish and repair our bodies. The discovery of the existence of food comes not by way of an *inference* based on the inner state of hunger; it is, rather an empirical discovery ... Just as we cannot prove that we inhabit a world in which food exists simply on the ground that we get hungry, so we cannot prove that an infinite Object [perfect happiness] of desire exists simply on the ground that we desire it. (1985, 18–19)

If Beversluis has correctly understood Lewis's argument, then his rebuttal of it seems completely reasonable. But given Lewis's thoughtfulness, I think we should wonder whether Beversluis has grasped Lewis's thought.

Following Wielenberg, who follows Steve Lovell (Lovell 2003), I believe that the Argument from Desire is best understood as one which is about the meaning of life and the idea of things ultimately not making sense. That Lewis is concerned in the two quotes above with the issue of making sense of things is indicated by his invocations of the notions of oddness and fraudulence for desires that go unsatisfied. Hence, given the existence of a desire for perfect happiness, which goes unfulfilled in this life, the argument concludes that life is ultimately absurd, if there is no afterlife in which the desire for perfect happiness can be satisfied. In the words of the philosopher and historian of comparative religion, Edwyn Bevan, of whose work we know Lewis thought highly (Lewis 2001c, 111):

> *if* [the universe] is rational in the ... sense [of the realization of value] ... then it must provide a satisfaction of the exigence of spirit ... [I]n a reasonable world exigencies would not arise which had not their proper satisfaction ... If [the universe] ... realizes no value ... then [it] ... would be absurd. (Bevan n.d., 367–9)

In response to Lewis, Wielenberg argues that a naturalist like himself is not without the resources to explain the existence of the desire for perfect happiness. The explanation Wielenberg proposes is evolutionary in nature. He reminds us that evolution will select those traits in organisms that lead to their survival and reproduction. Thus, if a particular desire comes to exist that is advantageous for survival and reproduction, it will, all else being equal, be preserved. But how might a desire for perfect happiness, where perfect happiness is not available either here on earth or in the afterlife (because there is no afterlife, according to naturalism), confer an evolutionary advantage? Wielenberg explains how it might in terms of Lewis's notion of Joy:

> The first important fact is that one of the main effects of Joy is that it prevents a person from deriving lasting contentment from earthly things. This fact is important because deriving lasting contentment from earthly things can be quite disadvantageous, evolutionarily speaking. Dissatisfaction can benefit us in the long run. This idea is evident in Ronald Dworkin's criticism of the use of psychotropic drugs as a "treatment" for ordinary unhappiness ... Dworkin labels the happiness produced in this way "Artificial Happiness" and observes that "[p]eople with Artificial Happiness don't feel the unhappiness they need to move forward with their lives." To see the evolutionary drawbacks of lasting contentment, consider a male human who is perfectly content as long as his basic needs (food, shelter, and sex) are satisfied. Once such needs are satisfied, he will have no motivation whatsoever to acquire additional wealth, power, status, or success; indeed, he will have no motivation to do anything at all, other than perhaps ensure

that his basic needs continue to be satisfied. Contrast this male with a second male who has the same basic drives but who *never* achieves lasting contentment ... Everything else being equal, the second male will likely do better than the first in the competition for limited resources ... Evolutionarily speaking, a good strategy is never to be entirely satisfied with one's lot in life. (2008, 116–17)

In sum, Wielenberg maintains there is a naturalistic explanation for our desire for perfect happiness which is evolutionary in nature: "By causing us to strive for the infinite, [Joy] prevents us from being entirely satisfied by the finite, and in this way causes us to survive and reproduce more successfully than we otherwise would" (2008, 117).

What might Lewis have said in response to Wielenberg? To begin, he most certainly would have insisted that lasting contentment (perfect happiness), were it had, would not be disadvantageous in itself, because happiness is intrinsically good, and anyone who experienced it would not care in the least that he no longer had to compete to survive and reproduce. Lewis believed that an existence wherein one survived perfectly happy without the need to struggle against others and one's environment would be ideal and, thus, better than an existence that included the need for competition and the pains that come with it. Moreover, Lewis thought that one is interested in surviving only if one believes one might or will be able to have a good enough hedonic quality of life in the future (where perfect happiness is the ultimate form of a good hedonic life). In other words, Lewis maintained it is the goodness of happiness and the desire for it (ultimately in its perfect form) that explain the desire to survive; it is not the desire to survive that explains the possession of the desire to experience (perfect) happiness. Hence, Lewis would have insisted that Wielenberg's evolutionary explanation of the existence of the desire for perfect happiness gets things backwards.

However, it is reasonable to think that Lewis would have had a good bit more to say in response to Wielenberg. For example, he likely would have gone on to point out that Wielenberg has, whether knowingly or unknowingly, simply assumed that desires *in terms of their mental nature* explain the occurrence of certain "survival" events in the material world. Yet, this explanatory role for the mental *as mental* is the very thing that naturalists (at least, the kind of naturalists with whom Lewis was concerned) deny is ultimately real. Hence, Lewis might well have posed a dilemma: If Wielenberg believes desires ultimately do not explain survival events in terms of their mental nature, then his response to the Argument from Desire is a ruse. If they do enter the explanatory story in terms of their mental nature, then Wielenberg is not a naturalist, but a supernaturalist, and Lewis would have asked him why an afterlife of perfect happiness is not possible.

To further clarify Lewis's position on the explanatory role of mental events, let us concede to Wielenberg (or any evolutionary naturalist), for the sake of argument, that desires as mental events are selected and preserved, given the supposed evolutionary advantage they bestow on their subjects. Lewis, it seems reasonable to suppose, would have made clear that it is nevertheless still the case on the naturalist's view that it is not possible to satisfy the desire for perfect happiness. Thus, while the evolutionary naturalist, as conceded, has provided an explanation for the existence of the desire for perfect happiness, his explanation in the end entails the ultimate absurdity of life because there is no way in which the desire for perfect happiness can be satisfied. Indeed, Wielenberg concedes this point (2008, 111–12), and then later adds that "I do not see that the mere fact that a view ... implies that the world is absurd ... constitutes a reason for thinking that the view in question is false" (2008, 118).

Lewis would have gone on to make clear that even though Wielenberg acknowledges the ultimate absurdity of things in terms of the desire for perfect happiness, he seeks an explanation for that desire because, like the rest of us, he is committed to making as much sense of things as is possible. But given this commitment, he should also be open to considering an explanation of the existence of the desire for perfect happiness which allows for its fulfillment. This, I take it, is the point Lewis was trying to make with the Argument from Desire. As McGrath writes, "Lewis's 'argument from desire' ... is essentially *suppositional*" (2014, 118) and seeks that "framework of interpretation [which] makes most sense of what is observed" (2014, 119). Because the existence of an afterlife in which perfect happiness can be experienced in relationship with God enables us to make life less odd and fraudulent (less absurd), an explanation of our desire for perfect happiness in terms of that afterlife and God is explanatorily superior to one provided by naturalism.[4]

What might a naturalist, Wielenberg or someone else, say in response to Lewis? He might again acknowledge that the impossibility of fulfilling the desire for perfect happiness is an ultimate absurdity on naturalism, but argue that it is an absurdity that makes sense within the naturalistic framework. That there are certain facts that ultimately do not make sense is something that makes sense (it is what one would expect), given the truth of naturalism.

Lewis, I believe, would have answered that a naturalist's acknowledgment that the impossibility of fulfilling the desire for perfect happiness is an ultimate absurdity concedes that theists and naturalists *share*, at least to some extent, an explanatory framework within which things would ultimately make more sense if that desire were capable of satisfaction. And because a view like theism makes possible the fulfillment of this desire within this shared explanatory framework, it is explanatorily superior to a view like naturalism that does not.

If a naturalist were to respond that Lewis's explanation of the possible satisfaction of the desire for perfect happiness requires the reality of questionable things like the *quale* of pleasure, mental explanations in terms of purposes, undetermined choices, the existence of souls, etc., then there would be disagreement between them about what realities can be invoked in a legitimate explanation. Lewis likely would have asked for an explanation for why we should doubt the existence of these realities. If a naturalist were to provide an explanation for their nonexistence that presupposes the truth of naturalism, Lewis would have asked why we should believe in naturalism. If a naturalist explained his belief in naturalism in terms of reasons, Lewis would, as we now know, have made clear that the invocation of reasons to explain a belief in naturalism would itself *make no sense* because naturalism itself excludes mental explanations in terms of reasons. If a naturalist were to concede the reality of these mental explanations, Lewis would then have wondered what explanation could be given for excluding other psychological realities (the *quale* of pleasure, purposeful explanations, undetermined choices, souls). In light of Lewis's conviction about the soundness of his overall critique of naturalism and defense of supernaturalism, he would have had us conclude that there is no good reason to exclude these additional psychological realities. Thus, because it is possible to explain both the existence of the desire for perfect happiness and its fulfillment in theistic supernaturalist terms, Lewis would have had us conclude that the theistic supernaturalist explanation of them is superior to a naturalistic one.[5]

Lewis believed we desire perfect happiness and that a theistic supernaturalist universe in which there exists an afterlife wherein this desire can be satisfied makes most sense of that desire. He knew all too well that the existence of an afterlife is needed because there is no perfect happiness in this life. And there is no perfect happiness in this life because there is evil. Lewis's treatment of the problem of evil is the subject of the next chapter.

notes

1   Yet, Lewis wrote:

> But why anything comes to be there at all [for science to investigate], and whether there is anything behind the things science observes—something of a different kind—this is not a scientific question ... Supposing science ever became complete so that it knew every single thing in the whole universe. Is it not plain that the questions, 'Why is there a universe?', 'Why does it go on as it does?' ... would remain just as they were? (2001b, 23)

> A passage like this suggests that Lewis had some intellectual connection with the cosmological argument.

2   Wesley Kort reminds us that Rudolf Otto, whose work on the numinous deeply influenced Lewis, was himself influenced by Friedrich Schleiermacher, "who made … the feeling of absolute dependence … grounds for understanding what religion is … " (2016, 46).

3   One might legitimately wonder how Lewis thought establishing that he had a Creator was sufficient to prove the existence of God. After all, God is traditionally thought of as more than Creator. He is supposed to be omnipotent (all-powerful), omnibenevolent, omniscient, etc. If we consider omnipotence (and that is all I can consider because of limitations of space), I think the short answer to this question is that Lewis thought of the power to create *ex nihilo* as a power that contributed to omnipotence, where omnipotence "means power to do all that is intrinsically possible … " (Lewis 2001f, 18). Because no created person has the power to create *ex nihilo*, he lacks a power that is part of the panoply of powers of an omnipotent being.

4   Earlier in this chapter, I pointed out that it seems Lewis believed that no material objects standing in relations with each other could cause the existence of a soul *ex nihilo*. In contradistinction from Lewis, the contemporary theistic philosopher William Hasker maintains that "a new individual [soul] … comes into existence as a result of a certain functional configuration of the material constituents of the brain and nervous system" (1999, 190). Hasker is reluctant to describe this as creation *ex nihilo*, because the power to create *ex nihilo* is a traditional attribute of God and something he is unwilling to attribute to a mere creature (1999, 196). But if the soul is a simple entity (it has no separable parts), as Lewis thought, it seems the coming into existence of a soul could be nothing other than *ex nihilo* in nature. The atheist Graham Oppy, under the guise of a more expansive conception of naturalism, is also open to the idea that "souls are *caused* to come into existence by brains achieving the right level of functioning" (2013, 55).

Though admittedly one must to some extent conjecture what Lewis would have said in response to Hasker and Oppy, he certainly believed that an atheistic naturalism like that suggested by Oppy is deeply problematic. Oppy maintains that if souls are caused to come into existence by brains achieving the requisite level of functioning, they are also "*caused* to go out of existence by brains ceasing to have that level of functioning" (2013, 55). Lewis would have made clear that the failure of the soul to survive death entails that the desire for perfect happiness can never be satisfied, and, therefore, that life is ultimately absurd. As Oppy states, "[w]hat Naturalism has that Theism does not have is a commitment to the non-existence of Heaven …. [A]ccording to Naturalism, there is no supernatural post-mortem realm in which we coexist with God … " (2013, 76). But, he adds, it does not follow that "Naturalism entails that our lives have no meaning … " (2013, 83).

Lewis would have conceded that a denial of an afterlife does not imply life has no meaning whatsoever, but made clear that naturalism does entail that our lives have no ultimate meaning insofar as they ultimately fail to make sense. And he undoubtedly would have added that it might be in order to avoid this absurdity that Hasker insists that "God could sustain the lives of human persons after their biological death" (1999, 233). Undoubtedly, Lewis would have also wondered about what recommends Hasker's view that souls are caused to come into existence by a certain functional configuration of the material constituents of the brain and nervous system over his own view that souls are created *ex nihilo* by God. After all, Hasker invokes God to sustain human persons in existence after death. Lewis likely would have added that if God must sustain human persons in existence post mortem in order for their lives to ultimately make sense, it makes just as much if not more sense to maintain that God creates souls *ex nihilo* and sustains them in existence in this pre-mortem life.

5 Timothy Mawson has suggested to me that a naturalist might argue that theistic supernaturalism is a conspiracy theory, where a conspiracy theory is an explanation of the data which can get in a significant number of facts, some of which on any more reasonable explanation would remain incongruous, accidental, or a matter of luck. For example, the theory that Lee Harvey Oswald worked alone to assassinate President John F. Kennedy might leave some facts dangling and apparently coincidental that are made sense of on the less plausible theory that the CIA and other intelligence forces collaborated to murder Kennedy. Lewis's theistic supernaturalist account of the argument from desire, a naturalist might argue, is a conspiracy theory. It can eliminate the incongruous fact that the desire for perfect happiness remains unsatisfied, but at the cost of invoking too many implausible realities in the form of purposeful explanations, choices, *qualia*, and souls, etc.

Lewis would likely have responded that anyone who formulates a theory about Kennedy's assassination does so on the basis of inferences and choices, the latter of which are explained by purposes. Hence, these kinds of mental realities do not only appear in a conspiracy theory. And that about which the theories are being developed also includes these kinds of mental realities. For example, to take seriously the idea that Oswald acted on his own presupposes that he made inferences and chose to do what he did for a purpose that plausibly included the idea that he and others would be happier if Kennedy were dead. Finally, Lewis would have gone on to argue that if the reality of what is mental in nature must be acknowledged in the ways just described, then the addition of souls which can survive death and have the possibility of experiencing perfect happiness in the afterlife hardly seems the stuff of a conspiracy theory.

the problem of evil

The one principle of hell is—"I am my own!"

(MacDonald 2001, 103)

It has been said, that there is of nothing so much in hell as of self-will.
For hell is nothing but self-will, and if there were no self-will there
would be … no hell.

(*Theologia Germanica* 1949, 208)

8.1 Statement of the Problem

C. S. Lewis stated the problem of evil in the following terms: "If God
were good, He would wish to make His creatures perfectly happy, and if
God were almighty, He would be able to do what He wished. But the
creatures are not happy. Therefore God lacks either goodness, or power,
or both" (2001f, 16). In short, if evil exists, God does not. If there is evil,
theism is false and atheism is true.

Another typical formulation of the problem of evil in support of
atheism is the following: If God is all-good (omnibenevolent), then he
wants to prevent evil. If God is all-knowing (omniscient), then he knows
how to prevent evil. If God is all-powerful (omnipotent), then he can
prevent evil. Therefore, God is either not all-good, or not all-knowing,
or not all-powerful, or not all three.

The two formulations of the argument for atheism from evil are quite
formal in nature. Lewis sometimes put the problem of evil in less formal
terms:

All stories will come to nothing: all life will turn out in the end to have
been a transitory and senseless contortion upon the idiotic face of
infinite matter. If you ask me to believe that this is the work of a

C. S. Lewis, First Edition. Stewart Goetz.
© 2018 John Wiley & Sons, Inc. Published 2018 by John Wiley & Sons, Inc.

benevolent and omnipotent spirit, I reply that all the evidence points in the opposite direction. Either there is no spirit behind the universe, or else a spirit indifferent to good and evil, or else an evil spirit. (2001f, 3)

Lewis acknowledged to his friend Dom Bede Griffiths that the problem of evil was behind his belief in atheism in his teens and twenties:

I think that though I am emotionally a fairly cheerful person my actual judgement of the world has always been what yours now is and so I have not been disappointed. The early loss of my mother, great unhappiness at school, and the shadow of the last war and presently the experience of it [war], had given me a very pessimistic view of existence. My atheism was based on it: and it still seems to me that *far* the strongest card in our enemies' hand is the actual course of the world: and that, quite apart from particular evils like wars and revolutions. The inherent "vanity" of the "creature", the fact that life preys on life, that all beauty and happiness is produced only to be destroyed—this was what stuck in my gullet. (2004b, 746–7)

One "solution" to the problem of evil would be to deny that evil exists. But Lewis would have none of this. He believed that pain is intrinsically evil, and it is its evilness that ultimately gives rise to the problem of evil. Given his view about the intrinsic evilness of pain, Lewis wrote the following to Edward Dell:

I don't think the idea that evil is an illusion helps. Because surely it is a (real) evil that the illusion of evil [should] exist. When I am pursued in a nightmare by a crocodile the pursuit and the crocodile are illusions: but it is a real nightmare, and that seems a real evil. (Whenever one says "This isn't a real so-and-so", is it not a real something else? e.g. if this is not a real pink rat it is a real delirium, if this pupil is not a real sufferer from headache he is a real liar—and so on). (2004b, 1010)

While Lewis did not shy away from raising and trying to answer the problem of evil, he clearly felt uncomfortable putting forth an explanation for the existence of people's pains and misfortunes. On one occasion, he recounted how his friend Charles Williams reminded him that God's displeasure had not been reserved for Job but for his friends, who were the "'comforters', the self-appointed advocates on God's side, the people who tried to show that all was well—'the sort of people' ... who wrote books on the Problem of Pain" (Lewis 2013b, 122). And in *The Problem of Pain* itself, Lewis acknowledged it was likely that

[a]ll arguments in justification of suffering [will] provoke bitter resentment against the author. You would like to know how I behave when I am experiencing pain, not writing books about it. You need not guess,

for I will tell you; I am a great coward … But what is the good of telling you about my feelings? You know them already: they are the same as yours. I am not arguing that pain is not painful. Pain hurts … To prove it palatable is beyond my design. (2001f, 104–5)

Though a self-proclaimed coward in the face of pain, Lewis nevertheless pressed ahead to deal with the problem raised by it, because he believed it was a legitimate topic for reasonable discussion. His thoughts about pain and God's reason for allowing it are the subject of the rest of this chapter. It is only fair that I tell the reader that I find Lewis's treatment of the problem of evil less than lucid at various points.

8.2   Human Beings and Evil

On Lewis's view, pain is real and, therefore, evil is too, because all pain is intrinsically evil. While Lewis believed evil is real, he also insisted that it cannot create anything but only "spoil something that Another has created" (2007, 520). In its role as a spoiler, evil is "contrary to God's will" (Lewis 2007, 163). But if evil spoils that which is created by God and is, therefore, contrary to his will, why did Lewis not remain steadfast in his original conclusion that the reality of evil proves the nonexistence of God? The answer is that he concluded a knowledge of what makes life worth living and life's purpose helps provide the answer to the problem of evil.

Like most theists, Lewis believed that in order to avoid the conclusion that the existence of evil shows a lack in the Creator's goodness, power, or knowledge (I will assume Lewis regarded omniscience as an essential component of the problem of evil, even though he left it unstated in his formal statement of the problem), it must be the case that the Creator, God, has a reason in the form of a justifying good that explains why He allows the occurrence of evil. As a former atheist, Lewis understood all too well that atheists typically believe it is reasonable to expect that theists state what the justifying good is. In philosophical terms, atheists believe it is reasonable to expect that theists be *theodicists*.

Some theists, who are commonly referred to as "skeptical theists" (Plantinga 1977), reject the idea that theists need to or should be theodicists. They maintain that because God is omniscient, His knowledge so vastly exceeds our own that it is ludicrous to think we could know through human reasoning alone God's reason for allowing evil. The recent history of this disagreement among theists and between theists and atheists about the need to provide a theodicy traces back more than thirty years to the philosopher William Rowe's discussion of the case of a long and painful death of a fawn in a forest fire (Rowe 1986; 1990). According to

Rowe, the fawn's suffering *appears* unjustified to us and provides us with a reason to believe in the non-existence of God.

In response to Rowe's paper, the skeptical theist Stephen Wykstra questioned whether Rowe's claim about the appearance of things is itself reasonable (Wykstra 1990). Wykstra suggested that the fawn's suffering can appear unjustified to us only if we have the epistemic wherewithal to understand the justifications God might have for allowing this suffering. Given that the contents of God's mind dwarf those of our own, Wykstra claimed it is reasonable to hold that God could have a justification for allowing the fawn's pain of which we, as would be expected, are unaware. In other words, Wykstra argued we should not be the least bit surprised that we do not know why God allows the fawn to suffer. Hence, rather than saying that the fawn's pain appears to us to be unjustified, Wykstra maintained we should hold that the justification for the fawn's suffering is not apparent to us, which, given the vastness of God's epistemic wherewithal compared with our own, is what we would expect. Furthermore, we should not be surprised not to know not only God's justification for allowing the fawn's suffering but also God's reason for allowing any evil. Thus, no evil appears to provide a reason to believe in God's nonexistence.

Lewis was not a skeptical theist, at least with respect to our own experiences of pain (I will return to the case of the fawn later in this chapter), because he believed we not only can, but do know the good that grounds the explanation for why God justifiably allows us to experience evil. He thought that this good is the purpose for which God created us, which is that we be perfectly happy, and the explanation for God's allowing us to experience evil is the possibility of our enjoying this good. Thus, the final chapter of *The Problem of Pain* is entitled "Heaven," and Lewis wrote that "no solution of the problem of pain which does not [put the joys of heaven into the scale against the sufferings of earth] can be called a Christian one" (2001f, 148). And Lewis believed a person would say of the joys of heaven "'Here at last is the thing I was made for.' ... If we lose this, we lose all" (2001f, 151), including the explanation for God's allowing us to experience pain.

That Lewis believed perfect happiness is our greatest good and the possibility of experiencing it is the justification for God's allowance of evil in our lives is evidenced by the fact that he used the idea of perfect happiness in his formulation of the problem of evil. But to understand how perfect happiness ultimately enters into an explanation for allowing *us* to experience evil,[1] Lewis believed we must first understand why the goodness of this happiness and the possibility of experiencing it require our possession of libertarian free will. Lewis wrote to Arthur Greeves that "God willed the free will of men and angels in spite of His knowledge that it [could] lead in some cases to sin and then to suffering: He thought Freedom worth creating even at that price" (2004b, 956). He stressed to Greeves that human freedom is worth creating, even though its possession opens up the possibility of experiencing pain. Though I am unable to cite book and page number, reading and rereading Lewis's thoughts on the problem of pain has left me with the impression that he also believed a world with self-conscious persons who could ultimately be perfectly happy *must* be a world in which they possess free will that makes possible the experience of pain. In other words, it seems to me Lewis believed God could not create self-conscious persons in heaven and have it over with. And in what follows, I will regularly assume that Lewis did believe this.

Why, then, must human beings have free will, if the use of it might produce experiences of pain? Lewis reasoned that because perfect happiness is God's *gift* of the *greatest good* an individual can experience, where that experience is the purpose for which a person was created, only those should receive this gift who make the requisite choice. To refresh ourselves about what that choice is, I think it is best first to remind ourselves what kind of choice Lewis thought excludes the chooser from perfect happiness. As I discussed in earlier chapters, he thought that those who choose to live for the maximization of their present happiness on their own terms and at the expense of the happiness of others (they seek to maximize their happiness in this way because they know that the greater their own happiness is the greater their own good) do not deserve to experience perfect happiness. The choice not to die to self deserves the withholding of perfect happiness. The following is a representative statement of his thought on this issue:

> Picture to yourself a man who has risen to wealth or power by a continued course of treachery and cruelty, by exploiting for purely self-ish ends the noble motions of his victims, laughing the while at their simplicity; who, having thus attained success, uses it for the gratification of lust and hatred and finally parts with the last rag of honour among thieves by betraying his own accomplices and jeering at their last moments of bewildered disillusionment. Suppose, further, that he does all this, not (as we like to imagine) tormented by remorse or even misgiving, but eating like a schoolboy and sleeping like a healthy infant—a jolly, ruddy-cheeked man, without a care in the world, unshakably confident to the very end that he alone has found the answer to the riddle of life, that God and man are fools whom he has got the better of, that his way of life is utterly successful, satisfactory, unassailable ... Can you really desire that such a man, *remaining what he is* (and he must be able to do that if he has free will) should be confirmed forever in his present happiness ... ? (Lewis 2001f, 122–3)

Who, then, will receive the gift of perfect happiness? Lewis believed it is the person who chooses to die to self, as the following quotations make clear:

> [A] crucifixion of the natural self is the passport to everlasting life. (Lewis 2001g, 172)

[A] thing will not really live unless it first dies ... [G]o on through that period of death into the quieter interest and happiness that follow ... (Lewis 2001b, 111)

Now the proper good of a creature is to surrender itself to its Creator ... When it does so, it is ... happy. (Lewis 2001f, 88)

8.3   The Irrelevance of Possible Worlds

Lewis held that the justification for allowing human beings to experience pain is ultimately connected to the good of perfect happiness, where the enjoyment of it can be had only if persons have the freedom to choose how they will become happy, to choose to die or not to die to self. Thus, Lewis articulated his theodicy in terms of the *actual individual* and his or her happiness.

"How else could it be treated?," one might ask. Perhaps surprisingly, many of those who have written about the problem of evil after Lewis have treated it in terms of *possible worlds* and what good or goods of them might justify God's creation of one world as opposed to another (Plantinga 1977). Though to the best of my knowledge Lewis never explicitly contrasted the possible worlds approach with his own, some points he made in contexts not directly concerned with the problem of evil support the view that he thought God is first and foremost concerned with the good of an actual person as opposed to the good of a possible world. For example, in a paper entitled "Membership," Lewis contrasted excessive claims made by the collective as opposed to those made by individuals, and wrote:

[The collective] is mortal; we [as individuals] shall live forever. There will come a time when every culture, every institution, every nation, the human race, all biological life is extinct and every one of us is still alive. Immortality is promised to us, not to these generalities. (2001g, 172)

From this comment, one can reasonably extrapolate that Lewis would have pointed out that possible worlds are abstract entities and, therefore, more akin to generalities or collectives, whereas the great good of perfect happiness that God promises is for actual individuals: "For it is not humanity in the abstract that is to be saved, but you—you, the individual reader, John Stubbs or Janet Smith" (Lewis 2001f, 152). It seems reasonable to conclude, then, that Lewis would have regarded a treatment of the problem of evil in terms of possible worlds as taking us in the wrong direction, because it fails to properly locate and identify the real problem.

One other consideration indicates that Lewis thought of the problem of evil and its solution primarily in terms of the actual individual.

Knowing that Lewis was a hedonist about happiness, someone might jump to the conclusion that he believed God, if He is genuinely good, would be obligated to create that world, if there is such, which has the most experiences of pleasure and fewest experiences of pain. However, Lewis maintained that thinking of the problem of evil in terms of the sum of human suffering, which is an abstraction, is misguided:

> Suppose that I have a toothache of intensity x: and suppose that you, who are seated beside me, also begin to have a toothache of intensity x. You may, if you choose, say that the total amount of pain in the room is now $2x$. But you must remember that no one is suffering $2x$: search all time and all space and you will not find that composite pain in anyone's consciousness. There is no such thing as a sum of suffering, for no one suffers it. When we have reached the maximum that a single person can suffer, we have, no doubt, reached something very horrible, but we have reached all the suffering there ever can be in the universe. The addition of a million fellow-sufferers adds no more pain. (2001f, 116–17)

Within any world that includes experiences of pain, there will be individuals having those experiences, and the issue will arise whether those individuals' experiences of pain are justified. And Lewis believed that no answer in terms of summed amounts of pain can be the least bit relevant to addressing that matter. Thus, it is a mistake to go down the explanatory path which suggests that God's justification for allowing us to experience evil is (or is something like) that our world contains more pleasure and less pain than any other world God might have created.

To help clarify Lewis's theodicy, consider a Christian theodicy recently developed by Plantinga in which he supposes God wanted to create a world with a certain level of goodness, and every world with that level of goodness contained incarnation and atonement (where incarnation is a prerequisite of atonement) (Plantinga 2004). Because atonement is about created persons being saved from the consequences of their sins, Plantinga, like Lewis, believes that atonement presupposes the possession of libertarian free will and the making of immoral choices by human beings.

What would Lewis have thought about incarnation and atonement as goods which justify God's allowance of evil? Though he did show some sympathy for the *felix culpa* idea ("Redeemed humanity is to be something more glorious than unfallen humanity would have been, more glorious than any unfallen race now is (if ... the night sky conceals any such)" (Lewis 2001c, 198)), the overall thrust of his thought makes it reasonable to hold he would have regarded this theodicy as mistaken. Thus, while Lewis believed achievement of the purpose of life required that human beings have the opportunity to exercise their free will, he also thought that had they exercised their free will rightly, there would have been no need for incarnation or atonement. As the philosopher Michael Peterson writes:

> For Lewis ... incarnation and atonement are necessary only given the fact of the human fall, but they are not absolutely necessary because God would [have carried] out his original plan for humanity even without the fall ... It was always possible, and always more desirable, [for human beings] not to sin. (2008, 184–5)

Although Peterson is right in claiming that Lewis would have rejected a theodicy of incarnation and atonement, he slightly misrepresents Lewis's view of the good that justifies God's allowance of evil. Peterson writes:

> Lewis would think it absurd to defend the counterfactual claim that, if humanity had not fallen, then we would not have the greatest good, which is God himself. Indeed, Lewis would disconnect incarnation and atonement, since incarnation may still have occurred in a nonfallen world ... Humanity did not need to fall into sin to get the greatest good of God himself ... (2008, 184).

According to Lewis's theodicy, however, the justifying good is not God himself but the possibility of experiencing the perfect happiness that comes from dying to self and yielding one's life to God to provide that happiness. The purpose for which we are created is perfect happiness, where this is experienced in the form of enjoying God. Lewis believed the purpose of life is not simply God Himself.

So Lewis thought we know God's justification for allowing human beings to experience pain. In the course of discussing Lewis's treatment of the problem of evil, Peterson asks whether Lewis believed there are pains that God could have prevented without thereby losing some greater good. Such pains would be considered gratuitous. Peterson argues that Lewis affirmed the occurrence of gratuitous pains and, thus, gratuitous evil (2008, 185–9). It seems to me, however, that we need to take extra care in reading Lewis at this point. If we understand the idea of gratuitous evil as evil that is not instrumental (a means) to any further good, then Lewis did believe in gratuitous evil. He believed that while God can bring good out of evil (use evil as a means to good) and in this way redeem the evil, it is not always the case that this occurs. For example, while one person might choose to respond positively to his pain and suffering (e.g., he becomes more loving toward others who suffer at the hands of the vicious), another might choose not to do so (e.g., he freely ends up embittered and hostile toward others), and in the case of the latter individual, the pain would prove to be gratuitous (assuming it is not a means to some other good). However, it does not follow from the fact that there are pains which are not means to some further good that those pains are also gratuitous in the different sense of not being at all connected with a justifying good. X might not be a means to, yet still be connected with, Y in the sense of being justified by Y. Lewis thought experiences of pain, while they might not be means to perfect happiness, were nevertheless justified by and connected with the possibility of experiencing that happiness through the free will whose wrong exercise produced them. Thus, while Lewis believed experiences of pain could be the result of wrong exercises of free will, he did not think free will itself is their justifying good. He regarded free will as no more than a necessary condition of experiencing perfect happiness, where the possibility of experiencing it is what justifies the pains resulting from wrong exercises of free will.

8.4   Lewis's View of the Fall

A moment ago, I mentioned Plantinga's appeal to incarnation and atonement to explain why God permits human beings to experience evil. These concepts are theological in nature, and they provide a natural bridge to a consideration of what Lewis thought of the Christian doctrine of the Fall of man (which Peterson touched upon in his discussion of Lewis's view of incarnation and atonement) and its relationship to the problem of evil. Lewis believed the true import of the idea of the Fall is that man abused his free will when he chose to try to maximize his happiness on his own terms (as opposed to choosing to trust God for its provision). Vis-à-vis experiencing perfect happiness, there were the alternatives of self or God, and man fell with his choice of self. Lewis believed that the fruit in the story of the Fall in the book of Genesis is part of a myth (and, given his view of myth, might or might not describe historical facts) about what is good and how it is pursued. However, he maintained it is not the fruit as such that is important, but the fruit in its capacity as a source of pleasure. Any other source of pleasure would in principle have worked just as well to convey the central idea of the Fall. Thus, Lewis stressed that "[w]hat exactly happened when Man fell [whether fruit was involved or not], we do not know ... " (2001f, 71). Indeed, we do not need to know how many human creatures were involved in the Fall, or how long they had been in a paradisal state (Lewis 2001f, 75). To stress what he considered the central import of wrongly exercised free will in the doctrine of the Fall, Lewis maintained that while we know the doctrine requires a creature which can think of itself as an "'I' and 'me'" (2001f, 72), it does not require the development of

> complex social conditions ... [or] great intellectual development ... [T]he terrible alternative [is between] ... choosing God or self for the centre

[as a source of happiness] ... [And the sin of choosing self] is committed daily by young children and ignorant peasants as well as by sophisticated persons, by solitaries no less than by those who live in society: it is the fall in every individual life, and in each day of each individual life, the basic sin behind all particular sins ... (2001f, 69–70)

8.5 Imaginative Metaphysics and Evolution

Lewis was a Christian who believed in the occurrence of biological evolution. And he saw no rational conflict in affirming both: "With Darwinianism as a theorem in Biology I do not think a Christian need have any quarrel" (Lewis 1986a, 63). In a letter to Bernard Acworth, the founder of the Evolution Protest Movement, in late 1944, Lewis wrote:

I am not either attacking or defending Evolution. I believe that Christianity can still be believed, even if Evolution is true ... Thinking as I do, I can't help regarding your advice (that I henceforth include arguments against Evolution in all my Christian apologetics) as a temptation to fight the battle on what is really a false issue ... (2004b, 633)

And Lewis was equally convinced of the legitimacy of science considered more generally. Thus, in response to Edward Dell's question about the place of science in American education, Lewis wrote:

One must not ... distort or suppress the sciences. [In the American educational scene] [i]t is rather, I suppose, a question of reducing them to their proper place—hypotheses (all provisional) about the *measurable* aspects of *physical* reality. Sometimes the adjustment between these hypotheses and the quite different pictures we get from Theology, Philosophy, and Art, has to be left in suspense—as discrepancies within the sciences themselves are left in suspense ... (2004b, 1010–11)

If there are sometimes discrepancies between what science says and what philosophy or theology says, we must live with the tension. But Lewis stressed in a letter to Miss Breckenridge that he believed there was no discrepancy between what we learn from evolutionary science about human origins and what we learn from theology about the Fall of man:

There is *no* relation of any importance between the Fall and Evolution. The doctrine of Evolution is that organisms have changed, sometimes for what we call (biologically) the better ... [and] quite often for what we call (biologically) the worse ... The doctrine of the Fall is that at one particular point one species, Man, tumbled down a moral cliff. There is neither opposition nor support between the two doctrines ... Evolution is not ... a doctrine of *moral* improvements, but of biological changes, some improvements, some deteriorations. (2004b, 962)

Lewis thought it important to stress that the theory of evolution in biological science is not a doctrine about *moral* improvement. He acknowledged that many people mistakenly think that it is, and, as a result, believe it conflicts with the idea, which is implicit in the Christian theological doctrine of the Fall of man, that things went morally from better (or neutral) to worse. Lewis insisted that those who affirm this conflict confuse the theory of biological evolution with what he referred to as the "Great Myth." The Great Myth is a philosophical doctrine concerning value about cosmic change in an upward or positive direction. He was convinced that the Great Myth gets particular inspiration from the development of technology, "the birth of the machines ... [and] the image of old machines being superseded by new and better ones. For in the world of machines the new most often really is better and the primitive really is the clumsy" (Lewis 1969, 10–11). The Great Myth takes this idea of improvement, imbues the theory of biological evolution with it, and then widens its scope even further to include the cosmos from its inception to its demise:

> Popular ... Developmentalism differs *in content* from the Evolution of the real biologists. To the biologist Evolution is a hypothesis. It covers more of the facts than any other hypothesis at present on the market and is therefore to be accepted unless, or until, some new supposal can be shown to cover still more facts with even fewer assumptions ... In the Myth, however, there is nothing hypothetical about it: it is basic fact ... Evolution is a theory about *changes*: in the Myth it is a fact about *improvements* ... In the popular mind the word "Evolution" conjures up a picture of things moving "onwards and upwards", and of nothing else whatsoever ... [F]or the scientist Evolution is a purely biological theorem. It takes over organic life on this planet as a going concern and tries to explain certain changes within that field. It makes no cosmic statement, no metaphysical statements, no eschatological statements ... But the Myth knows none of these reticences. Having first turned what was a theory of change into a theory of improvement, it then makes this a *cosmic* theory. Not merely terrestrial organisms but *everything* is moving "upwards and onwards" ... To those brought up on the Myth nothing seems more normal, more natural, more plausible, than that chaos should turn into order [and] death into life ... (Lewis 1967, 85, 86)

Lewis proceeded to put a bit of mythical flesh on the ideational bones:

> The drama proper is preceded ... by the most austere of all preludes; the infinite void and matter endlessly, aimlessly moving to bring forth it knows not what. Then by some millionth, millionth change— what tragic irony!—the conditions at one point of space and time bubble up into that tiny fermentation which we call organic life.

the problem of evil

At first everything seems to be against the infant hero of our drama ... But life somehow wins through. With incalculable sufferings ... against all but insuperable obstacles, it spreads, it breeds, it complicates itself; from the amoeba up to the reptile, up to the mammal ... [T]here comes forth a little, naked, shivering, cowering biped, shuffling, not yet fully erect, promising nothing: the product of another millionth, millionth chance. His name in this Myth is Man ... He becomes the Cave Man with his flints and his club ...

But these were only growing pains. In the next act he has become true Man. He learns to master Nature ... More and more he becomes the controller of his own fate. (Lewis 1967, 86–7)

Lewis believed it was important to remind people that the Great Myth is imaginative metaphysics. It is philosophy and not science. Hence, when the doctrine of the Fall suggests a decline for human biological life from a better to a worse state, from a less to a more painful existence, it is in conflict with the doctrine of the Great Myth and not with the scientific theory of biological evolution, because the latter is, strictly speaking, about nothing more than change as such, irrespective of any question about its value.

With the development of the Great Myth, there was a change in philosophical perspective "from a cosmology in which it was axiomatic that 'all perfect things precede all imperfect things' to one in which it is axiomatic that 'the starting point ... is always lower than what is developed' ... " (Lewis 1964, 220). Lewis described how, when he was a boy, he believed that Darwin discovered evolution, "and that the far more general, radical, and even cosmic developmentalism ... was a super-structure raised on the biological theorem" (Lewis 1964, 220). But as he matured intellectually, Lewis became convinced that his "boyish" view had things backwards. The idea of cosmic development in a positive direction could be found in intellectuals like Keats, Wagner, Goethe, Herder, Leibniz, Kant, Bergson, Chardin, and others. What happened was that in light of the Great Myth, a search ensued for empirical phenomena that would support it. Such was found in evolutionary biology. Again, Lewis stressed that he did not question the facts of evolutionary biology: "I do not at all mean that these new phenomena are illusory" (Lewis 1964, 221). But the picking and choosing of facts to support the Great Myth is possible because "Nature has all sorts of phenomena in stock and can suit many different tastes" (Lewis 1964, 221). Given that nature itself contains facts that are compatible with a multiplicity of philosophical views, Lewis insisted that a philosophical view like the Great Myth "reflects the prevalent psychology of an age almost as much as it reflects the state of that age's knowledge" (1964, 222). He believed that if the planet Earth were to survive long enough with human beings, there would undoubtedly be a philosophical view that would supersede the Great Myth. So while a philosophical view like the Great Myth "will not be set up without evidence … the evidence will turn up [only] when the inner need for it becomes sufficiently great" (Lewis 1964, 222–3).

8.6 Evil before the Existence of Human Beings

Given Lewis thought biological evolution occurred and other forms of sentient life existed and experienced pain before the existence of human beings, what did he think explained this evil? Lewis once again turned to the idea of free will, but not that of human beings. Instead, he suggested that there might be angelic beings who misused their free will to introduce evil into the world before human beings existed. In a letter to Ruth Pitter, Lewis wrote:

> The pre-human earth already contained suffering. This is why (like our fathers) we must believe in the fall of the angels long prior to the fall of man. Our fall consisted in joining the wrong side in a battle [which] had already begun. I'm inclined to think that the mutual preying of irrational creatures (at least creatures on more or less the same level) *is* evil. [Could] it be without pain? (2004b, 754)

In what he wrote to Pitter, Lewis reiterated what he had written in *The Problem of Pain* about the origin of evil: on the assumption that God originally created the universe without suffering (because of His goodness), evil must be explained in terms of free will. Lewis was well aware that some would deride the idea that evil in the pre-human world of animals was the result of the free choices of fallen angelic beings. In his treatment of the problem of evil, Plantinga also acknowledges that many people find the idea of angelic beings causing evil preposterous, but responds that while this is sociologically interesting, it is argumentatively irrelevant (Plantinga 1977, 62). As best as he knows, writes Plantinga, there is no evidence against the existence of such beings. And Lewis agreed.

8.7 Evil and Beasts

All of the foregoing has left unaddressed the question of whether it would be just for God to allow beasts, who do not possess free will and, thereby, cannot sin, to have experiences of pain for which they are not responsible. Is God justified in allowing Rowe's fawn and other such animals, both before and after the supposed fall of human beings, to experience pain? Lewis believed so, though I find his reasoning confusing, and perhaps in the end inconsistent.

Some of what Lewis wrote suggests that he was a skeptical theist with regard to animal pain. That is, in certain writings he seems to have expressed the belief that we do not know God's reason for allowing animals to experience pain, and that we should not be surprised by our ignorance. We should not be surprised because "[w]e know neither why they [beasts] were made nor what they are [what is their nature] ... [so] everything we say about them is speculative" (Lewis 2001f, 133). Lewis marveled "that God brings us into such intimate relations with creatures of whose real purpose and destiny we remain forever ignorant. We know to some degree what angels and men are *for*. But what is a flea for, or a wild dog?" (2007, 1376–7). In writing about how serious readers extend their intellectual horizons through the eyes of others, Lewis wrote that "I regret that the brutes cannot write books. Very gladly would I learn what face things present to a mouse or a bee; more gladly still would I perceive the olfactory world charged with all the information and emotion it carries for a dog" (1961a, 140). Given our ignorance of how a beast sees the world and the purpose of its existence, Lewis insisted that "we must never allow the problem of animal suffering to become the centre of the problem of pain ... because it is outside the range of our knowledge" (2001f, 132–3).

Given our ignorance of the nature and purpose of beasts, one would expect Lewis would have claimed that their experience of evil does not appear to us to be unjustified (which is not to say that it appears to be justified). However, at points, he wrote as if at least some of the pain which animals experience appears unjustified. For example, he stated that there is an appearance of divine cruelty in the kingdom of the beasts. Nevertheless, given the supposed goodness of God, he concluded that this appearance must be an illusion and false (Lewis 1970, 168; 2001f, 133). But how can the suffering of beasts appear unjustified, when we do not know what the nature of and purpose for their existence are? At best, it seems we are justified in claiming that it is not apparent to us what the justification of their pain is, assuming there is one. In discussing animal pain Lewis seems to have confused the appearance of a *lack* of a justification with the lack of an *appearance* of a justification. To make his position consistent, it is reasonable to conclude he should have said that a theist is not in a position to claim either that the pains of beasts appear justified or that they appear unjustified. At most, he should have said it appears that at least some beasts experience pain.

Regardless of what Lewis thought about the appearance of evil among beasts, he was (once again) not averse to engaging in informed "guess-work" (Lewis 2001f, 133) about how the experience of evil by beasts might be justified. At the heart of this guesswork was the supposition that the majority, or perhaps all, of the animals which do experience pain are not self-conscious subjects of experience. To illustrate his conjecture, he made use of an example involving the occurrence of three successive sensations A, B, and C (I will assume they are experiences of pain), to which I made reference in Chapter 2. Self-conscious beings (souls) are aware of A occurring in themselves and passing away to be replaced by the occurrence of B in themselves, and the occurrence of B in themselves passing away to be replaced by the occurrence of C in themselves. They are aware of themselves having the experience of ABC. But what if a subject of A, B, and C were not self-conscious? It would have experience A, then have experience B, and then have experience C. What it would not have is the awareness of itself having either the experience of A, the experience of B, or the experience of C, or the experience of itself having ABC. There would be a succession of experiences and perceptions but no experience or perception of succession. There would be three experiences of pain, but "no co-ordinating self which can recognise that 'I have had [three] pains'" (Lewis 2001f, 136). Lewis conceded that we cannot imagine such sentience without self-awareness, "not because it never occurs in us, but because, when it does, we describe ourselves as being 'unconscious'" (2001f, 136). He concluded that his guesswork about the nature of animal consciousness was consistent with the fact that we regard beasts as "incapable either of sin or virtue: therefore they can neither deserve pain nor be [morally] improved by it" (Lewis 2001f, 132).

If Lewis was right about beasts not being self-conscious (I will leave aside the possibility that a few are) and, therefore, not aware they are experiencing the pain that they are going through, then, it seems he should have concluded the following: while the pain beasts experience is intrinsically evil, there is nothing morally problematic with God's permitting them to experience it. To understand why Lewis should have reached this conclusion, consider what he said about the possibility of immortality for beasts, where by "immortality" he was thinking of life in heaven. Lewis wrote that the real difficulty about supposing there is immortality for beings that are not self-conscious is that the idea itself "has almost no meaning ... " (2001f, 141). He made his point in terms of a newt:

> If the life of a newt is merely a succession of sensations, what should we mean by saying that God may recall to life the newt that died today? It would not recognise itself as the same newt; the pleasant sensations of any other newt that lived after its death would be just as much, or just as little, a recompense for its earthly sufferings (if any) as those of its resurrected—I was going to say "self", but the whole point is that the newt probably has no self ... There is, therefore ... no question of immortality for creatures that are merely sentient. Nor do justice and mercy demand that there should be, for such creatures have no painful experience. Their nervous system delivers all the *letters* A, P, N, I, but since they cannot read they never build it up into the word PAIN. (Lewis 2001f, 141–2)

But if a newt that is experiencing pleasure now does not, because it lacks self-consciousness, recognize itself as the same newt which earlier experienced pleasure (indeed, it does not recognize *itself* as experiencing pleasure, period), then presumably a newt that is experiencing pain now does not recognize itself as the same newt which earlier experienced pain (because, as with pleasure, it does not recognize *itself* as experiencing pain, period). But then not only does it seem that the idea of immortality makes no sense for such a creature, it also seems that the idea of hell lacks any sense for such a creature. And if this is the case, then it seems that questions about the justness or unjustness of hell for beasts cannot arise, just as Lewis wrote that questions about the justness or unjustness of heaven could not arise for them. And if they cannot arise about hell (presumably the worst form of existence), it is hard to see how they could arise about any less-than-hellish (less than worst) experience of pain on earth (assuming earth is not hell; but see the next section for Lewis's view of hell). In short, because a newt lacks the self-awareness that *it* is experiencing pain, where this self-awareness is necessary for intelligible questions to arise about the justice or injustice of its experiencing hellish pain, it seems to follow that no injustice is done to a newt (or newt-like creature) by letting it experience pain in this world.

Just as important for the present discussion, however, is the fact that if Lewis was correct in his claims about the non-self-conscious nature of a newt's experiences of pleasure and pain, then it seems his belief in the need to introduce an angelic fall (Lewis often referred to this fall in terms of Satan) to explain the existence of evil by pre-human beasts was not clearly justified. Given, as Lewis suggested, that the experience of pain by beings which lack self-consciousness is neither just nor unjust, there seems to be no need to introduce an angelic fall for the purpose of explaining God's justification for allowing this pre-human experience of pain. Lewis regarded the introduction of Satan at this point as simply "a wider application to the principle that evil comes from the abuse of free will. If there is such a power [as Satan], as I myself believe, it may well have corrupted the animal creation before man appeared" (Lewis 2001f, 138). But Lewis believed free will played an important role in justifying the experience of pain by human beings on the assumption that they are self-conscious and created for perfect happiness. Absent self-consciousness and this purpose for beasts, there seems to be no need to invoke the free will of an angelic (or any other similar) being to justify beastly experiences of pain, even though there would be such a need (on Lewis's view) to invoke free will to justify the experience of pain by angelic beings themselves (assuming that, like human beings, they are self-conscious and created for perfect happiness).

8.8 Hell

If Lewis was right, non-self-conscious animals cannot experience heaven, and they cannot experience hell. But things are different with self-conscious human beings. Lewis thought they can justly end up in hell. Why did he believe this? Here we must hearken back to Lewis's view of the importance of death to self in relationship to the purpose of life. In Lewis's mind, we are created for the purpose that we be perfectly happy and our experience of pleasure in this life tempts us to try to maximize our happiness as we see fit. This demands that we make a choice either to die to self and ultimately receive the gift of perfect happiness for which we were created or to reserve the right to pursue that happiness on our own terms. And as we have already seen, Lewis believed that those who choose to reserve the right to pursue happiness on their own terms are justly denied the experience of perfect happiness. Lewis was convinced all of this "has the support of reason" (2001f, 120).

But what is the relationship between not experiencing perfect happiness and hell? Lewis dealt with the topic in his book *The Great Divorce* by having the reader identify choosing to pursue happiness on one's own terms with choosing earth, and choosing to die to self with choosing heaven. Given these identities, he wrote: "I think earth, if chosen instead of Heaven, will turn out to have been, all along, only a region in Hell: and earth, if put second to Heaven, to have been from the beginning a part of Heaven itself" (Lewis 2001e, ix). With regard to the latter alternative, Lewis was suggesting that while we are created for perfect happiness, one might understand this world as an outer region of heaven because it includes experiences of pleasure. As one moves "further up and further in" (Lewis 1984, 201) to heaven, one will ultimately reach that place where there is nothing but experiences of pleasure. Similarly, earth has experiences of pain, and if one chooses to pursue pleasure on one's own terms, then one can view earth as an early stage of hell. So not experiencing perfect happiness can be considered a state of hell.

Lewis, however, was careful not to get involved in speculation about what hell is like. He reasoned that we know more about heaven than we do about hell because we were made for heaven and not hell (Lewis 2001f, 127, 129, 152). For Lewis, then, given we know the purpose for which we were created, it is plausible to consider anything less than perfect happiness as, to some greater or lesser degree, hell. So hell most fundamentally is not heaven, the place of our deepest satisfaction: "[F]rom this point of view … we can understand hell in its aspect of privation" (Lewis 2001f, 152). In personal correspondence with a student at Cambridge named Searles, Lewis imagined hell as a scrap-heap and added

> [w]hether that scrap-heap is annihilation or some kind of decayed consciousness is a point I won't dogmatise on. Our Lord's words usually

stress the negative side of it, not what the lost souls get but what they miss [perfect happiness]. Perhaps we had best leave it at that. (Lewis 2007, 1149)

Nevertheless, because Lewis thought earth can plausibly be regarded as a region of hell, we know he must have believed that hell positively characterized is an existence that includes pain, where pain is God's megaphone to let us know that something is wrong. After all, wrote Lewis, God "shouts in our pain" (2001f, 91).

But is the idea of a person being in hell just? Lewis believed it is natural to work with the concept of hell in terms of positive retributive punishment. And he thought it is just for those who will not choose to die to self to be excluded from heaven. But he also pointed out to his readers that while Jesus sometimes spoke of hell as a sentence imposed by a tribunal, he also described it in terms of men preferring darkness as opposed to light (Lewis 2001f, 124). Lewis thought that these two different ways of describing hell amounted to the same thing (he wrote that they "mean" the same thing, which seems not to be the case), and he understood the latter depiction of hell as a choice to have happiness on one's own terms. In other words, Lewis thought existence in hell is not a punishment inflicted by someone else but the result of a choice to have happiness in one's own way. The mark of hell is "the ruthless, sleepless, unsmiling concentration upon self ... " (Lewis 1961b, ix). As the "Big Ghost" in *The Great Divorce* asserts, "I only want my rights" (Lewis 2001e, 28), which are the rights to pursue happiness as he deems suitable. Thus, wrote Lewis, "[w]e must picture Hell as a state where everyone is perpetually concerned about his own dignity and advancement, where everyone has a grievance, and where everyone lives the deadly serious passions of envy, self-importance, and resentment" (Lewis 1961b, ix).

Ultimately, then, on Lewis's view, while those in hell are never perfectly happy, they "are, in one sense, successful, rebels to the end ... [so] that the doors of hell are locked on the *inside*" (Lewis 2001f, 130). Having read Edwyn Bevan's *Symbolism and Belief*, in which Bevan wrote that while the wrongdoer "does not will the pain[,] he is in a sense imposing it on himself by willing that to which the pain is connected by a moral nexus" (Bevan n.d., 240), Lewis concluded that hell is "simply the working out of the soul's evil to its logical conclusions ... " (Lewis 2007, 504). And Lewis believed this is what is retributively just.

note

1   I stress for *us*, here, for two reasons. First, to make clear that Lewis believed we know what justifies *our* experience of evil as self-conscious persons, as opposed to that of the beasts. Second, Lewis wrote that God created us not primarily for the purpose that we might love Him (though he said we were

created for that too), but that He might love us (Lewis 2001f, 40–1). This might create the worry expressed by Baier (which I discussed in Chapter 3) that as artifacts we are reduced to mere gadgets, domestic animals, or slaves. Lewis stressed that while perfect happiness is the purpose for which God created us, we can ultimately be perfectly happy only on terms (principally, dying to self and loving God) that make us lovable by God ("when we are such as He can love without impediment, we shall in fact be happy" (Lewis 2001f, 41). So even if Lewis thought our happiness was secondary to God's being able to love us, he most certainly held it was not disregarded because God's being able to love us ultimately amounts to his being able to offer us the gift of perfect happiness.

an enduring mind

There is thus a tendency in the study of Nature to make us forget the most obvious fact of all. And since the sixteenth century, when Science was born, the minds of men have been increasingly turned outward, to know Nature and to master her. They have been increasingly engaged on those specialised inquiries for which truncated thought is the correct method. It is therefore not in the least astonishing that they should have forgotten the evidence for the Supernatural. The deeply ingrained habit of truncated thought—what we call the "scientific" habit of mind—was indeed certain to lead to Naturalism, unless this tendency were continually corrected from some other source.

(Lewis 2001c, 65–6)

Throughout this book I have aimed to provide the reader with a detailed account of the philosophical thought of C. S. Lewis. That thought remains relevant to contemporary philosophical discussions more than fifty years after his death. To illustrate how, I conclude with two recent contributions to a page of *The Wall Street Journal* under the title "Terms of Enlightenment." The authors Frank Wilczek, a physicist at the Massachusetts Institute of Technology, and Steven Pinker, a psychologist at Harvard University, were asked to give their views about which scientific term or concept should be more widely known in 2017. Wilczek selected the concept of complementarity, which

is the idea that there can be several different ways of describing a single system, each useful and internally consistent, but mutually incompatible ... Consider the concept of legal responsibility. Science, on the face of it, suggests that human beings are physical objects, whose behavior is fully determined by physical laws. That is a very useful perspective to take if, for example, we want to design reading glasses or drugs. But from this perspective, no one really controls his or her own behavior. The strictly physical description of human beings isn't a useful way to describe the way that we act in society. The perception

C. S. Lewis, First Edition. Stewart Goetz.
© 2018 John Wiley & Sons, Inc. Published 2018 by John Wiley & Sons, Inc.

that we exercise will and make choices is based on a coarser but more useful description of our being, which comes naturally to us and guides our legal and moral intuitions. (Wilczek 2016)

Pinker believes the concept that deserves wider recognition is the Second Law of Thermodynamics, which

states that in an isolated system (one that is not taking in energy), entropy always increases over time ... In 1915, the physicist Arthur Eddington wrote, "The law that entropy always increases holds, I think, the supreme position among the laws of nature." Why the awe for the Second Law? I believe that it defines the ultimate purpose of life, mind and striving: to deploy energy and information to fight back the tide of entropy and carve out refuges of beneficial order ... An underappreciation of the Second Law lures people into seeing every unsolved social problem as a sign that the world is being driven off a cliff. (Pinker 2016)

What would Lewis have said in response to Wilczek and Pinker? It is plausible to think he would have stressed that Wilczek is confusing naturalism with science, and while the former maintains that human beings are physical objects whose behavior is fully determined in accordance with physical laws, the latter does not. It is naturalism, Lewis would have stressed, and not science that excludes the reality of choice and undermines morality. Hence, he would have added, the explanatory descriptions of science are thoroughly compatible with purposeful explanations of our choices and morality. These different kinds of explanation are about different parts of reality. They are not different explanations of the same reality. Lewis would have concluded that the idea of complementarity is not only mistaken but also not needed for describing human beings.

Lewis would likely have found it peculiar that Pinker, who is a naturalist, writes in terms of the ultimate purpose of life. Such language suggests the idea of an artificer who created human beings for a purpose, which is something Pinker rejects. Lewis would have emphasized that what is not peculiar is Pinker's linking of the concept of the purpose of life to the idea of what is beneficial to us, where the latter is the idea of what contributes to our happiness. However, Lewis would have made clear that because Pinker holds that a perfectly beneficial order for us is not achievable in this or any other world, he is wrong to chide people who believe that this world is being driven off a cliff. If one accepts the truth of naturalism, our world is headed over a cliff because our desire for perfect happiness cannot be achieved.

Finally, Lewis would have reminded us that we can think and reason about the assertions of Wilczek and Pinker only because we are rational beings. And he believed that if we start our philosophy with the fact that we are able to think and reason, we will be on an intellectual journey to genuine enlightenment about the nature of ourselves and the universe we inhabit. Lewis thought that if we give the fact that we reason the attention it deserves, we will understand that we are supernatural beings who inhabit a universe that is at bottom supernatural in nature. He concluded that once we recognize this fact, we will understand that there is good reason to take seriously the idea that God exists and has available for us the perfect happiness that makes life worth living.

bibliography

Annas, Julia. 1993. *The Morality of Happiness*. Oxford: Oxford University Press.

Anscombe, Elizabeth. 1981. "A Reply to Mr. C. S. Lewis's Argument that 'Naturalism' is Self-Refuting." In *The Collected Philosophical Papers of G. E. M. Anscombe*: vol. 2, *Metaphysics and the Philosophy of Mind*, 224–32. Minneapolis: University of Minneapolis Press.

Aristotle, 1962, *Nicomachean Ethics*, translated by Martin Ostwald. Indianapolis, IN: The Bobbs-Merrill Company.

Armstrong, David. 1978. "Naturalism, Materialism and First Philosophy." *Philosophia*, 8: 261–76.

Augustine, St. 1961. *Confessions*, translated by R. S. Pine-Coffin. New York: Penguin Books.

Augustine, St. 1999. *The Enchiridion of Faith, Hope, and Love*, translated by Bruce Harbert. Hyde Park, NY: New City Press.

Ayer, A. J. 1977. *Part of My Life: Memoirs of a Philosopher*. London: Harcourt Brace Jovanovich.

Ayer, A. J. 2008. "The Claims of Philosophy." In *The Meaning of Life*, 3rd ed., edited by E. D. Klemke and Steven Cahn, 199–202. Oxford: Oxford University Press.

Baggini, Julian. 2004. *What's It All About? Philosophy and the Meaning of Life*. New York: Oxford University Press.

Baier, Kurt. 2000. "The Meaning of Life." In *The Meaning of Life*, 2nd ed., edited by Elmer Daniel Klemke, 101–32. New York: Oxford University Press.

Balfour, Arthur J. 2000. *Theism and Humanism*, edited by Michael W. Perry. Seattle: Inkling Books.

Barfield, Owen. 1989. *Owen Barfield on C. S. Lewis*, edited by G. B. Tennyson. Middletown, CT: Wesleyan University Press.

Barkman, Adam. 2009. *C. S. Lewis & Philosophy as a Way of Life*. Allentown, PA: Zossima Press.

Bennett, J. A. W. 1992. "The Humane Medievalist." In *Critical Essays on C. S. Lewis*, edited by George Watson, 52–75. Aldershot: Scolar Press.

Bering, Jesse. 2006. "The Folk Psychology of Souls." *Behavioral and Brain Sciences* 29: 453–62.

Bevan, Edwyn. n.d. *Symbolism and Belief*. London: George Allen & Unwin.

Beversluis, John. 1985. *C. S. Lewis and the Search for Rational Religion*. Grand Rapids, MI: Eerdmans.

Boswell, James. 2008. *The Life of Samuel Johnson*, edited by David Womersley. London: Penguin Classics.

Brontë, Charlotte. 1997. *Jane Eyre*. New York: Signet Classic.

Campbell, Keith. 1980. *Body and Mind*. Notre Dame, IN: University of Notre Dame Press.

Carpenter, Humphrey. 1997. *The Inklings: C. S. Lewis, J. R. R. Tolkien, Charles Williams, and Their Friends*. London: HarperCollins.

Carroll, Sean. 2016. *The Big Picture: On the Origins of Life, Meaning and the Universe Itself*. London: Oneworld.

Chalmers, David J. 1996. *The Conscious Mind: In Search of a Fundamental Theory*. Oxford: Oxford University Press.

Chesterton, G. K. 2007. *The Everlasting Man*. Mineola, NY: Dover.

Cleveland, Timothy. 2005. "Different Worlds, Different Bodies: Personal Identity in Narnia." In *The Chronicles of Narnia and Philosophy*, edited by Gregory Bassham and Jerry L. Walls, 180–92. LaSalle, IL: Open Court.

Conan Doyle, Sir Arthur. 1930. *The Complete Sherlock Holmes*. New York: Doubleday.

Cottingham, John. 2016. "Theism and Meaning in Life." *European Journal for Philosophy of Religion*, 8: 47–58.

Crane, Tim. 2016. "Bewitched," *The Times Literary Supplement*, No. 5891. February 26, 4.

Dennett, Daniel. 1991. *Consciousness Explained*. Boston: Little, Brown and Company.

Descartes, René. 1958. *Descartes' Philosophical Writings*, translated by Norman Kemp Smith. New York: The Modern Library.

Duriez, Colin. 2015. *The Oxford Inklings: Lewis, Tolkien, and Their Circle*. Oxford: Lion.

Dyer, Justin Buckley and Micah J. Watson. 2016. *C. S. Lewis on Politics and the Natural Law*. Cambridge: Cambridge University Press.

Feinendegen, Norbert and Arend Smilde. 2015. The "Great War" of Owen Barfield and C. S. Lewis: Philosophical Writings, 1927–1930. *Inkling Studies Supplement*, No. 1.

Fetherston, Patience. 1988. "C. S. Lewis on Rationalism: (unpublished notes)." *Seven*, 9: 87–9.

Feynman, Richard. 1998. *The Meaning of It All*. Reading, MA: Perseus Books.

Fox, Robin Lane. 2015. *Augustine: Conversions and Confessions*. New York: Basic Books.

Frazer, James George. 2006. *The Golden Bough*. Sioux Falls, SD: Nu-Vision Publications, LLC.

Gelernter, David. 2016. "Machines that Will Think and Feel." *The Wall Street Journal*, March 19–20, C1–2.

Gilson, Etienne. 1960. *The Christian Philosophy of Saint Augustine*, translated by L. E. M. Lynch. New York: Random House.

Goetz, Stewart. 2005. "Frankfurt-Style Counterexamples and Begging the Question." In *Midwest Studies in Philosophy*, edited by John Martin Fischer, Peter A. French, and Howard K. Wettstein, 29: 83–105. Malden, MA: Blackwell.

Goetz, Stewart. 2015a. *A Philosophical Walking Tour with C. S. Lewis: Why It Did Not Include Rome*. New York: Bloomsbury.

Goetz, Stewart. 2015b. "Substance Dualism." In *The Ashgate Research Companion to Theological Anthropology*, edited by Joshua R. Farris and Charles Taliaferro, 125–37. Burlington, VT: Ashgate.

Goetz, Stewart and Charles Taliaferro. 2011. *A Brief History of the Soul*. Oxford: Wiley-Blackwell.

Green, Roger Lancelyn and Walter Hooper. 1974. *C. S. Lewis: A Biography*. London: Collins.

Green, Roger Lancelyn and Walter Hooper. 2003. *C. S. Lewis: A Biography*. Rev. ed. London: HarperCollins.

Gresham, Douglas. 2005. *Jack's Life: The Life Story of C. S. Lewis*. Nashville, TN: Broadman & Holman.

Haldane, J. B. S. 1928. *Possible Worlds*. New York: Harper and Brothers.

Hasker, William. 1999. *The Emergent Self*. Ithaca, NY: Cornell University Press.

Honderich, Ted. 1993. *How Free Are You? The Determinism Problem*. New York: Oxford University Press.

Hume, David. 1962. *On Human Nature and the Understanding*, edited by Antony Flew. New York: Collier Books.

Humphrey, Nicholas. 2011. *Soul Dust*. Princeton, NJ: Princeton University Press.

Irwin, T. H. 1996. "Rethinking Happiness and Duty." In *Aristotle, Kant, and the Stoics*, edited by Stephen Engstrom and Jennifer Whiting, 63–101. Cambridge: Cambridge University Press.

Jackson, Frank. 2002. "Epiphenomenal Qualia." In *Philosophy of Mind: Classical and Contemporary Readings*, edited by David J. Chalmers, 273–80. Oxford: Oxford University Press.

Johnson, Samuel. 1969. *The Rambler*. In *The Yale Edition of the Works of Samuel Johnson*. vol. V, edited by W. J. Bate and Albrecht B. Strauss, No.150, August 24, 1751. New Haven, CT: Yale University Press.

Kant, Immanuel. 1956. *Groundwork of the Metaphysic of Morals*, translated by H. J. Paton. New York: Harper and Row.

Kenny, Anthony. 2013. "Faith in Lions." *The Times Literary Supplement*, No. 5751. June 21, 3–4.

Kim, Jaegwon. 1996. *Philosophy of Mind*. Boulder, CO: Westview Press.

Kim, Jaegwon. 2005. *Physicalism, Or Something Near Enough*. Princeton, NJ: Princeton University Press.

Kort, Wesley A. 2016. *Reading C. S. Lewis*. Oxford: Oxford University Press.

Kreeft, Peter. 1989. "C. S. Lewis's Argument from Desire." In *G. K. Chesterton and C. S. Lewis: The Riddle of Joy*, edited by Michael H. Macdonald and Andrew A. Tadie, 249–72. Grand Rapids, MI: Eerdmans.

Kreeft, Peter. 1994. *C. S. Lewis for the Third Millennium*. San Francisco: Ignatius Press.

Levine, Joseph. 2001. *Purple Haze: The Puzzle of Consciousness*. Oxford: Oxford University Press.

Levine, Joseph. 2002. "Materialism and Qualia." In *Philosophy of Mind: Classical and Contemporary Readings*, edited by David J. Chalmers, 354–361. Oxford: Oxford University Press.

Levy, Neil. 2014. *Consciousness and Moral Responsibility*, Oxford: Oxford University Press.

Lewis, C. S. 1924. "The Moral Good—Its Place among the Values." CSL/MS–76. Wheaton College, Wheaton, IL: The Marion E. Wade Center.

Lewis, C. S. 1936. *The Allegory of Love*. Oxford: Oxford University Press.

Lewis, C. S. 1939. *Rehabilitations and Other Essays*. Oxford: Oxford University Press.

Lewis, C. S. 1942. *A Preface to Paradise Lost*. New York: Oxford University Press.

Lewis, C. S. 1954, *Poetry and Prose in the Sixteenth Century*. Oxford: Oxford University Press.

Lewis, C. S. 1955. *Surprised by Joy*. New York: Harcourt.

Lewis, C. S. 1961a. *An Experiment in Criticism*. Cambridge: Cambridge University Press.

Lewis, C. S. 1961b. *The Screwtape Letters*. New York: Macmillan.

Lewis, C. S. 1962. "*Ex Libris.*" *The Christian Century*, 79, June 6, 719.

Lewis, C. S. 1964. *The Discarded Image: An Introduction to Medieval and Renaissance Literature*. Cambridge: Cambridge University Press.

Lewis, C. S. 1967. *Christian Reflections*. Grand Rapids, MI: Eerdmans.

Lewis, C. S. 1969. *Selected Literary Essays*, edited by Walter Hooper. Cambridge: Cambridge University Press.

Lewis, C. S. 1970. *God in the Dock*. Grand Rapids, MI: Eerdmans.

Lewis, C. S. 1982. *On Stories: And Other Essays on Literature*. New York: Harcourt Brace.

Lewis, C. S. 1984. *The Last Battle*. New York: HarperCollins.

Lewis, C. S. 1986a. *Present Concerns*. New York: Harcourt.

Lewis, C. S. 1986b. *Reflections on the Psalms*. New York: Harcourt.

Lewis, C. S. 1988. *The Four Loves*. New York: Harcourt.

Lewis, C. S. 1991. *All My Road Before Me*. New York: Harcourt.

Lewis, C. S. 1992a. *Letters to Malcolm: Chiefly on Prayer*. New York: Harcourt.

Lewis, C. S. 1992b. *The Pilgrim's Regress*. Grand Rapids, MI: Eerdmans.

Lewis, C. S. 1996. "Introduction." In *St. Athanasius: On the Incarnation*, translated and edited by a Religious of C. S. M. V., 3–10. New York: St Vladimir's Seminary Press.

Lewis, C. S. 2000. *C. S. Lewis: Essay Collection and Other Short Pieces*, edited by Lesley Walmsley. London: HarperCollins.

Lewis, C. S. 2001a. *A Grief Observed*. New York: HarperSanFrancisco.

Lewis, C. S. 2001b. *Mere Christianity*. New York: HarperSanFrancisco.

Lewis, C. S. 2001c. *Miracles*. New York: HarperCollins.

Lewis, C. S. 2001d. *The Abolition of Man*. New York: HarperSanFrancisco.

Lewis, C. S. 2001e. *The Great Divorce*. New York: HarperSanFrancisco.

Lewis, C. S. 2001f. *The Problem of Pain*. New York: HarperSanFrancisco.

Lewis, C. S. 2001g. *The Weight of Glory and Other Essays*. New York: HarperCollins.

Lewis, C. S. 2002. *Poetry and Prose in the Sixteenth Century*. Oxford: Clarendon Press.

Lewis, C. S. 2003a. *Out of the Silent Planet*. New York: Scribner.

Lewis, C. S. 2003b. *Perelandra*. New York: Scribner.

Lewis, C. S. 2003c. *That Hideous Strength*. New York: Scribner.

Lewis, C. S. 2004a. *The Collected Letters of C. S. Lewis:* vol. I; *Family Letters, 1905–1931*, edited by Walter Hooper. New York: HarperSanFrancisco.

Lewis, C. S. 2004b. *The Collected Letters of C. S. Lewis:* vol. II; *Books, Broadcasts, and The War, 1931–1949*, edited by Walter Hooper. New York: HarperSanFrancisco.

Lewis, C. S. 2007. *The Collected Letters of C. S. Lewis:* vol. III; *Narnia, Cambridge, and Joy, 1950–1963*, edited by Walter Hooper. New York: HarperSanFrancisco.

Lewis, C. S. 2013a. "'Early Prose Joy': C. S. Lewis's Early Draft of an Autobiographical Manuscript." *Seven*, 30. 13–49.

Lewis, C. S. 2013b. *Image and Imagination*. Cambridge: Cambridge University Press.

Lewis, C. S. 2014. *The Pilgrim's Regress: Wade Annotated Edition*, edited by David C. Downing. Grand Rapids, MI: Eerdmans.

Lewis, Warren Hamilton. 1933. *Memoirs of the Lewis Family: 1850–1930*, vol. IV. Leeborough Press. The Marion E. Wade Center, Wheaton College, Wheaton, IL.

Lewis, Warren Hamilton. 1934. *Memoirs of the Lewis Family: 1850–1930*, vol. V. Leeborough Press. The Marion E. Wade Center, Wheaton College, Wheaton, IL.

Lewis, Warren Hamilton. 1982. *Brothers and Friends: The Diaries of Major Warren Hamilton Lewis*, edited by Clyde S. Kilby and Marjorie Mead. San Francisco: Harper and Row.

Lewis, Warren Hamilton. n.d. C. S. Lewis: A Biography. Unpublished typescript in the Marion E. Wade Center, Wheaton College, Wheaton, IL.

Logan, Stephen. 2010, "Literary Theorist." In *The Cambridge Companion to C. S. Lewis*, edited by Robert MacSwain and Michael Ward, 29–42. Cambridge: Cambridge University Press.

Lovell, Steve. 2003. "Philosophical Themes from C. S. Lewis." Ph.D. dissertation, University of Sheffield.

MacDonald, George. 2001. *George MacDonald: An Anthology*, edited by C. S. Lewis. New York: HarperSanFrancisco.

Mackie, J. L. 1990. "Evil and Omnipotence." In *The Problem of Evil*, edited by Marilyn McCord Adams and Robert Merrihew Adams, 25–37. Oxford: Oxford University Press.

Markos, Louis. 2015. *C. S. Lewis: An Apologist for Education*. Camp Hill, PA: Classical Academic Press.

Marsden, George. 2016a. *C. S. Lewis's Mere Christianity: A Biography*. Princeton, NJ: Princeton University Press.

Marsden, George. 2016b. "'Mere Christianity' Still Gets a Global Amen." *The Wall Street Journal*, March 25, A9.

McGrath, Alister. 1988. *Justification by Faith*. Grand Rapids, MI: Zondervan.

McGrath, Alister. 2014. *The Intellectual World of C. S. Lewis*. Malden, MA: Wiley-Blackwell.

McGrath, Alister. 2016. "Telling the Truth through Rational Argument: C. S. Lewis on the Reasonableness of Christian Faith." In *C. S. Lewis at Poets' Corner*, edited by Michael Ward and Peter S. Williams, 3–22. Eugene, OR: Cascade Books.

Meilaender, Gilbert. 1998. *The Taste for the Other*. Grand Rapids, MI: Eerdmans.

Meilaender, Gilbert. 2010. "On Moral Knowledge." In *The Cambridge Companion to C. S. Lewis*, edited by Robert McSwain and Michael Ward, 119–31. Cambridge: Cambridge University Press.

Mill, John Stuart. 1964. *The Autobiography of John Stuart Mill*. New York: Signet Classics.

"More Anti-Lewisite." 2016. lewisiana.nl/haldane/.

Nozick, Robert. 1974. *Anarchy, State, and Utopia*. New York: Basic Books.

Oberman, Heiko A. 1993. "The Pursuit of Happiness: Calvinism between Humanism and Reformation." In *Humanity and Divinity in Renaissance and Reformation*, edited by John W. O'Malley, Thomas M. Izbicki, and Gerald Christianson, 251–83. Leiden: E. J Brill.

O'Connor, Timothy. 2013. "Do We Have Souls?" https://www.bigquestionsonline.com/2013/01/08/have-souls/.

Oppy, Graham. 2013. *The Best Argument against God*. New York: Palgrave Macmillan.

Papineau, David. 1993. *Philosophical Naturalism*. Oxford: Blackwell.

Papineau, David. 2002. *Thinking about Consciousness*. Oxford: Clarendon Press.

Peters, Ellis. 1990. *The Heretic's Apprentice*. New York: Warner Books.

Peterson, Michael L. 2008. "C. S. Lewis on the Necessity of Gratuitous Evil." In *C. S. Lewis as Philosopher: Truth, Goodness and Beauty*, edited by David Baggett, Gary R. Habermas, and Jerry L. Walls, 175–92. Downers Grove, IL: InterVarsity Press.

Pinker, Steven. 2016. "Terms of Enlightenment: On the Second Law of Thermodynamics." *The Wall Street Journal*, December 28.

Plantinga, Alvin. 1977. *God, Freedom, and Evil*. Grand Rapids, MI: Eerdmans.

Plantinga, Alvin. 1997. "Methodological Naturalism." *Perspectives on Science and Christian Faith*, 49: 143–54.

Plantinga, Alvin. 2004. "Supralapsarianism, or 'O Felix Culpa'." In *Christian Faith and the Problem of Evil*, edited by Peter van Inwagen, 1–25. Grand Rapids, MI: Eerdmans.

Purtill, Richard. 2004. *C. S. Lewis's Case for the Christian Faith*. San Francisco: Ignatius.

Reppert, Victor. 2003. *C. S. Lewis' Dangerous Idea: In Defense of the Argument from Reason*. Downers Grove, IL: InterVarsity Press.

Rey, Georges. 1997. *Contemporary Philosophy of Mind*. Oxford: Blackwell.

Rorty, Richard. 1979. *Philosophy and the Mirror of Nature*. Princeton, NJ: Princeton University Press.

Rosenberg, Alex. 2011a. *The Atheist's Guide to Reality: Enjoying Life without Illusions*. New York: W. W. Norton & Company.

Rosenberg, Alex. 2011b. "Why I Am a Naturalist." *The New York Times*. September 17.

Rowe, William. 1986. "The Empirical Argument from Evil." In *Rationality, Religious Belief, and Moral Commitment*, edited by Robert Audi and William J. Wainwright, 227–47. Ithaca, NY: Cornell University Press.

Rowe, William. 1990. "The Problem of Evil and Some Varieties of Atheism." In *The Problem of Evil*, edited by Marilyn McCord Adams and Robert Merrihew Adams, 126–37. Oxford: Oxford University Press.

Ruse, Michael. 1998. *Taking Darwin Seriously*. Amherst, NY: Prometheus Books.

Ruse, Michael and Edward O. Wilson. 1993. "The Approach of Sociobiology: The Evolution of Ethics." In *Religion and the Natural Sciences*, edited by James E. Huchingson, 308–11. Fort Worth, TX: Harcourt Brace Javonovich College.

Ryle, Gilbert. 1949. *The Concept of Mind*. New York: Barnes & Noble.

Sarot, Marcel. 2011. "The Cardinal Difficulty for Naturalism: C. S. Lewis' Argument Reconsidered in Light of Peter van Inwagen's Critique." *Journal of Inklings Studies* 1: 41–53.

Sayer, George. 1994. *Jack: A Life of C. S. Lewis*. Wheaton, IL: Crossway Books.

Sayers, Dorothy L. 1987. *The Mind of the Maker*. New York: Harper One.

Schakel, Peter J. 1984. *Reason and Imagination in C. S. Lewis*. Grand Rapids, MI: Eerdmans.

Sidgwick, Henry. 1966. *The Methods of Ethics*, 7th ed. New York: Dover Publications.

Sinnott-Armstrong, Walter. 2009. *Morality without God*. New York: Oxford University Press.

Smilde, Arend. 2011. "What Lewis Really Did to *Miracles*: A Philosophical Layman's Attempt to Understand the Anscombe Affair." *Journal of Inklings Studies* 1: 9–24.

Stroud, Barry. 2004. "The Charm of Naturalism." In *Naturalism in Question*, edited by Mario De Caro and David Macarthur, 21–35. Cambridge, MA: Harvard University Press.

Taylor, Richard. 1992. *Metaphysics*, 4th ed. Englewood Cliffs, NJ: Prentice-Hall.

Theologia Germanica. 1949. Translated by Susanna Winkworth. New York: Belgrave Press.

Tillyard, E. M. and C. S. Lewis. 1939. *The Personal Heresy*. London: Oxford University Press.

Timpe, Kevin. 2013. *Free Will: Sourcehood and its Alternatives*. London: Bloomsbury.

Van Inwagen, Peter. 2011. "C. S. Lewis' Argument Against Naturalism." *Journal of Inklings Studies* 1: 25–40.

Van Riel, Gerd. 1999. "Does Perfect Activity Necessarily Yield Pleasure? An Evaluation of the Relation between Pleasure and Activity in Aristotle, *Nicomachean Ethics* VII and X." *International Journal of Philosophical Studies* 7: 211–41.

Wain, John. 2015. "Nevill Coghill and C. S. Lewis: Two Irishmen at Oxford." In *C. S. Lewis & His Circle: Essays and Memoirs from the Oxford C. S. Lewis Society*, edited by Roger White, Judith Wolfe and Brendan N. Wolfe, 239–47. Oxford: Oxford University Press.

Walsh, Chad. 1949. *C. S. Lewis: Apostle to the Skeptics*. New York: Macmillan.

Walsh, Milton. 2008. *Second Friends: C. S. Lewis and Ronald Knox in Conversation*. San Francisco: Ignatius Press.

Ward, Michael. 2016. "Panel Discussion: What Can Twenty-First Century Apologetics Learn from C. S. Lewis?." In *C. S. Lewis at Poets' Corner*, edited by Michael Ward and Peter S. Williams, 25–52. Eugene, OR: Cascade Books.

Ward, Michael. 2017. *THE ABOLITION OF MAN: C. S. Lewis's Classic Essay on Objective Morality; A Critical Edition by Michael Ward*. Wheaton, IL: Teller Books.

White, Nicholas. 2006. *A Brief History of Happiness*. Oxford: Blackwell.

Whitehead, Alfred North. 1958. *The Function of Reason*. Boston: Beacon Press.

Wielenberg, Erik J. 2008. *God and the Reach of Reason: C. S. Lewis, David Hume, and Bertrand Russell*. Cambridge: Cambridge University Press.

Wielenberg, Erik J. 2014. *Robust Ethics: The Metaphysics and Epistemology of Godless Normative Realism*. Oxford: Oxford University Press.

Wilczek, Frank. 2016. "Terms of Enlightenment: on Complementarity." *The Wall Street Journal*, December 28.

Williamson, Timothy. 2011. "What Is Naturalism?" *The New York Times*, September 4.

Wilson, E O. 2014. *The Meaning of Human Existence*. New York: W. W. Norton.

Wolf, Susan. 2013. "The Meaning of Lives." *In Exploring the Meaning of Life*, edited by Joshua Seachris, 304–18. Oxford: Wiley-Blackwell.

Wolf, Susan. 2015. "Science and the Search for Meaning." sciencemag.org, Vol. 347, Issue 6218: 137–8.

Wolterstorff, Nicholas. 2008. *Justice: Rights and Wrongs*. Princeton, NJ: Princeton University Press.

Wykstra, Stephen J. 1990. "The Humean Obstacle to Evidential Arguments from Suffering: On Avoiding the Evils of 'Appearance'." In *The Problem of Evil*, edited by Marilyn McCord Adams and Robert Merrihew Adams, 138–60. Oxford: Oxford University Press.

Zaleski, Philip and Carol Zaleski. 2015. *The Fellowship: The Literary Lives of the Inklings; J. R. R. Tolkien, C. S. Lewis, Owen Barfield, Charles Williams*. New York: Farrar, Straus and Giroux.

index

C. S. Lewis, First Edition. Stewart Goetz.
© 2018 John Wiley & Sons, Inc. Published 2018 by John Wiley & Sons, Inc.